The French in Early Florida

Florida A&M University, Tallahassee
Florida Atlantic University, Boca Raton
Florida Gulf Coast University, Ft. Myers
Florida International University, Miami
Florida State University, Tallahassee
University of Central Florida, Orlando
University of Florida, Gainesville
University of North Florida, Jacksonville
University of South Florida, Tampa
University of West Florida, Pensacola

The French
in Early Florida

In the Eye of the Hurricane

JOHN T. MCGRATH

University Press of Florida

GAINESVILLE · TALLAHASSEE · TAMPA · BOCA RATON
PENSACOLA · ORLANDO · MIAMI · JACKSONVILLE · FT. MYERS

LIBRARY OF CONGRESS CATALOGING-IN-PUBLICATION DATA
McGrath, John T., 1956–
The French in early Florida: in the eye of the hurricane /
John T. McGrath.
p. cm.
Includes bibliographical references and index.
ISBN 0-8130-1784-X (alk. paper)
1. Florida—History—Huguenot colony, 1562–1565. 2. French—Florida—
History—16th century. I. Title.
F314.M19 2000
975.9'01—dc21   99-056332

The University Press of Florida is the scholarly publishing agency for the
State University System of Florida, comprising Florida A&M University,
Florida Atlantic University, Florida Gulf Coast University, Florida
International University, Florida State University, University of Central
Florida, University of Florida, University of North Florida, University of
South Florida, and University of West Florida.

University Press of Florida
15 Northwest 15th Street
Gainesville, FL 32611–2079
http://www.upf.com

In memory of Joan McLaughlin McGrath

CONTENTS

ILLUSTRATIONS AND MAPS

Illustrations

Maps

ACKNOWLEDGMENTS

At different points many people have contributed to this effort by offering their ideas and advice. I would like to specifically thank Gayle Brunelle, Chester De Pratter, Barbara Diefendorf, Paul Hoffman, Amy Turner Bushnell, and Bertrand van Rumbeke for their knowledge and encouragement. Additionally, I owe a considerable debt to the several anonymous scholars who evaluated the manuscript at different stages.

I would also like to extend my appreciation to the librarians at the Widener Library at Harvard University and the Mugar Library at Boston University, as well as the staff of the St. Augustine Historical Society, all of whom rendered cheerful and knowledgeable assistance.

At Boston University's College of General Studies, I would like to thank Dean Brendan Gilbane, Jay Corrin, Michael Kort, and Bill Tilchin, who gave me reliable support and ideas. I should also mention the invaluable stimulus that I have gotten from my students, who inspire me every day with their determination and energy, and who make my job the best job in the world.

On the home front, I send my appreciation and love to my daughter, Katie, and son, Sam, for their patience and cheerfulness. Most of all, this could never have been either begun or completed without the amazing technical support provided by my wife, Ellie, as well as her constant encouragement.

More years ago than I care to admit, Mr. Roger Duncan of the Belmont Hill School helped me to understand that writing well is hard work. To him, my deepest gratitude.

Finally, I would like to mention my mother, Joan McLaughlin McGrath, whose courage, kindness, and love of history set a lifelong example for me, and to whom I dedicate this book.

1

Introduction

The Reformation era featured some of the most complex and confusing developments in European history. Startling transformations of politics and diplomacy reflected deep-seated changes in cultural values, social organization, and economic structure. Among the most significant historical themes of this period were the birth of Protestantism, the widespread use of the printing press, the growth of capitalism, and the first expansion of Europe into the "New World" of America. Chains of cause and effect that defy easy generalizations link these momentous developments together, in both obvious and subtle ways, making it sometimes difficult to clearly distinguish one from another.

In the period between Columbus's landing in the Bahamas and the permanent establishment of English settlers in Virginia, the kingdom of Spain dominated European activity in America, while the Portuguese enjoyed a sometimes contested sphere of influence in Brazil. It was not until the end of the sixteenth century that the English, Dutch, and French were in a position to initiate colonial conquests of their own.[1] It is not difficult to understand why the English and Dutch were latecomers in this quest for territory in the New World. In the former case, English maritime capabilities were extremely limited until the beginning of the reign of Elizabeth I in 1558, and even then English maritime activity in the New World was circumscribed until the 1580s by a formal alliance with Spain.[2] In the case of the Dutch, it is even easier to see why they undertook no significant overseas colonial projects until the very end of the sixteenth century. Only at that point had their extended and ultimately successful revolt freed the northern part of the Low Countries from Spanish control, whereupon these Calvinist northerners quickly emerged as a major colonial power.[3]

In comparison to the English and Dutch, it is considerably less obvious why the French seemed to lag behind their Iberian rivals in maritime enterprise. A brief glimpse of their activities during the sixteenth century might lead one to conclude that the French limited their activity in America to a few isolated and ineffective forays. If this is indeed true, how and why did this happen? One can discern without too much effort that it could not have been because they lacked maritime expertise or resources; the French certainly had an adequate supply of the physical means to compete for overseas empire. Did they suffer from a lack of will, and if so, why?

The traditional and seemingly most logical answer can be found in the serious French domestic and political problems of the sixteenth century. Early in the century, the ongoing war with Spain claimed a disproportionate share of French royal resources and was a horrible complication on the European diplomatic scene. For these reasons, it was difficult for the French Crown to take an active role in sponsoring an overseas empire, especially during the reign of François I (1515–47). Even more discouraging to French designs was the fact that, after 1562, the kingdom suffered through thirty-five years of religious and civil war; when they had an opportunity to create a colonial empire, their soldiers and sailors were too preoccupied with fighting among themselves to take advantage of it.[4]

As with many things in history, the reality of the situation was not so simple. In fact, the French did make significant efforts to lay claim to American territories during the sixteenth century. While European problems undeniably had a critical impact on the scope and range of their overseas activity, it is hardly accurate to say that such considerations prevented them. The French Crown provided both direction and material support for colonial claims in Canada during the 1530s, in Brazil in the 1550s, and on the southeast coast of North America during the following decade. In particular, the latest of these efforts, which created the outposts at Charlesfort and Fort Caroline in the present-day United States, represented the most ambitious and significant overseas effort that the French had ever attempted at that time.

Despite what many historians have claimed, this episode was hardly a minor historical footnote carried out by a few disenfranchised Protestants fleeing religious persecution.[5] Organized, financed, and militarily supported by the French Crown, it represented an attempt to lay claim to the southern part of the relatively unknown east coast of North America, an area Europeans often referred to in its entirety as "Florida." What emerges as the most interesting feature of this effort is not that it took place, or even the magnitude of its intentions, which is also widely ignored. What is most astonishing is the way in which it failed.

In regarding these events from a long-term perspective, one might see the French effort in Florida as a hopeless effort to challenge the mighty Spanish American empire. This explanation is quite unsatisfactory, since it views the outcome as a foregone conclusion and treats this colonizing effort as little more than a curiosity. In doing so it trivializes the intentions of the French in Florida, the Spanish reaction to their presence, and the factors responsible for the outcome. This book explains the circumstances surrounding this staggering French defeat in Florida and what it meant for subsequent historical events.

While it is essential to examine the long-term forces at work—such as the development of the Spanish American empire and the course of the French Wars of Religion—these can tell us only so much. In the case of the French in Florida, individual decisions also had a major impact upon the final result. What is just as important as the long-term historical forces themselves is the way in which the central characters in this drama perceived these forces and how they reacted to them. Only by appreciating the perspectives of the actors themselves—individuals such as Pedro Menéndez, Jean Ribault, René Laudonnière, Gaspard de Coligny, Catherine de Medici, and Philip II of Spain—can we appreciate the deeper historical significance of what ultimately took place in Florida.

One cannot understand these events without being aware of the viewpoints of the main decision makers, and in this case a crucial variable was the incompatibility of the respective legal claims of Spain and France to the New World. While there were many points of disagreement during this era between these two powers, one of the most insoluble was the lack of consensus about what defined "Spanish" territory in the New World. That the Spaniards and French refused even to attempt a resolution of this important issue reveals much about the conflicts that splintered the European continent during the Reformation and remains critical to our understanding of the causes and fate of this Florida initiative.

An additional important factor that affected the course of events in Florida was that the major actors possessed imprecise knowledge of the situations that confronted them. The timeliness and reliability of available information were more often than not severely flawed because of difficulties in transportation and communication. Those who directed the events were forced to act on the basis of knowledge that was sometimes incomplete, out-of-date, and mistaken. When combined with the pervasive assumptions of the Reformation era—for example, those of Spanish Catholics about French Protestants or widespread optimism about the possible existence of a "Northwest Passage" to Asia—we can see that key decisions surrounding these events were often affected by uncertainty, misinformation, and confusion.

To explain why specific people committed specific acts, one must look as much as possible through their eyes and appreciate the basis on which they were able to make decisions. While it is impossible, more than four centuries later, to understand such perspectives completely, it is possible to come up with a deeper, more meaningful, and more helpful understanding of what happened to this French colonial initiative. Ultimately, the French in Florida created a situation in which they became victims of powerful, capricious, and merciless forces that fell well beyond their control. The hurricane-force winds that doomed this bold effort stand as a stark metaphor for the violent uncertainty that characterized Europe during the Reformation era.

This is a story of the highest drama. The Spaniards' destruction of the French outpost in Florida did not unfold according to any predictable formulaic script. It is a tale whose actors displayed as much stupidity as brilliance, as much cowardice as heroism, and as much greed as idealism; there were plenty of all of these to go around, and no one person or side had a monopoly on any of them. Above all, these events show that the people involved in them were no more immune to human limitations than anyone else.

This French defeat (or Spanish victory, depending upon how one chooses to look at it) had immense consequences both for later European involvement in the New World and upon subsequent European affairs. This study, besides providing a badly needed accurate reconstruction of these events, will also cast light upon how these events affected long-term historical developments. The story that follows has never been told accurately in full, largely because of the way that earlier historians have used the existing source materials. Published narrative accounts comprise much of our evidence, and these have not always been handled carefully and critically; these sources are often contradictory and misleading, and they must be placed within the historical context that created them.

This book relies heavily upon such published contemporary accounts and upon the correspondence of the people who participated in these events. Even a cursory comparison of these sources reveals frequent and serious contradictions, not only about why these events occurred but even about their nature. This is especially true with the portrayals of the violent encounters that took place after both Ribault's and Menéndez's fleets arrived in Florida in the late summer of 1565. There has been, and still is, considerable disagreement about exactly what transpired during the Spanish flight to St. Augustine, the capture of Fort Caroline, and, in particular, the bloody finale at Matanzas Inlet.[6]

Because of this situation, a few words are necessary here about the ways I have used these sources. As a guiding principle, I have evaluated each work with a healthy skepticism about the intentions of its author and the circumstances that surrounded its composition and publication. Sixteenth-century authors were probably even less objective than authors are today, and perhaps considerably less so. After all, it was during this era that the printed word first emerged as a powerful influence upon the viewpoints of the growing population of literate Europeans, and publishers throughout the European continent were eager to employ the new weapon of publishing in their ideological battles.[7] The case under consideration provides an excellent example of the hazards involved in taking such published sources at face value.

Despite their limitations, such sources also often contain splendid detail and even insightful analysis of the events described. In most of the testimonies that survive, complete fabrication of events is rare, though they often suffer from the more common weaknesses of exaggeration and genuine confusion. However, if one uses them carefully in conjunction with other, more objective, evidence, it is possible to arrive at a close approximation of what actually happened in Florida. In turn one can comprehend the reasons behind these events, as well as appreciate their often-neglected importance. Additionally, the eyewitness accounts are able to convey the historical flavor of these events in a way that a modern author cannot.

Spanish and French sources represent different viewpoints and the different experiences of their writers, and one can make certain generalizations about them that are relevant here.[8] The Spanish accounts reveal a fundamental misunderstanding of the French actions and intentions in Florida, influenced by their own unique sense of imperial mission and the righteousness of their cause. The French accounts were mostly written by Calvinists and Catholic moderates in the wake of the French defeat. For the most part, French writers insist on regarding these events in sharp contrasts, which distorts our understanding of the events by making moral judgments upon them.

It was the French sources, not the Spanish ones, that have had the most influence upon later historical writing, both because the former were more numerous and because they directly stimulated a considerable body of late sixteenth-century French and English historical writing. In particular, we can easily determine that many contemporary chroniclers accepted at face value the two accounts authored by the French survivors Nicolas Le Challeux and Jacques Le Moyne de Morgues.[9] This has led to confusion, since much of what these authors reported was invented and exaggerated. These two sources cannot and must not be used without skepticism, and the appendix explains the way in which this author has employed them as evidence.[10]

Even taking such limitations into account, all of the surviving first-hand accounts are immensely valuable sources when used carefully, and they provide us with details unavailable in archival records or in other written accounts. Fortunately for history, most of these authors were insightful observers and skilled writers. Together and separately they convey a participant's perspective that is invaluable to our understanding of these events. The following study makes liberal use of passages from contemporary histories and letters, in order to facilitate the reader's appreciation of the perspectives of the people who took an active role. Although there still remain some parts of this story that require interpolation or even speculation, it is possible to recreate the events in a way that helps us to better understand this unusual chapter in the history of European colonization.

In terms of organization, I have tried to proceed roughly chronologically. Chapters 2 through 4 focus on the conditions that created this opportunity, and I examine a number of important topics that are relevant. Some of these are long term, and some are more immediate. The former category includes sixteenth-century French maritime development, the prior Spanish interest and involvement in Florida, the range of geographical ideas about America current in Europe at the time, and the diplomatic relationship between these two Crowns, which includes the different perspectives on the legitimacy of their different claims to territories in the New World. More immediate topics that contributed directly to this effort include the political and personal situation of Admiral Gaspard de Coligny, who held ultimate responsibility for the French effort; the growth of religious and political divisiveness in France prior to 1562; and the multifaceted career of Jean Ribault, the original leader of this venture.

Chapters 5 through 8 present a narrative history of the French effort between 1562 and the fall of 1565. I examine not just the events themselves but the contemporary developments in both Europe and America that were affecting them at the time. These chapters outline the uncertainties and logistical problems faced by the French leadership, as well as the reasons why the Spanish authorities had little choice but to respond in the brutal and unequivocal manner that they did. In chapter 9, I describe the aftermath of this affair in a context of the problems and priorities of these two European powers during this critical era in European history and in light of the later course of European colonization in the New World. Finally, the appendix examines the relative credibility of the written sources in regard to certain key events and also gives a brief outline of the way that historians from the sixteenth century to the present have portrayed these events and how their efforts have affected our understanding.

This is an episode in history that has never been accurately and thoroughly reconstructed—never mind satisfactorily explained—and one that is all too easy to obscure through oversimplification. Unlike the chroniclers of the Reformation era, I have tried to give an evenhanded, objective interpretation of these dramatic events, in a way that makes them understandable for what they were. In doing so, I show how the French in Florida, though they faced almost insuperable obstacles, came tantalizingly close to inflicting a staggering defeat on their hated Spanish rivals. The reasons for their failure have as much to do with human frailties and downright bad luck as they do with the many long-term, "deterministic" factors that are usually attributed as causes. While there can be little question that this French initiative was risky and perhaps even overly ambitious, the way in which it met its ultimate fate was anything but predetermined, and this story gives us a revealing glimpse at the brutal, desperate, and complicated world of the sixteenth century.

2

Terra Florida

In June 1565, the highest representatives of the two most powerful European states met in the Gascon seaport of Bayonne. King Philip II of Spain was represented by his most trusted associate, the Duke of Alva, who would soon achieve lasting infamy for his "Council of Blood" in the Spanish Netherlands. Queen Mother Catherine de Medici, undertaking a royal tour of the provinces with her son, fourteen-year-old King Charles IX, represented France along with veteran diplomats. Each side brought to the table a lengthy list of topics for discussion. The "Bayonne Interview," as it later became known, was intended to clear the air about several crucial matters of mutual interest to these two kingdoms.[1]

In 1559 the Treaty of Cateau-Cambrésis had officially ended sixty-five years of intermittent warfare between Spain and France. At that time, the French king, Henri II, had accepted less than favorable terms in order to gain external peace that would allow him to devote attention to his growing domestic problems. In particular, he needed to concentrate on curbing the growth of French Calvinism, which was threatening the unity of his realm. After largely disappointing military campaigns during the previous two years, Henri had agreed to stop the aggression of his armies in Italy, Germany, and the Low Countries by accepting the Cateau- Cambrésis treaty.

To mark the peace, the French and Spanish royal houses arranged diplomatic marriages, as was customary at the time. In one of the strange turns of history so characteristic of the Reformation era, Henri met a fatal accident in a jousting tournament during the wedding celebrations that July.[2] This catastrophe threw France into chaos, since Henri's heirs were neither fully mature nor very capable. For two years, his eldest son,

François II, ruled as a virtual puppet of the powerful Guise family. The Guises, a cadet branch of the House of Lorraine, claimed direct descent from Charlemagne and had emerged as the champions of orthodox Catholicism in France. Charles, the Cardinal of Lorraine, and François, the Duke of Guise, had previously maneuvered Henri into marrying young François to their niece, Mary Stuart of Scotland. Though not entirely successful in their efforts, this orthodox faction pressured the king to strengthen religious persecution against France's growing Calvinist population during the two years of François's brief reign.[3]

While Henri had enjoyed some success in controlling the quarrelsome factions among the French nobility, his sons lacked their father's diplomatic skill and his decisiveness. By the end of 1559, rival French nobles, fearing the political maneuverings of the Guise family, began to assert their opposition at the French court. Some of them, including Prince Louis of Condé, Queen Jeanne d'Albret of Navarre, and Admiral Gasspard de Coligny, formed an alliance in the name of French Calvinism, which added an explosive variable into an already combustible situation. As religious repression increased during François's reign, the leadership of these individuals formed what became known as the Huguenot party. Aided by John Calvin's carefully directed evangelization effort from Geneva, the number of Protestants quickly expanded in France, and by the end of 1561, when the sickly King François died, Calvinists composed as much as 10 percent of the French population.[4] It was not long after this, in March 1562, that the Duke of Guise's massacre of Calvinist worshippers at Vassy, east of Paris, plunged France into outright civil war. Interrupted only by a series of ineffective peace treaties, eight somewhat distinct conflicts, known collectively as the French Wars of Religion, ravaged the kingdom until 1598. Perhaps no era in French history has been grimmer.

In the first war, Huguenot armies commanded by Condé and Coligny lost both major battles, first at Rouen and later at Dreux.[5] By March 1563, Catherine forced the Calvinists to accept conditions known as the Peace of Amboise, which essentially reversed the religious conditions imposed by a royal edict of January 1561. While the earlier edict had forced French Calvinists to worship outside city walls—a stipulation that had led directly to the Vassy massacre—the Amboise settlement now required that Calvinism could be permitted only discreetly within certain towns, in order to minimize the opportunities for provocation. However, in the long term this peace settled nothing. Atrocities committed by Calvinists and Catholics alike continued during the uneasy peace that followed, and by the middle of 1565 the conditions that had been imposed upon the defeated Huguenots were contributing to rising tension within France.

Many of the matters to be discussed at Bayonne revolved around a general issue of grave concern to the Spaniards, namely, Catherine's religious policy toward Protestants.[6] Philip blamed Protestant agitation among the nobility and the towns of northern France for his difficulty in maintaining order in his own Netherlands possessions. This commercially dynamic and ethnically diverse region, which included Antwerp, had become the economic nerve center of Philip's empire during the middle decades of the sixteenth century. From Philip's point of view, the growth of Calvinism—aided and abetted by French refugees—threatened the social and political stability of this part of his kingdom.[7] At Bayonne, through the Duke of Alva, the Spanish king demanded that his mother-in-law make good on her past promises to rid her realm of heresy.

A more specific issue on the duke's agenda had to do with a large French military expedition that had been reported outfitting in Normandy. According to Spanish intelligence, as many as a thousand French troops were set to launch a strike against Florida, which Spanish kings had considered their possession since 1493. Philip and the duke were also both aware of a French fort on the east coast, which they understood to have been established for the purpose of attacking the Spanish silver fleet as it returned to Spain. The readying of this French fleet—reportedly composed of Protestants and led by noted corsair leaders—seemed to leave little doubt of French hostility. Alva had prepared an official complaint to present to Catherine at Bayonne, to warn her of the dire consequences of such colonial aggression.

However, by the time the Bayonne meeting got under way in June, the Spaniards had received a report that the French fleet had already departed.[8] As a result, the duke decided not to present his complaint to Catherine; after all, there was a more direct means of dealing with this latest French affront. Alva was fully aware that Philip was planning other measures to counteract the French threat to Florida, decidedly nondiplomatic ones. Even as the French and Spanish representatives were meeting, two separate Spanish armadas were preparing for departure, one in Asturias and one in Cadiz. Under the overall command of Spain's most experienced Indies captain, Pedro Menéndez de Avilés, a total of more than twenty ships would shortly sail to a rendezvous in the Canary Islands. Together they planned to stop at Spanish ports in the Indies to pick up supplies and additional soldiers, then sail north to attack the French outpost of Fort Caroline. If all went according to plan, they could capture the fort and remove the French before their reinforcements arrived. Menéndez's force of soldiers, civilian settlers, and officials could then establish the permanent outpost in Florida that had eluded the Spaniards, despite several attempts, since the time of Ponce de León more than forty years before.

The respective French and Spanish interests in Florida at that time were complex and were continuing to evolve. In looking at the background of this conflict, we can discern a fundamental disagreement over the legitimacy of a French presence in the New World. Though opportunities arose before, during, and even after the Bayonne meeting where the two powers could have discussed these differences, they did not take advantage of them. The results of this were, in hindsight, unsurprising. Not only did this mean that neither side had an accurate idea of what the other was trying to accomplish in America, but each side felt justified to defend what it considered to be its territory. Exacerbating this problem was the long-standing mutual suspicion between these two ancient rivals, who were only too eager to credit the other with the worst of intentions. Perhaps most important, neither wanted to be seen as backing down to the demands of the other.

In this environment, as the Spaniards and the French each reacted to perceived aggression by the other, hostilities became inevitable. By the time the Bayonne meeting was concluded, in late June 1565, two large and heavily armed war fleets were under way to Florida—one Spanish, under Menéndez, and the other French, led by Jean Ribault. By then there was little chance of a peaceful settlement of the issues. The final outcome would rest on an unlikely combination of circumstances, well beyond the control of either the French or the Spaniards, and the result would have a large impact on the future course of North American colonization, in ways that neither the French nor the Spanish could possibly have anticipated in 1565.

*　　*　　*

In 1493, the year after Columbus's landing in the Bahamas, Pope Alexander VI, a Spaniard, issued a series of four papal bulls that essentially divided the world into spheres of Spanish and Portuguese influence. Known as "the Papal Donation," these pronouncements led to direct negotiations between the two monarchies the following year. In 1494 Spain and Portugal concluded the Treaty of Tordesillas, which established a slightly different and more formal "line of demarcation" for their explorers and merchants to observe. Although the two Iberian kingdoms continued to squabble over the exact boundaries of this colonial world well into the sixteenth century, each founded its imperial policies on Tordesillas, which relied on papal sanction for its legitimacy.

Other European monarchies drew different conclusions about the meaning of the Papal Donation and the Tordesillas treaty. Even before the end of the century, the English king, Henry VII, had supported John Cabot's voyage across the North Atlantic, which reached Newfoundland. Basques, Portuguese, Bretons, Normans, and Englishmen soon followed Cabot, and all were regular visitors to the rich fishing banks of the northwest Atlantic by early in the century. Meanwhile, other European monarchs ignored or resented the putative Portuguese/Spanish division of the world.[9]

Perhaps the French king, François I, best expressed this lack of general acceptance of the Tordesillas arrangement. He certainly had political reasons for rejecting some of its terms; François's long reign (1515–47) was most noted for an intense rivalry with the Hapsburg emperor, Charles V, whose hereditary lands included Spain, the Netherlands, Austria, much of Italy, and various other parts of Europe. By virtue of the Papal Donation and the Treaty of Tordesillas, Charles also laid claim to all of the New World save those areas that had been awarded to the Portuguese. During the height of his competition with Charles, François made the apocryphal but well-known assertion that "I would like to be shown the article in Adam's will that divides the New World between my brothers, Emperor Charles V and the King of Portugal, and excludes me from the succession. The sun shines on me just as it does on them."[10]

François I has often been referred to as France's "Renaissance King." He ruled during a period of French economic and demographic expansion that featured a strengthening of France's commercial position with other European states, which included the development of French maritime activity and overseas trade. One particularly powerful stimulus for this was the growth of the city of Rouen into an international trading and manufacturing center early in the sixteenth century. The Rouennais textile industry created a demand for foreign products that included silks and dyes from outside of Europe. To facilitate such long-distance trade, the construction of the new port of Le Havre-de-Grâce gave the merchants of Rouen access to a well-fortified deep-water port capable of handling larger vessels. The Le Havre project, directed by the king himself, involved the creation of an entirely new town, which soon became one of the busiest ports on Europe's Atlantic coast.[11]

In particular, François consistently disputed Spanish and Portuguese claims that France was forbidden from the "spheres of influence" awarded in 1493 and formalized the following year at Tordesillas. During the decade of the 1530s, he succeeded in persuading Pope Clement VII to make clear that the donation of 1493 referred only to known lands and that it did not preclude the discovery of new ones, by the French or anyone else.[12] By then French Atlantic maritime tradition already held that many parts of the New World had been first seen by mariners from such ports as Dieppe and Saint-Malo. Later, François's overseas policy in negotiations with Spain and Portugal relied upon the guiding principle of "effective occupation," as he asserted that permanent settlement was the only legitimate basis for claiming new lands.[13] By the 1530s, labels such as "Terre des Bretons" and "Nova Francia" were beginning to appear on European maps of North America, even those composed by Italians, Germans, and Spaniards.[14]

In 1522 an Italian sailing in François's service, Giovanni da Verrazzano, conducted one of the most significant voyages of exploration of this era. François had granted a royal commission to Verrazzano, who had extensive family and business connections to the French city of Lyon, giving him explicit instructions to search for a western passage to the Indies.[15] Verrazzano's reconnaissance and mapping of most of the east coast of North America gave François and his successors a claim to have "discovered" North America first, which provided much of the basis of French royal policy on the issue four decades later.

While Spanish and Portuguese kings maintained close centralized control of their overseas fleets, in contrast, the private sector played a greater role in maritime ventures in sixteenth-century France. Sizable fleets of French mariners, known as "corsairs," financed by wealthy merchants and nobles in Atlantic ports such as Dieppe, La Rochelle, and Bayonne, traded and raided throughout Atlantic waters. Depending on the political situation at the moment, François sometimes awarded these fleets "letters of mark" (*lettres de marque*), which permitted them to appropriate, at their own discretion, compensatory damages from the shipping of hostile nations.[16] Letters of mark were in fact thinly disguised licenses for piracy that granted the bearer, in case of capture, the status of prisoners of war instead of common criminals. Hence these documents, at least in theory, could enable French sailors to avoid a summary hanging and guarantee that their captors would turn them over to authorities for a diplomatic judgment of their fate.

Whether they possessed such licenses or not, the French corsair fleets maintained a de facto independence from state control. Detailed documentation of their activities is hard to come by, though, since they seldom kept written records of their voyages and often fabricated their destinations in order that some of their more questionable activities—such as outright piracy—would be harder to detect.[17] These corsairs demonstrated increasing initiative and effectiveness during the first half of the sixteenth century, and their activities often caused serious diplomatic problems. French ambassadors could speak truthfully when they met frequent Portuguese and Spanish complaints by responding that they neither knew about nor could control the actions of the Atlantic fleets.[18]

Despite the Le Havre project and occasional letters of mark, the French merchant community was largely dissatisfied with the level of François's support for their trade, and they often complained that their rights were neglected in favor of obscure political and diplomatic considerations.[19] The career of the most powerful and successful French shipowner during François's reign, Vicomte Jean d'Ango of Dieppe, probably best exemplifies this. Ango's corsair fleets regularly traded with Brazil and West Africa from the 1520s to the 1540s; on one occasion in 1529, his captain, Jean Parmentier, even led three ships through the Indian Ocean to Sumatra.[20] Ango experienced bewildering changes in the level of support afforded him by François. Occupied by his struggle with Charles V, the king felt that he could not afford to provoke the Portuguese into open warfare, and so he backed down and refused to support Ango's interests. Several times during the 1520s and 1530s François granted Ango royal letters of mark against the Portuguese, and each time he revoked them when confronted with Portuguese diplomatic protests. At one point, in utter frustration, one of Ango's private fleets imposed a blockade of Lisbon harbor to try to wring monetary compensation from the Portuguese Crown for damages done by Portuguese ships. In 1545, with François's encouragement, Ango played a large part in a major naval expedition against England, furnishing ships and men as part of an attempt to discourage English reinforcement of Calais. The effort suffered unexpected misfortunes, and the king never reimbursed Ango for his considerable expenses. Involved during his last years in costly and ultimately fruitless legal efforts to obtain satisfaction from the Crown, Ango died bitter and debt-ridden in 1551. His experience typifies the inconsistent and often confrontational nature of relations between François and the French maritime community.

During the first half of the century, French mariners had two primary destinations in the New World: the fishing areas in the north, especially around the mouth of the St. Lawrence River, and Brazil. French sailors had established contact with both regions by or near 1500, and during the sixteenth century the French Crown itself undertook brief but significant projects in each.

During the 1530s, François directly supported Jacques Cartier's voyages to the northern area. While the Portuguese and Basques, in particular, had become regular visitors to these areas for fishing and whaling, they had never sought to establish anything more permanent than coastal trading stations. Cartier, while making the first exploration up the St. Lawrence, attempted to implant a permanent French colony, their first in the New World, even though the Spaniards technically laid claim to the same areas. While this French initiative never posed any direct threat to existing Spanish trade or settlements, Cartier's presence provoked Emperor Charles V into making formal complaint in 1540 and 1541.[21] The latter was apparently most concerned that the French might find a waterway that would enable them to contest his control of Mexico, which may actually have been among Cartier's objectives. Ultimately, though, the withdrawal of the outposts Cartier had established on the St. Lawrence made the disagreement moot.[22] Nevertheless, this attempt gave the French another reason to claim first discovery, if not effective occupation, of that part of North America. Though they made no further formal claims on present-day Canada during the rest of the century, fishing and trading fleets from many parts of Europe continued to frequent this Spanish-claimed region. By early in the following century, Cartier's experience stimulated the French Crown to direct a later effort, that of Samuel de Champlain.

Brazil was the other region where the French Crown tried to stake a claim in the New World. This vast territory, discovered accidentally by the Portuguese in 1500, had acquired a special place in the hearts and minds of both the French merchant community and the larger public. For most of the sixteenth century, it was the best-known and most romanticized part of the Americas. The name "Brésil," originally applied to a mythical island of Irish legend, began to appear on medieval *mappae-mundi* by the fourteenth century. The Portuguese, who had first called the land Sancta Cruz, renamed it Brazil early in the sixteenth century and referred to the useful dark hardwood that grew there as "brazilwood" (*bois du brésil*). By the middle of the century, Europeans often associated the land of Brazil with fantastic creatures and peoples, including Amazons, cannibals, and beasts of legend. In sixteenth-century France, "Brésil" became virtually interchangeable with "America," in large part due to the fact that it was the most visited and most widely publicized part of the New World.[23]

French Atlantic mariners, especially Normans, had established the practice of trading on Brazilian shores for almost half a century prior to Henri's accession to the throne of France. On return voyages from West Africa, they often called at the Brazilian coastline, where they traded directly with the local populations for supplies of brazilwood, useful in the production of the colorful dyes increasingly utilized in Norman and Flemish textile manufacturing.[24] Although brazilwood was bulky, the heavy demand for it had made such voyages highly profitable for the merchant backers of such enterprises. As its linens assumed the role of the kingdom's leading source of foreign exchange, the Rouen textile industry was gaining in relative importance throughout Europe. Rouennais merchants sold their linen in numerous parts of Europe, Spain being the largest market, as Rouen became France's busiest international marketplace.[25]

Even by midcentury, the French presence on Brazilian shores equaled or exceeded that of the Portuguese. One reason for this was that Portuguese kings considered Brazil less promising than their other colonial possessions in Africa and Asia, and they accordingly devoted fewer of their precious resources to its exploitation. As a result, Portuguese forts and trading stations in Brazil were initially few, undermanned, and loosely administered.[26] Even after the Portuguese Crown made its first serious attempts to administer this vast territory in the late 1540s, French fleets continued to profitably trade for woods and dyes through a series of coastal trading stations. Both the need and the opportunity for a permanent French presence in Brazil was becoming apparent.

Henri II had become king of France in 1547, and it was he who first actively encouraged interest in Brazil. His relations with the merchant community were considerably more positive than François's had been. Unlike his father, whose preoccupation with the Hapsburgs and European diplomacy seemed at odds with the welfare of his merchant subjects, Henri seemed to regard overseas trade as an economic opportunity instead of a political liability. Even during the beginning of his reign, when his foreign policy was relatively cautious, he appreciated the great economic potential of Atlantic commerce. Henri consistently approved a higher level of royal expenditures for the marine infrastructure, especially for shipbuilding and the construction of harbors, which showed his commitment to the promotion and protection of Atlantic enterprise.[27]

One of the most dramatic spectacles of Henri's reign was the Rouen procession in September 1550 in honor of the king's entrance to that city. Considered by some to have been the most magnificent of all French Renaissance entries, its most extraordinary aspect was the attention devoted to Brazil.[28] A Brazilian village and forest were re-created on the riverbank, complete with genuine flora and fauna. Several dozen Tupinamba Indians, along with Norman mariners attired in Brazilian costumes, staged a mock battle for the entertainment of the king and his court. The extravagance of this event well indicates the importance of Brazil for the Rouennais and the earnestness of their efforts to attract royal support for their interests there.

Shortly afterward, in June 1551, Henri dispatched the navigator Guillaume Le Testu to the coast of Brazil for a mission of reconnaissance. The ship *Salamandre* sailed as far south as 26° latitude, some distance beyond Rio de Janeiro.[29] After carefully mapping the coast and surviving a skirmish with two Portuguese vessels, the *Salamandre* returned to Dieppe in July 1552. In April 1556, based on his observations, Le Testu completed his atlas, *La cosmographie universelle,* which he dedicated to Gaspard de Coligny, who had become Admiral of France shortly after the *Salamandre*'s return in 1552.[30]

King Henri had a clear interest in Brazil's possibilities, as evidenced by his support of the Le Testu voyage, though precisely why is more difficult to determine. It may be that he had no particular specific goal in mind for Brazil aside from a general desire to create a New World colony. Certainly the maintenance of a French presence on Brazilian shores could pave the way for a formal claim to the area, based on the principle of effective occupation. This would enable him to use the same argument as his father had, that lands first occupied by Frenchmen belonged to the French Crown.

Yet there were also a number of more material reasons why a king of France might have been interested in this area. Perhaps the most obvious was the need to protect the brazilwood trade, which had continued to prosper. As the Portuguese military presence increased, Henri may have feared attacks against the French trading stations and the interruption of this profitable commerce. A half century of active French involvement in the Brazil trade and a growing domestic need for American products had perhaps readied Henri to either pursue a formal claim to Brazil or establish a military capability in the area that could defend French commerce. Also, a well-fortified French presence in Brazil may have been related to diplomatic considerations between France and Portugal. The two king-doms maintained a tense official truce during Henri's reign, and in any future negotiations a strong military base there could prove useful.

There is another possible reason for the French king's interest in Brazil at this time. After the discovery of the massive Andean silver deposits at Potosí in 1545, the estuary of the Rio de la Plata had rapidly become an active outlet for both legal and illegal trade coming out of the South American interior. The possibilities of overland commerce with the newly settled regions of Bolivia and Paraguay, as well as rumors of fur-ther "mountains of silver" yet to be discovered, had aroused the interest of not only Spaniards but the Portuguese and French as well.[31] It is en-tirely possible that Henri desired to establish a base in Brazil that could facilitate commerce and exploration in the Rio de la Plata area.

Whatever the possible combinations of motives that Henri may have had, in 1555 he acted on them in the most decisive colonial initiative of his reign. Three years after Le Testu's return, the king commissioned Nicolas Durand de Villegagnon, a Knight of Malta and the Vice Admiral of Brittany, to establish an outpost in Guanabara Bay, in the vicinity of present-day Rio de Janeiro.[32] In November of that year, Villegagnon dis-embarked there commanding a mostly civilian labor force of around six hundred men. He then set to work on an island commanding the en-trance to the bay, constructing a stone fortress which he christened Fort Coligny in honor of the admiral. The effort was largely in vain, however, since in the meantime the admiral himself had been taken prisoner at the siege of St. Quentin in 1557, and because of the negotiations surrounding the Treaty of Cateau-Cambrésis, King Henri never made any practical use of his new American outpost. While Villegagnon was in France seek-ing military reinforcement in early 1560, Fort Coligny's civilian defend-ers bravely resisted a Portuguese naval siege before finally surrender-ing.[33] The Portuguese replaced the French outpost with a Jesuit mission, and the loss of Fort Coligny was a crippling setback for French royal designs in Brazil for the rest of the century.

Though the squandered opportunity in Guanabara Bay discouraged further claims to that area, French interest in the New World remained active. Admiral Coligny, who was gradually resurrecting his influence at court after 1561, began to look elsewhere to establish a New World base for the French Crown. By then, the admiral had a very limited choice of where he might launch a new American effort, and as the new decade opened, Coligny turned his attention toward the coast of North America.

*　*　*

One of the most important factors that motivated Europeans in their exploration of America during the sixteenth century was the promise of vast wealth. Spanish *conquistadores,* spurred on by rumors of gold, treasure, and fabulously rich kingdoms, explored and subjugated millions of square miles of South and North America while claiming them for the growing Spanish Empire. Most of these quests were disappointing failures, ranging from Ponce de León's search for the Fountain of Youth, to Coronado's hunt for the Seven Cities of Cibola, to numerous attempts to find the fabled El Dorado. Occasionally, though, there was a success. Hernán Cortès's dramatic defeat of the Aztecs in 1521 gave the Crown an opportunity to create the Viceroyalty of New Spain, which finally enabled the first truly lucrative Spanish colonization of the Americas. During the next decade, Francisco Pizarro, while consciously emulating Cortès, achieved the destruction of the vast Incan Empire, which resulted in the establishment of a second Spanish viceroyalty, known as Peru.

Besides the spectacular treasures seized by Cortès and Pizarro, their conquests led to an even richer long-term exploitation of American resources. As Spaniards began to settle the territories of New Spain and Peru, they also discovered vast reserves of precious metals in both areas. During the 1540s they first exploited the rich silver deposits at Zacatecas, in northern Mexico, and shortly thereafter, they located the legendary Potosí silver reserves in the Bolivian Andes.

It is difficult to overestimate the impact of these discoveries upon the subsequent development of America, as well as upon the economy of Europe for the next hundred years. Among other important effects, they dramatically transformed the nature of the Spanish presence in America. The colonies were no longer a drain on Spanish resources, as had generally been the case prior to the 1540s. The flow of wealth was now reversed, as Spanish monarchs began to rely upon American resources to support their activities in Europe. Of the New World commodities exploited, precious metals from Mexico and Peru were far and away the most important after midcentury and comprised a rapidly increasing share of colonial exports. Especially when German firms began employing new mining technologies, using locally available mercury, the production of American silver increased exponentially during the 1550s.[34] After more than half a century of colonial frustration, America had finally revealed treasures that would have satisfied even Christopher Columbus.

Two organizations in Seville controlled most aspects of Spanish colonial trade in America.[35] The Casa de Contratácion, an institution created by royal decree in 1503, was primarily an administrative body that awarded trade privileges, granted licenses, approved emigration, and in other ways determined who and what could travel between Europe and the Indies. Working closely with the Casa was the *consulado*, the guild of firms that held royal license to conduct business in the Indies. Both of these organs were dependent upon the king, through his royal Council of the Indies, for their authority. In doing so, both were ultimately obligated to abide by royal policy.

Even by early in the century, in order to facilitate their control, the Casa had begun to formalize a convoy system between the two areas. These convoys, known as *flotas*, dramatically expanded in size after the discoveries at Zacatecas and Potosí.[36] Soon the Spanish Crown increased its direct involvement in colonial trade. After 1561 a series of royal decrees increased the level of King Philip II's regulation of the flotas, and he began to provide armed warships to escort the outgoing and returning fleets. Such convoys not only minimized the opportunities for smuggling but also lessened the danger from the ubiquitous corsairs, many of them Normans and Bretons, who stalked Atlantic waters in search of easy riches. By then, most Spanish private ships were arranging their sailing schedules so that they could attach themselves to the flotas, and generally only speedy dispatch boats dared to sail the Atlantic unaccompanied.

As the planning and organization of these vital fleets became more precise, a definite regular pattern emerged by the 1560s, featuring one and sometimes two annual sailings to and from Europe.[37] After leaving Seville in the fall or spring, the outbound flotas divided in the West Atlantic and proceeded separately to their respective destinations: Nombre de Dios in Panama, and Veracruz on the east coast of Mexico. At these points the fleets loaded the silver and other colonial cargo that awaited them. Fully loaded with the fruits of empire, these ships then departed from Nombre de Dios in January and from Veracruz in February. The two groups made a rendezvous in Havana, in order to have a unified return journey to Spain. As a general rule, the recombined fleet loaded and departed from Havana as efficiently as possible—ideally by late spring—in order to minimize hazardous weather. During the sixteenth century, the precise date varied according to factors beyond the control of even the Spanish Crown.

Coordinated timing was essential for the success of what had developed into a complex operation. Tropical weather posed the greatest threat to the successful convergence of the fleets from Mexico and

Panama. For the New Spain flota, seasonal wind patterns made it necessary to wait until early in the year to cross the Gulf of Mexico. Meanwhile, torrential rains often delayed the arrival of the treasure in Nombre de Dios by making roads and mountain trails to the harbors in Panama and Peru impassable. This meant that there was seldom much time to spare in Havana, because of the threat of the hurricane season that could begin as early as June. The earlier the assembled ships could leave Havana, the better were their chances of avoiding catastrophic weather.

For all practical purposes, because of winds and currents, fleets could set out from Havana for Europe only by going north. From Havana, the southwest trade winds and the Gulf Stream afforded a route that—in decent conditions—could take a convoy quickly past the treacherous Florida Keys and through the Bahama Channel (or Florida Strait), which separated the Florida peninsula from the Bahama archipelago. Once the flota was past this narrow alley, farther north along the North American coast they encountered trade winds that permitted a relatively reliable and safe cross-ocean sailing to the East. As an additional advantage, this route enabled the fleet to stop at the Azores to resupply and pick up additional naval protection for the last leg of the journey.

The combination of prevailing currents, seasonal weather, and navigational hazards meant that during the sixteenth century, to use the words of one modern historian, "it was easy to get into the Caribbean, but hard to get out."[38] By early in the century, European sailors had learned that the Bahama Channel provided the only practical exit. This first three hundred miles out of Havana always remained the primary obstacle to a flawless return journey, since the channel, besides its vulnerability to hurricanes, was bordered by dangerous shoals and reefs on both sides. The combination was frequently fatal. Yet the flotas invariably had little choice but to run the gauntlet on this initial stretch, and the convoy sailings improved their success rate. While Spanish authorities had to accept certain losses to shipwrecks, they could lessen these by insisting on group sailings where the presence of many other ships could rescue at least some of the crew and cargo. Given the unpredictability of the weather, the flota system as it had developed provided the best chance for the successful and timely arrival of the American treasure back to Europe, where the king's bankers and other creditors eagerly awaited it.

It has been estimated that the Spanish convoy system carried 95 percent of the value of colonial goods exported to Spain during the second half of the sixteenth century, including virtually all of the legally exported gold and silver.[39] As the volume of American silver production expanded in the 1560s, so too did the volume of shipping. The average value of silver exported between 1551 and 1560 was 32,375 pesos annually, with an average of 120 Spanish ships making the crossing from America to Spain. Despite a trade recession for most of this decade, both figures still amounted to more than a 50 percent increase from the 1540s. A quantum leap in the value of silver exports occurred during the 1560s: from 1560 to 1610, the average level exported from America was about 290,000 pesos annually, an increase of more than 900 percent over the 1550s.[40]

* * *

Since Florida's discovery by Ponce de León in 1513, Spain had accomplished little in the territory. Ponce himself was fatally wounded there in 1521 and probably died without realizing that Florida was not an island. By that time, Cortès's achievements in Mexico, and the first circumnavigation of the globe, completed by the survivors of Magellan's expedition, stimulated the imaginations of Spanish explorers, merchants, and administrators about the possibilities of more fabulous riches they might find in the New World.

One of the most important ideas concerned the Atlantic coast of North America. By 1521 coastal explorations had given birth to rumors among Spanish settlers in the Caribbean of a prosperous and temperate northern land awaiting discovery. Some Spanish explorers, identifying it as the Indian land of Chicora, believed that this territory, located at the same latitude as Andalucia in Spain, held immense potential as both a source of wealth and a site for civilian settlement.[41] In 1526 Emperor Charles V granted the first royal license to settle this coast to Lucas Vásquez de Ayllón, a wealthy official in Hispaniola. Ayllón sponsored an early exploratory voyage along the coast and helped publicize this area's potential, and his settlement expedition, when it finally got under way in 1526 after some delays, had multiple purposes: Ayllón intended to search for a sea passage through North America, to evangelize among the Indians, and to establish a permanent Spanish base.[42] However, the outpost he founded in present-day South Carolina did not survive more than a few months, victimized by a lack of food and by internal dissension. Though Ayllón's expedition failed, the hope persisted that somewhere along this coast might be found a "land of milk and honey."[43]

Yet later attempts amply demonstrated the difficult obstacles that the eastern part of North America presented. Pánfilo Narváez's disastrous expedition of 1528 had resulted in massive losses of soldiers but little inland penetration aside from Cabeza de Vaca's remarkable odyssey through the Gulf Coast region. Later, between 1539 and 1543, Hernando de Soto's expedition through what is today much of the southeastern United States had given Spaniards the widely held impression that Florida was "full of bogs and poisonous fruits, barren, and the worst country that is warmed by the sun."[44]

The Crown's hesitancy to further exploit this area is shown by its refusal of a later application for exploration and settlement rights in 1544. What could not be won by the sword, however, might be won by the cross, and in 1549 the viceroy of New Spain sponsored a mission of evangelization in the area around Tampa Bay. This, too, met with disastrous results, as the local inhabitants well remembered the depredations of de Soto and his predecessors. They entrapped the Dominican missionary Luis Cancér and another friar, killing and eating them as horrified Spaniards watched from the helpless safety of an offshore boat. Not surprisingly, the survivors abandoned this evangelization effort, and further curiosity about Florida was minimal for a number of years.

It was only late in 1557 that Spanish interest in the area revived, when authorities agreed to a plan to make a permanent settlement at Punta de Santa Eleña, near the border of present-day Georgia and South Carolina and close to where the Frenchman Jean Ribault would establish Charlesfort in 1562. The royal instructions included two stated purposes: to convert the local inhabitants to Christianity and "so that the Spaniards who reside in those lands and go out to them may be benefited and may become established in them and may have homes and means of living."[45] A seaborne reconnaissance of the Gulf Coast by Guido de las Bazares returned a favorable report of the area, and at the beginning of 1559, the viceroy of New Spain, Luis de Velasco, dispatched Tristán de Luna y Arellaño, a veteran of the Coronado campaign, as the newly appointed governor of Florida. Luna was expected to establish and administer his new settlement as a district of New Spain, and Spanish authorities hoped that he could make this colony agriculturally self-sufficient within a short period of time.

The lack of firm knowledge of the longitudinal distances is evident from the concept that the planners embraced. Velasco assigned Luna to lead a mixed group of soldiers and civilians to near present-day Pensacola by ship. From there, they were to blaze a trail from the Gulf of Mexico to the Atlantic Ocean while establishing permanent settlements along the way. If successful, Luna's expedition would not only create

Spanish outposts on both coasts but just as importantly it would open up a strategic overland path that the cattle ranchers of northern Mexico could use to drive their herds all the way to the Atlantic. This initiative might solve another problem, as well: it could enable some of the Spanish treasure shipments to bypass the treacherous waters around the southern tip of Florida. Instead, Mexican silver shipments could be dispatched overland along this route and meet up with the *flota* near Punta de Santa Eleña. It is evident from the viceroy's original instructions that the planners believed that the major obstacle to such a scheme would be the crossing of the Mississippi River, and they vastly underestimated the tremendous distance (1,600 miles) involved.[46]

Luna's declaration of intent expressed a newly optimistic view of Florida's possibilities, one that echoed Ayllón's earlier claims: "The expedition is of great importance and it will be much to your honor and benefit, sir, both for you and for the gentlemen, *hidalgos,* and other persons who may go upon it, for the land is large, good, healthful, and fertile."[47]

In the documents relating to the planning of this expedition, there was little mention of any strategic or military purpose. Only after Luna had embarked, in May 1559, was there a direct reference to the threat posed by the French. At that time Velasco sent Philip a written account of his preparations that emphasized a secondary benefit to be gained:

> One of the good effects that, God helping, this expedition will have will be this: if a port is colonized on the east coast of La Florida, which is from one hundred to one hundred and thirty leagues from the port of La Havana and lies midway of the Bahama Channel, where all the ships are forced to go which come to Tierra Firme, Nombre de Dios, and New Spain, I believe that when it is known by the corsairs who are accustomed to pass these parts that there are Spanish ships and people on both sides of the Bahama Channel to impede their passing and assist each other from La Florida to La Havana and from La Havana thither, they will not go by here, and the route will be assured as far as the Azores Islands, which is of much importance.[48]

Luna's expedition had severe problems from the outset, suffering loss of life and supplies when a hurricane struck as the colonists disembarked. Soon after, Luna relayed to Velasco his new intention to alter the scope of his assignment. In light of his problems, he felt that he would be able to establish an inland settlement only if he received additional supplies and personnel. But even by December 1559, after news had reached Spain of the initial difficulties, Philip wrote to Luna:

> As you know from having been told, it was fitting and very nec-
> essary to make a strong settlement at the Punta de Santa Eleña,
> which is in that land of La Florida, in order to make an effort from
> there by means of preaching and good treatment to bring the people
> of that land to our holy Catholic faith, and in order that the ships
> which come from New Spain and other parts of the Indies to these
> kingdoms and make port there may find shelter instead of being
> lost on account of there being no settlement at all at the Punta: and
> also to prevent people from France and any other foreign kingdom
> from entering there to settle or take possession in our lands. . . . For
> notwithstanding that we are at peace with France, we have learned
> that Frenchmen, under the pretext of going to Los Bacallaos [the
> North Atlantic fishing areas], may possibly be desirous of going to
> that land of La Florida to settle in it and take possession of our
> lands.[49]

Therefore, Philip continued, Luna must abandon any intention of settling inland and proceed with the original plan of reaching and settling
the east coast. But Luna had become geographically disoriented by the
difficult terrain, and internal dissension had rendered his party immo-
bile. Despite Philip's exhortation, he failed to reach the Atlantic coast or
to establish a permanent Spanish outpost anywhere else. Finally, in 1561,
Viceroy Velasco ordered the navigator Angel de Villafañe to sail to Punta
de Santa Eleña and establish a coastal beachhead, but because of supply
problems, Villafañe, too, was unable to establish a permanent presence.
The attempt had failed, and by September 1561, Philip himself was ex-
pressing doubt "whether it would be expedient to continue populating
. . . Florida, or not."[50]

The land they called Tierra Florida lay only a few hundred miles from
the site of Columbus's first landing, but it had proved to be as intractable
a region for Spanish colonization as anywhere in all of the Americas. This
reality presented Philip with a serious dilemma. If experience had shown
that Florida was a difficult location to plant a civilian settlement, it was
equally clear that he must protect the waterway it controlled. By 1561
Florida's strategic value was increasing, as the annual flotas were rapidly
becoming the economic lifeline of Spain. Meanwhile, Philip's inability to
arrive at a satisfactory agreement with France over navigation to the

Indies meant that the presence of French corsairs in Atlantic waters continued to cause him to worry.

The Age of Conquistadores had ended, and the decade of the 1560s marked the beginning of a new era for Spanish America. After Philip II's accession to the throne in 1556, the American land area that had been explored and conquered by the Spaniards would never become significantly larger. In the young king's vision of empire, the New World served a different purpose than it had for his father. Instead of expansion, Philip's concerns in America centered around the exploitation and protection of the vital resources that were already claimed.[51]

Amid the turbulence of the Reformation, Philip could put his New World resources to immediate use in the Old World. Specifically, the fountain of silver that was beginning to flow across the Spanish Atlantic highway enabled the king to ready his armies for hostilities against his growing list of European enemies. By giving Philip the liquidity he needed to hire soldiers, build ships, and buy guns, this lucrative colonial system was providing the essential fuel for his European war machine.

*   *   *

While the Spaniards had to adapt as best they could to the natural obstacles that hindered their treasure fleets, they were also forced to react to man-made ones. By the late 1550s, during a decade of especially frequent and destructive French corsair raids, Spanish authorities clearly recognized the necessity of more security. Whatever may have been the previous negotiations and "understandings" his diplomats had wrested from the French in previous years, these were clearly ineffective. Even with the formal peace after 1559, Philip knew that he must guard against French interlopers who might threaten the economic foundations of his empire. Quite clearly, dealing with this potential threat would have to become, and remain, an urgent priority.

These French attacks, however spectacular and damaging they might occasionally be, were part of a larger and more difficult problem. The French merchants who financed the corsair fleets saw the Spanish colonies in the New World as lucrative markets for their trade, and these same fleets that sometimes attacked shipping and towns also brought the settlers needed trade goods, such as textiles, wines, African slaves, or iron tools. Moreover, the French usually offered these at more competitive prices than those for sale by the licensees of the Casa. Because the high prices and limited selections available by legal trade frequently exasperated Indies colonists, local officials could not always prevent smuggling by foreigners; in fact, they sometimes tacitly encouraged such illegal trade.[52] This was not only because the availability of cheaper trade goods helped to make life more bearable for the often discontented settlers, but it was also because allowing peaceful trade removed the incentive for the corsairs to attack. Most of the time, the profit motive overruled national antagonisms or religious tensions among these French interlopers, who were glad to engage in commerce rather than violence when given the choice.

For the Spanish authorities, the question of trade and navigation in the Indies, especially for French vessels, required significant clarification. The 1544 treaty between France and Spain at Crépy-en-Laonnois, which followed two years of renewed war in Italy, had originally contained a separate article that specifically permitted French ships to trade in New World Spanish possessions. While opposition to such a license by vested interests in Seville prevented ratification of this article, eventually the treaty did contain a clause more generally permitting French commerce in Spanish possessions.[53] This arrangement did not last long, though. A year later, because of increased French corsair strikes, Emperor Charles V demanded that François I formalize a total ban on French ships in Spanish-claimed waters. Not wishing to jeopardize the delicate peace that he needed, François acquiesced to Charles's demand. One result of this was that, since the agreement said nothing about Portuguese areas, French corsairs shifted much of their attention to the South Atlantic, West Africa, and Brazil.[54]

The periodic Franco-Spanish war that had started in 1494 experienced its last and bloodiest phase between 1552 and 1559. This had the unfortunate result that, at almost exactly the same time that the flow of American silver to Europe was rising dramatically, French attacks on Spanish Atlantic shipping intensified.[55] Even though war or peace was not always the crucial factor in whether French interlopers would seize a share of Spain's colonial trade, the renewed outbreak of hostilities had immediate and dramatic results in the New World. During the summer of 1555, Protestant captain Jacques Sores, operating with a royal letter of mark, sacked the port of Havana, committed various atrocities, defiled a church, and killed a number of Spanish subjects. Though he had arrived too late to capture the silver fleets in Havana's harbor, his corsairs held complete control of the town for more than a month before departing. A few weeks after his departure, another French corsair seized the same port with little resistance, complaining later that Sores "had left nothing to pillage."[56]

Had there remained any question, Sores's raid made the Spanish Crown painfully aware of the vulnerability of their colonial possessions. Continuing French attacks after 1555 made certain that they did not forget it. The power of French corsairs had never been greater in the Atlantic than it was during the second half of the decade, as they menaced the shipping lanes along the European coast, lurked around the Canaries and Azores, and extended their reach throughout the Caribbean to the shores of South America.[57] To the Spaniards, the aggressions of French corsairs in the waters around Havana and Florida represented an unacceptable threat to fleets that were already embattled by the elements.

*　*　*

The first five years of Henri II's reign had seen a period of truce with Spain, and the young king's attitude toward the corsairs' activities had begun on a cautious note.[58] Initially he refused to issue letters of mark against the Portuguese, honoring his father's suspension of such a year prior to his death. But once war recommenced with Spain in 1552, the carnage that followed in Italy, on the Rhine, and in the Low Countries was perhaps the most destructive of a war that had already spanned four generations.

For Henri, the independent corsair fleets represented one of his most effective weapons to contest the might of the Hapsburgs. Henri resumed the issuance of letters of mark, once more making the Atlantic a particularly active arena for French strikes against Iberian shipping. In the years between 1552 and 1559 French corsair activity reached new levels in terms of both frequency and effectiveness, and by the beginning of the 1560s, the growth of Protestantism among many members of the Norman and Rochellais seafaring communities added an especially ominous note to these developments.[59]

By the middle of the decade, diplomats from both kingdoms were again trying to find a way to stop the war without either side losing face. In 1556 they had hammered out the details of a document known as the Truce of Vaucelles, designed to interrupt the hostilities while they negotiated a more permanent treaty. During the discussions for this truce, the problem of the French presence in the Spanish-claimed parts of the New World became a major issue. In the Spanish diplomatic position with France, there had long been a distinction between the protection of areas of settlement in America and the Spanish claim to all of the lands awarded them by the Papal Donation of 1493. While officially maintaining that France had no legitimate claim to any parts of the New World—

which was an irreconcilable difference of opinion at that point, since it was flatly denied by the French—the more immediate concern of Spanish negotiators at Vaucelles was that the French not harass and disrupt their commerce in the Indies.

Sores's sack of Havana and the continuing corsair strikes and smuggling had prompted urgency in this matter. Because of their outrage over Sores's raid and other French corsair aggressions, Spanish diplomats forced Admiral Coligny and the other French representatives at Vaucelles to grudgingly surrender to their demands on this point.[60] In its final form, the Vaucelles agreement completely banned French shipping in the Spanish Indies, except in special circumstances, which the Spaniards insisted would help encourage peaceful relations. It stated that "the subjects of the king of France or others by their instigation should not navigate, trade, or engage in commerce in the Indies belonging to [Philip II of Spain] without his express assent and permission."[61] Despite this major French concession, the truce was not officially ratified in Spain, and thus the carefully negotiated outlines it drew were never legally binding for those involved. Even had it been so, it is doubtful how much impact the stipulation banning American trade would have had as a practical matter. The corsair fleets had never been especially concerned with diplomatic considerations, while the French Crown had repeatedly shown itself helpless to enforce its will against their violations of royal commands.

In other words, although the Truce of Vaucelles had led to some overdue official discussions of the issue of French incursions, it blatantly failed to ensure the safety of Spanish commerce in the Indies. Corsair attacks continued in the Caribbean on a regular basis, as they had in previous years. For the most part these took place outside of Crown control; after the truce broke down, even Henri himself became involved in aggressive actions in American waters. In September 1558, he personally initiated an expedition involving the dispatch of 1,200 men to Panama to intercept the silver shipments, with additional plans to plunder Veracruz, Santo Domingo, and Havana.[62] However, at almost the last minute the king canceled his involvement because of the ongoing peace negotiations of Cateau-Cambrésis. A smaller independent force eventually took its place, under the command of the colorful Norman corsair François Le Clerc (more commonly known as *Jambe de Bois*, or, by the Spanish, *Pie de Palo*). In 1560 Le Clerc, whose career was notable for a string of dramatic and costly failures, caused great destruction in Panama while trying to intercept the bullion shipment as it traveled overland toward the Atlantic coast.[63] Other smaller-scale French raids and attacks on ports and ships throughout the Caribbean continued to take their toll on Spanish commerce; the corsairs directed many of these against the returning silver fleet after its departure from Havana. Even prior to 1559, Philip II had personally expressed the fear that French incursions in Florida would threaten his precious shipping lane through the Bahama Channel.[64]

The repercussions of the failed French initiative in Brazil affected the relationship between the two Crowns, as well. The Spaniards had learned of the outpost in Guanabara Bay even earlier than the Portuguese, by 1556, and feared it would be used as a corsair base to interfere with their trade around the Rio de la Plata estuary. In 1559 their diplomats at Cateau-Cambrésis had apparently insisted that Villegagnon's colony in Brazil be recalled because they considered it to be a threat to their shipping. In 1561 Spanish negotiators were worried about French naval preparations involving Coligny and Villegagnon, which they feared were intended to "attack the ships coming from Peru."[65] The French ambassador subsequently assured the Spaniards that Villegagnon had possession of a letter of mark only against the Portuguese (which he never utilized), and this apparently allayed the Spanish fears for the moment. Yet this incident caused Spanish authorities to believe it likely that the French would attempt to reestablish an outpost in South America, which added to the already pervasive mistrust and suspicion.

In such a context it is not difficult to understand why the French and Spaniards found the issue of freedom of French trade to the Indies to be so difficult, and why, ultimately, the formal treaty accepted at Cateau-Cambrésis in the spring of 1559 contained no adequate agreement dealing with it. The French negotiators—who did not include Coligny, who was then a prisoner in the Spanish Netherlands—maintained François I's earlier principles. They asserted the right to claim lands that were first discovered and settled by Frenchmen, and they denied the validity of the Spanish interpretation of Tordesillas that claimed unequivocal Spanish possession of all the lands "donated" to them by that treaty.[66] The Spaniards insisted that the French recognize Tordesillas and, moreover, apparently insisted on the prohibition of any activity they themselves interpreted as contrary to their own interests. This included not only hostile actions by corsairs but any unlicensed trade whatsoever. Ultimately, the 1559 treaty generally permitted merchants from each kingdom to conduct business according to the laws of the land in question, but the negotiators never arrived at anything that specifically defined what rights, if any, that French subjects might enjoy in Spanish-claimed American territories.

With the main part of the treaty completed and accepted by both sides in June 1559, separate negotiations specifically concerning the Indies continued well into 1561. The same problems as before hindered a solution, and the negotiators agreed only upon a broad guiding principle that the French would obey Spanish laws. However, no written agreement—in 1559 or later—ever mentioned specific American territories by name.[67]

By the end of 1561, these negotiations over rights in the New World appeared repetitive and pointless, though it is possible that each side felt that some progress had been made toward a workable understanding. The Spaniards had certainly made clear to the French that they would have no patience with any French illegal activities in their American possessions. On their part, the French had definitely agreed to respect Spanish law, but they had done so without having to specifically renounce all future interests in the Americas. Perhaps most importantly, after 1561 they still refused to consider themselves completely excluded from claims in the New World, as they had always refused to.

The obvious problem was that there was no clear agreement as to where such a zone of limitations began or where it ended, since none of the negotiations connected to Vaucelles or Cateau-Cambrésis had resulted in a written agreement that named specific locations from which French ships were forbidden.[68] The Spaniards, officially at least, continued to maintain that their realm included all of the Americas with the exception of that portion granted to the Portuguese by the Treaty of Tordesillas in 1494. In their view, they had conceded nothing in these negotiations, while winning a promise that French corsairs would stop harassing their ships and settlements.

Yet the French did not feel that such discussions were a total diplomatic defeat, since they had never agreed to completely ban their ships from American waters, nor had they ever agreed to renounce their principle of "effective occupation." While they could have suffered no illusion as to the Spanish point of view, they had escaped without having to formally agree to prohibit further French exploration in the New World.

Perhaps the crux of the issue is what defined the idea of "possession." As historian Patricia Seed has pointed out, each European colonial power in the sixteenth century felt uniquely justified to lay claims to the "New World," and each supported these claims on the basis of different historical, cultural, legal, and even linguistic traditions.[69] Both the

Spanish and Portuguese had vehemently rejected any French claim on the South American continent, and Mexico and the Caribbean were by then "effectively occupied" under the jurisdiction of the viceroy of New Spain, so that it would have been very difficult for the French to justify the presence of their ships in these areas.

In areas to the north, the situation was less clear. In Florida, and points north, there had never been any permanent and successful Spanish settlement, a fact that Coligny and the French Crown may well have chosen to interpret as an absence of a meaningful or effective Spanish claim to territory. After 1561 it was anything but clear where the eastern coast of North America fit into these two opposed concepts of "legitimate colonization." In fact, neither the French nor the Spanish negotiators had much understanding of, or even seemed very interested in, the other's point of view. It seems that they had "agreed to disagree" on the matter, and the results would be tragic.

3

Gaspard de Coligny and the New World

The tumultuous years that followed the unexpected death of Henri II marked a turning point in French history. Precisely when the French people needed decisive leadership, both religious and political developments shattered French unity. Tension and conflict threatened the kingdom from both within and without, as France staggered into a thirty-six-year era of instability. Admiral Gaspard de Coligny emerged as one of the most important individuals of this period, leaving an indelible imprint on its crucial historical developments. It is difficult to appreciate his intentions in the New World without taking into consideration his role in the environment of domestic upheaval then taking place within France.

The Crown's difficulty in maintaining consistent policies during this period stemmed from two particular problems. First, the growth of French Protestantism was posing a severe threat to national unity. Though reformist ideas had reached France as early as the 1520s, a cohesive and unified reformation movement began in earnest only in 1555. In that year, John Calvin began an organized evangelization effort from Geneva, which successfully unified various strains of existing religious nonconformity in France. This movement continued to grow, despite intermittent persecution, until around 1562. By that time, possibly more than 10 percent of the French population had converted to Calvinism, with high concentrations in particular regions and towns including Normandy and the south of France.[1]

This growth of religious divisiveness complicated the other main destabilizing factor in French affairs, which was the competition for political influence among various factions of the French nobility.[2] While King Henri had enjoyed a certain level of success in exerting his authority over antagonistic noble families, his untimely death led to a breakdown of

1. Gaspard de Coligny,
Admiral of France (courtesy
of the Bibliothèque
Nationale, Paris).

whatever delicate balance he had achieved. Ultimately, the combination
of religious dissent and noble factionalism resulted in the first of the
French Wars of Religion, which started in March 1562—only a few weeks
after the first French expedition to Florida had set sail.[3]

To properly understand the French effort in Florida, one must place it
in a context of the developing French domestic crisis in the years leading
up to 1562. The complex forces that affected Coligny's situation give us
some idea of both his intentions and his priorities in the New World.
While there is room to question whether the colonization of Florida was
Coligny's idea in the first place, there can be no doubt that his influence
was the decisive factor in making it a reality. During this critical era, both
court and religious intrigue entangled Admiral Coligny at the center of
events, and he became the de facto leader of the Huguenot party until his
assassination in 1572. A man of undisputed leadership qualities, he had
combined pragmatism and principle to rise into the highest ranks of the
French nobility during Henri's reign.[4] In doing so, he had earned the

respect, if not necessarily the friendship, of the most powerful members of the royal court, including the king himself.

In November 1552, King Henri had appointed Coligny, related to the powerful Montmorency family, as Admiral of France. At this time, the admiralty was a relatively recent institution, and the title of Admiral had not yet assumed the meaning that it currently has, that is, a position as a senior naval commander. Instead, it appears that the primary responsibility of the Admiral of France was the defense of the kingdom's coasts; as such, the office was usually more concerned with land-based operations than maritime ones, and the qualifications evidently did not include personal expertise in maritime affairs.[5] Most of Coligny's prior military experience had been on land, and, in fact, as far as we can determine, Coligny himself never set foot on an oceangoing vessel during his entire lifetime. His appointment was a great honor as well as a great opportunity, springing him into the top ranks of the French nobility and giving him access to the highest levels of power and prestige. During his twenty years of service, his accomplishments were many. In addition to being a trusted advisor to the royal family, he served energetically as an army commander and as a diplomat, and he was instrumental in organizing the ill-fated Brazil colony that bore his name.

One of Coligny's most important tasks in service to his king was acting as the chief French negotiator for the 1556 Truce of Vaucelles, which put a momentary stop to the recurring violence of the Franco-Spanish war. However, shortly after Vaucelles went into effect, while Coligny was recuperating from an illness at his estate outside Paris, the agreement disintegrated, largely due to the ambitions of Coligny's chief rivals, the Guise family of the House of Lorraine, over territories in Italy.[6] The reeruption of hostilities created an immediate crisis for the French, who found themselves in a wide-ranging conflict in numerous theaters of war against new Spanish King Philip II and his allies. During the next three years, military clashes broke out not just in Italy but also on the German frontier and in Flanders. In the north, the French suffered a series of disastrous defeats, most notably at St. Quentin in Picardy in the summer of 1557. In this battle, besieging Spanish troops overwhelmed the French and forced Coligny to surrender the city. Along with many other members of the high French nobility, the admiral was taken prisoner, and he was held in captivity until the spring of 1559. This made it impossible for him to reinforce the outpost he had ordered established in Brazil, which was largely responsible for its demise. His captivity also prevented him from taking part in the negotiations that finally led to the Treaty of Cateau-Cambrésis in the spring of 1559.

Meanwhile, the only significant French victory in this last phase of the war was the 1558 capture of Calais from Spain's English allies, an event that would cost Coligny dearly. For one thing, French control of this strategic Channel port, the last remaining English continental possession after the Hundred Years' War, soon led to significant diplomatic tensions between France and England. This proved to be a particularly unwelcome development for Coligny and other Huguenot leaders, since in coming years it would hinder their ability to procure English aid for their cause. What may have been even worse for the admiral was the fact that his bitter rival, François, the Duke of Guise, had engineered the triumph, and as a result, the duke and his orthodox Catholic faction earned the lion's share of royal favor at court.[7] When Henri unexpectedly died in 1559, the Guise family was positioned to exert a great deal of control over the affairs of young King François II. For Coligny, the result of this power shift was that, after his release from captivity in early 1559, his influence at the French court was minimal during the span of François's eighteen-month reign.

Religion always played a crucial role in sixteenth-century events, and thus it is not surprising to find that it also had a major impact on this Florida project. In sixteenth-century France, as elsewhere in Europe, the religious element was complex, as it was entangled by social, political, and diplomatic developments. After King Henri's death, religious nonconformity among many French nobles hastened the disintegration of the balance of power at court, which became one of the most critical causes of the French Wars of Religion.[8]

Admiral Coligny's experience provides an excellent case in point. He appears to have been considerably more tolerant than most men of his era; from the early part of the 1550s, he had been an outspoken opponent of religious persecution, and by 1555 he had been described as "the glorious initiator of the principle of religious liberty."[9] The admiral's adoption of Calvinism was a gradual and intensely spiritual process that had barely begun by 1555 at the earliest, and as acknowledged by most historians, Coligny did not openly declare his religious sympathies until after his release from captivity in 1559 or 1560.[10] Even then, his tenuous political position made him refrain from criticizing the intensified religious persecutions in France during 1559 and 1560.[11] Thus, it is hardly accurate to say, as some historians have, that Coligny's main motive for settling

Brazil between 1555 and 1560 was to establish a "Huguenot refuge" from religious persecution.[12] A similar motive has also been attributed to the Florida expeditions, a claim that likewise lacks evidence. As we shall see, however, there can be little doubt that the admiral's developing religious sympathies had a tremendous effect upon his standing at the French court, both before and during the reign of King Charles IX, and this in turn had much to say about why and when he decided to send French settlement expeditions to Florida.

As noted, Coligny's political influence immediately after King Henri's death was limited, since his rivals, the Cardinal of Lorraine and the Duke of Guise, exerted great influence upon their son-in-law and Henri's successor, François II. Coligny refused to openly clash with the Catholic Lorraine faction, choosing to accept a less visible and influential role in the setting of royal policy. Instead of reacting militantly against the repressive religious policy of the Crown, the admiral adopted a mediator's role between orthodox forces and more radical Protestants led by Prince Louis of Condé. While doing so, he began to cultivate a relationship of mutual trust and respect with Queen Mother Catherine de Medici, the Italian-born widow of the late King Henri. When Condé's faction attempted to seize the young king in the ill-fated Tumult of Amboise of March 1560, purportedly to protect him from the influence of the Guises, Coligny refused to sanction this action, which bore political fruit for him shortly afterward.[13]

The religious issue continued to divide the most powerful figures in France, and it always remained the most serious obstacle to political unity during this era. In addition to hard-line Catholics and radical Calvinists, there were those, like Catherine and her Chancellor Michel L'Hôpital, who hoped to achieve some sort of doctrinal compromise by incorporating moderate reforms into the French Gallican Church organization.[14] To try to develop a dialogue, Coligny and L'Hôpital proposed that the kingdom's notable persons hold a public discussion. As a result of this initiative, during August 1560, many—but not all—of the realm's leading nobles agreed to hold an assembly at the royal palace at Fontainebleau. On this occasion, Coligny astonished the assembled notables—and guaranteed his return to royal influence—by pleading that public worship be granted to Protestants. According to a contemporary account of the address given by Coligny, the admiral is supposed to have stated to the king and his mother, Catherine: "The greatest desire that we [French Calvinists] have, after the service of God, is to always remain in your obedience and in that of the magistrates empowered on your behalf, in rendering to you all the subjection and all the duties that trusted and loyal subjects owe to their prince."[15]

As Junko Shimizu has remarked, "his speech presented a new concept: that religious dissent and political loyalty could be compatible."[16] The pragmatic and moderate tone of Coligny's address, and his insistence upon political loyalty, won him Catherine's respect and friendship.

Subsequent events further reinforced their relationship and enabled Coligny to attain more influence. In October, the admiral refused to intervene in the imprisonment of Condé, whom royal agents had implicated in yet another conspiracy against the Guises. Coligny's loyalty indicated to Catherine that he refused to be driven by the more politically radical faction of the Huguenot movement, and this helped him to extend his personal influence even further with the queen mother.[17]

In the autumn of 1560, the rapidly declining health of the young king again threatened the political balance within the realm, and the admiral found himself in a unique position to take advantage of it. As it became apparent that François's brother, ten-year-old Charles, would have to take the throne, Coligny refused to allow himself to become embroiled in court intrigue, and instead he wisely remained at his estate at Châtillon. When the king died on December 17, the admiral was able to assume a mediator's position, alongside Catherine, that gave him far more influence on royal policy than he had enjoyed during the previous two years.[18]

By French law, the minor status of the new king, Charles IX, necessitated a regency government, and a meeting of the venerable institution of the Estates-General was called to determine its composition. Traditional practice held that the Estates-General would award the position of Regent to the closest adult relative of a minor king, that is, the "first prince of the blood." In this case, this was Condé's brother, Antoine Bourbon, the king of Navarre, who had recently abandoned the Huguenot cause to establish an alliance with the Guises. However, in large part because of Coligny's plea for unity and toleration, the Estates-General approved Catherine instead of Bourbon as Regent during the summer of 1561, which amounted to a stunning political reversal for the Guises.[19] Quite rapidly, after three years of virtual political impotence, Coligny had become Catherine's most trusted advisor, while she had become his political protector.

During the rest of the year, these two figures struggled to keep the kingdom from splitting apart by staking out the political middle ground, while the religious question continued to polarize the nobility of France into two distinct groups. On one side, the pro-Catholic "Triumvirate" of Constable Montmorency, the Duke of Guise, and Marshal St. André tried to ensure the continuance of the orthodox religious policies of François II and Henri II, while on the other side, the Huguenot party emerged as an opposition faction. The Prince of Condé, who could barely restrain his personal antagonism toward the Guises, led this latter group of nobles, who hoped to achieve a royal recognition of Calvinism and a denunciation of the Guises as traitors to the Crown. In contrast to them, Coligny took a more moderate approach, even as many Huguenots looked to him for leadership. Using his now considerable influence at court, he lobbied for a royal decree of religious toleration within the realm and sought a workable compromise solution, all the while emphasizing the critical need for French national unity.

While Coligny and Condé promoted different solutions to the domestic religious problem, they had similar ideas about foreign policy. Early in the regency period, both were receptive to initiatives offered by Elizabeth Tudor's more Protestant officials, such as Nicholas Throckmorton and William Cecil, who feared a Guise-inspired conspiracy on behalf of Mary Stuart to seize Elizabeth's throne.[20] The "Triumvirate," meanwhile, looked elsewhere for a foreign alliance. The Guise family had opened relations with Spain almost immediately following the death of François II, asserting a common goal of eliminating heresy from their respective realms, which became the focal point of the Bayonne interview four years later.[21]

The Colloquy of Poissy, which finally met after some delay in September 1561, was intended to see if theologians on both the Catholic and Protestant sides might reconcile their differences. Catherine and Coligny hoped that this meeting might ultimately lead to the adoption of needed reforms in the Gallican Catholic Church by finding a middle ground on some of the most contentious issues. However, neither side was willing to compromise at all, and the colloquy quickly devolved into a disagreement over the always irreconcilable issue of transubstantiation.[22] Despite the failure of the theologians present at Poissy to make any progress, during the autumn of 1561 Coligny continued to press his personal influence with Catherine over the less theological and more political issue of religious toleration, desiring to achieve a peaceful arrangement which would allow Calvinists to worship. Meanwhile, Protestant leaders throughout France began to look toward him as their spokesman in trying to impose their agenda into royal policy.[23]

The "Edict of January" proclaimed by the queen regent on the seventeenth of that month was one result of his efforts. Although it fell short of a complete royal recognition of religious freedom, it did, for the first time, grant French Calvinists the legal right to conduct religious services. The edict was intended as a conditional measure and required that Protestants conduct services only in public places, but outside town walls. While Catherine further emphasized that under no circumstances should Protestantism be permitted to jeopardize the interests of France or the Catholic Church, her edict contained the first official acknowledgment of the existence of Calvinism in the realm. While the January Edict certainly did not grant the Protestants what they were seeking, it satisfied the Catholics even less. Catholic nobles, led by the Triumvirate, bitterly resented Catherine's moderation in the matter.[24]

Such were the delicate circumstances that immediately preceded the first French expedition to Florida. Coligny felt pressure from both the orthodox Catholic party and the more radical Huguenots: while one was accusing him of heresy and disloyalty, the other accused him of being too politically ambitious at the expense of his faith. In the meantime, both sides were becoming impatient and skeptical of any possibility of avoiding violence. Coligny, joining Catherine in a plea for national unity, stubbornly maintained his moderate views in an increasingly desperate attempt to avoid civil war.

*   *   *

The Protestant movement reached its apex in France shortly after the death of François II in December 1560. During the next two years Coligny strongly encouraged reform movements throughout the kingdom, especially in Normandy. This is important because most of the participants in the Florida ventures starting in early 1562 were Protestants, primarily from areas within a short distance of the Norman harbors of Le Havre and Dieppe.[25] Thus to understand the respective roles of Coligny and Protestantism in these expeditions, one must consider the growing impact of Calvinism on these Norman maritime communities in the period immediately preceding Ribault's first voyage. While doing so it is instructive to recall the principle that Coligny had enunciated at Fontainebleau: that Calvinism and political loyalty were not incompatible. In fact, one can best understand these Florida missions as an attempt to prove this principle by action.

Frequent commercial relations with Protestant countries had exposed Normandy to reformist ideas more extensively than other parts of France prior to this time. Regular contacts with Geneva, Germany, England, and

Lyon brought Protestant ideas and printed material into Norman ports as early as the 1520s, while the experiences of certain nobles who had served in wars in Germany and Italy provided an additional source of reformist influence. But even in Normandy, Protestant conversions were initially sporadic and lacked unity, and prior to 1557, the number of Norman Protestants was relatively small. Those who embraced the reform were predominantly wealthy merchants involved in international commerce and a few of the educated nobility.[26]

The year 1557 saw the first stirrings of a cohesive Calvinist movement in Normandy with the arrival of the first Calvinist minister in Rouen. However, the Rouen parlement, already active in the repression of heresy, successfully discouraged the spread of Calvinism and other Protestant teachings through legislation and prosecution and began to exert its influence in other parts of Normandy as well.[27]

By the end of the decade the port city of Dieppe had emerged as the leader of the Calvinist movement in Normandy, and during the 1560s it rivaled La Rochelle as the leading outpost of French Protestantism. Yet even in that city there had been only slow progress during the decade of the 1550s. Prior to 1557 Protestantism had little impact on its inhabitants, primarily because of the parlement of Rouen's firm enforcement of religious orthodoxy throughout the province. Although quantitative data attesting to the spread of Calvinism is as scarce for Normandy as for elsewhere in France, local historians have provided us with relevant details of the spread of Genevan-directed Calvinism in Dieppe after 1557.[28]

The first Dieppois Calvinists were textile merchants with connections to England, who, in 1557, began to smuggle Bibles across the Channel in shipments of textiles. News of this development reached Calvin in Geneva, who initiated contact with the wealthy cloth merchant Hélène Bouchard that August by dispatching the bookseller Jean Venable to Dieppe with a "number of Bibles and other books." Venable, under Mme. Bouchard's protection, led the first Calvinist preaching in September of that year.[29] Yet initially he had only ten or twelve followers, and Calvinism remained a clandestine movement for the next couple of years.

The first actual Calvinist ministers arrived in Dieppe in late 1558, in the persons of M. de La Porte, dispatched from Geneva for permanent service as a pastor, and John Knox, accompanying de La Porte while on his way to Scotland. Knox remained in Dieppe for six weeks and had a powerful effect on conversions in the city. In particular, the Scotsman encouraged many urban notables, among them a number of magistrates, to publicly declare their adherence to Calvin's teachings. By April 1559

Calvinism in Dieppe had shed much of its secrecy and in doing so began to attract renewed attention from the Rouen parlement, which began a sporadic series of anti-heresy campaigns that lasted until the end of the first War of Religion.[30]

Coligny, who was a major landowner in Normandy, visited Dieppe in July 1560 and took an active role in the religious developments there, especially through his encouragement of public Protestant worship. His influence helped to spread Calvinism among the less educated sectors of Dieppe's population, including the mariners and laborers. One important result of Coligny's brief visit was that, as one contemporary chronicle recounted, "those who had been previously incorrigible, rude, and given to their base appetites, and notably the mariners, became docile and disciplined, abstaining from blaspheming the name of God, each reinforcing the next one, abhorring the houses of ill-repute, the prostitutes, the fancy attire, and games of cards and dice, detesting the frequenting of taverns; this could never have been accomplished previously, whatever the King had commanded on several occasions, under great punishments."[31]

Coligny promised Norman Calvinists that he would press the issue of legal public worship at the Assembly of Fontainebleau during the following month, and his experiences in Normandy seem to have influenced him greatly in his determination to contest the advocates of religious repression.[32] In the months following Fontainebleau, the municipal leadership of most of the important ports of Normandy, including Le Havre and Honfleur, publicly declared their support for Coligny's pro-toleration policies.[33]

It has been noted that, in Dieppe, the nobility converted to Calvinism later than elsewhere in Normandy, that is, only after 1560.[34] After this point the movement gained wider social appeal, and among Norman maritime towns Dieppe emerged at the forefront of the reform movement. Other ports, notably Harfleur, Le Havre, Fécamp, and Honfleur, began to have appreciable Calvinist sympathies only after 1561, but these towns, like Dieppe, remained strong outposts throughout the Wars of Religion and afterward.[35] Calvinism's penetration in Brittany, meanwhile, was limited to inland areas around Rennes and Nantes as late as 1562, and the faith never took significant hold in the western parts of the province, even among the maritime communities there.[36]

In analyzing the spread of Norman Calvinism, we can identify three distinct stages. Prior to 1557, Protestant influence came mostly from outside France and found the most fertile ground among the higher classes of society. Its manifestations included Lutheran and Swiss teachings as well as Calvinism, and before this time it is inaccurate to speak of a Calvinist movement as such in Normandy.

That would begin during the two years following 1557, when the first Calvinist minister arrived in Rouen. Dieppe became the leader of the movement in Normandy, although Calvinism was still not practiced openly. The appeal of the new religion, moreover, was limited mostly to the wealthy commercial classes, although nobles and workers in other parts of Normandy had begun to embrace the new religion by the end of this period.

The third stage took place between 1559 and 1562, following the arrival of Knox and de La Porte in Dieppe. It was characterized by fairly explosive growth, not only in Dieppe but also in various cities and towns of the province. Calvinism displayed a widening appeal in terms of its social composition, especially because of the influence of Coligny and the emergence of Calvinism as a more unified movement with support throughout France. Increasing repression challenged this growth during the last months of François II's reign at the end of 1560. Yet French Calvinism remained unified and defiant in the face of the opposition, particularly in such strongholds as Dieppe and other ports. The year 1562 was probably the high point in terms of numbers of Norman Calvinists; by the time of the massacres at Vassy, in March, a large majority of the inhabitants of Dieppe had probably converted to Calvinism.[37]

These converts included much of the maritime community, although probably not all of it. Protestant shipowners and ships' officers may have encouraged conversions among Norman sailors during the 1560s, but the success of the movement was far from uniform.[38] Those who relied upon the sea were on the whole less affluent and less literate than urban workers in the province, which presented an obstacle to firsthand examination of the Scriptures. Moreover, the sailing community had a strong tradition of superstition and ritual in their spiritual lives, in large part because of their vulnerability to disasters such as shipwrecks and other acts of God. This factor also presented an impediment to their embrace of the "purified Christianity" of Calvinism.

Still, the continuous exposure of many of these sailors to the Protestantism of England and other parts of northern Europe encouraged conversions. A heavily Calvinist commercial and social leadership began to dominate the affairs of French Atlantic maritime communities—particularly in La Rochelle and Dieppe—and even prior to 1562 Calvinism had become a strong influence upon the common mariners and their families.

An additional and important incentive for them to convert was their resentment of the Iberian powers' claim to the New World, which hindered French commercial and maritime interests. Since the Papal Donation of 1493, Spain and Portugal relied heavily on this religious justification to exclude the French from New World areas. In those parts of France that had a vested interest in American commerce, such as Normandy, conversions to Calvinism may have been strengthened by a reaction against the perceived Roman support for these Spanish and Portuguese claims. This resentment perhaps contributed more to an anti-Catholic sentiment than to a pro-Genevan one, and if so, while it may have increased such individuals' militance, Calvinism's effect on their religious piety remains questionable. One may tentatively conclude that by 1561, while Calvinism was probably widespread among Norman mariners, its spiritual depth remained shallow.[39]

Thus, it would appear that the penetration of Calvinism spread only among the top layers of Norman society prior to 1560. Yet shortly afterward—by the fall of 1561, when Ribault was preparing his first voyage to Florida—many members of Normandy's maritime community had converted. At the same time, some Norman orthodox urban leaders and nobles, often acting on behalf of the Guises, were leading a backlash against "heresy," which further contributed to widespread discontent among the Protestants in the province.[40] By then, Admiral Coligny was an acknowledged leader of the movement both in France as a whole and in Normandy especially, and his ability to energize and encourage participants in the missions to Florida had become considerable. A vast and capable reservoir of Norman Protestants—ranging from mariners and soldiers, such as Ribault, to artisans, such as the carpenter Nicolas Le Challeux—were by then ready to heed his call. As we will see, the growth of Norman Calvinism had a significant impact upon the intent and composition of these missions, and Coligny provided the link between them.

*   *   *

A recurrent feature of the early European interest in the New World was the search for a "passage to the Indies." As late as the early seventeenth century, navigators, explorers, cartographers, and diplomats were still debating the size and shape of the Americas.[41] A look at European cartographic development provides us with some tantalizing clues about the purposes of this mission.

From the time of John Cabot, if not before, European explorers and fishermen of various nationalities had reached the northern parts of the

Americas, including Labrador, Newfoundland, and Nova Scotia. Meanwhile, for more than two decades after Columbus's first transatlantic voyage, Spanish explorers had concentrated their attentions upon the Caribbean littoral and the northern coasts of South America, as, among others, Juan de Solís and then Ferdinand Magellan had coasted the southern continent prior to 1522. After the survivors of Magellan's first circumnavigation reported how difficult it was to find a passage around Cape Horn to reach the Pacific, Spain looked elsewhere for a more reasonable western passage. By 1524 the Spanish Crown had assigned the Portuguese pilot Estevão Gomes to reconnoitre the coast of North America.

Before Gomes, a veteran maritime explorer, could get under way, the French beat him to the punch when the Florentine Giovanni da Verrazzano, in service to François I, sailed along the North American coast in 1524. During this four-month voyage he contributed enormously to European knowledge of the Americas by recording his observations of the extent and direction of the coast of present-day North America.[42] Ironically, while Verrazzano's voyage made a major contribution to European knowledge of the New World, it was one of his misperceptions that may have had the most impact on subsequent developments. While sailing along the Outer Banks of the present-day Carolinas, Verrazzano mistook Pamlico Sound for an arm of the "Great South Sea" reported by Balboa a decade before. Although he was accurate about most of the information that he presented, he unwittingly added confusion to the unknown question of the width of the continent itself, and as a result of his error, a significant number of Europeans began to accept the existence of what became known to cartographers as "the Verrazzanian Sea."

During the sixteenth century, the possible existence of an alternative route to the Indies attracted increasing attention from Europeans of various nationalities. It took decades for Europeans to realize that Verrazzano's description of this coastline was imperfect, while the existence of the so-called Verrazzanian Sea provided much of the stimulus for later French and English searches for a "South Sea Passage" by which they could reach the Pacific.[43] Even the Spaniards, whose geographic awareness had presumably benefited from the Ayllón expedition, as well as the inland explorations of de Soto and Coronado in the late 1530s and 1540s, did not consider such a route to the East as an impossibility. After they had developed harbors on the west coast of Mexico, which diminished their own need for a "western passage," they continued to worry that others might find such a route. In fact, Pedro Menéndez himself had expressed to the king his fear that the French had found precisely such a passage, linking the St. Lawrence with Mexico, in his 1565 memorandum to the king advocating a Spanish presence in Florida.[44]

After midcentury, it was the French and English, who had less solid claims to American territories, who were most interested in finding a trading route to Asia through North America. At that time, European geographic knowledge was only beginning to emerge as a field of inquiry that was based on observation, and theoretical concepts inherited by both the classical world and biblical tradition continued to exert a significant influence upon it. Many Europeans continued to believe in the possible existence of both a "Northwest Passage" and a Verrazzanian Sea, which were often linked together.[45] Verrazzano's conviction that North America featured a narrow isthmus somewhere to the north of Florida exerted a strong influence on many mapmakers, geographical theorists, and cosmographers well into the second half of the century.[46] Later maps often depicted North America as comprising two large mainland areas joined only by a narrow land bridge separating the Atlantic from an arm of the great South Sea, while French mariners from Normandy and Brittany, who frequented the Gulf of St. Lawrence for fishing and trade, continued to popularize this belief in their maps and charts.[47]

According to this geographical concept, the larger mainland areas connected by this narrow isthmus were inevitably given separate labels. Cortes's conquest in the early 1520s had established the Spanish dominion of Nueva España (New Spain), whose Pacific coast had been reached shortly afterward, confirming the longitudinal narrowness of this area. It had long been known that the Gulf Coast of Nueva España swept out to the east, leading to the Florida Peninsula, before heading to the northeast. Yet the explorations launched inland by conquistadores after the 1520s had proved confusing at best. It was not certain, for example, how much territory the Coronado and de Soto expeditions had covered in common, if any. Did the Mississippi River lead to the South Sea? Or was it connected somehow to the St. Lawrence? The answers to such questions were uncertain.[48]

Thus by midcentury, the size, shape, and character of mainland America was still the focus of great disagreement, which would linger for many years. While Magellan's voyage had revealed the size of the earth beyond much question, Europeans also recognized that there was a serious obstacle to a direct route to the East. Whether there was a passage through the continent was one question that explorers would continue to try to answer. Another question concerned the quality of this land and its

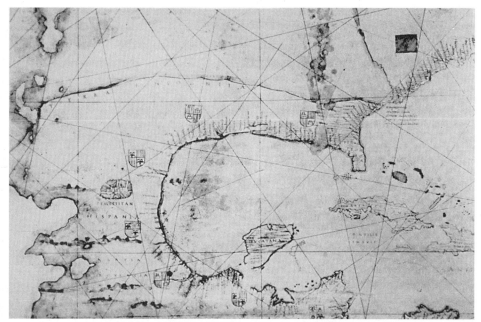

2. Map drawn in 1529 by Gerolamo da Verrazzano (brother of Giovanni da Verrazzano), depicting North America and featuring the mythical "Verrazzanian Sea" (courtesy of the Vatican Library).

inhabitants. Some Europeans viewed North America as merely an obstacle to the East, of dubious value in and of itself, while others, perhaps influenced by Ayllón's description of a "New Andalucia," still hoped to discover promising places for settlement. For others, there remained the hope that North America might contain great civilizations and vast riches awaiting exploitation.

The labels given to sixteenth-century cartographic representations reveal much about the way in which Europeans envisioned America. In claiming newly discovered lands, both French and Spanish discoverers bestowed names upon them, as a means of giving such areas a colonial identity.[49] By midcentury, the labels "Terra Francesca" or "Tierra Francisca," which Verrazzano had first used in honor of François I, began to appear on maps made by not only the French but also those of Italian, Portuguese, and even Spanish cartographers.[50] On such maps, North America's southern extremity, usually located in an approximately correct latitudinal position, was most often labeled as *Terra Florida*. For example, the cosmographer Sebastian Münster, whose various editions of *Cosmographie Universelle* were among the most widely read geographical

3. North America as featured in Guillaume Le Testu's 1556 atlas, dedicated to Admiral Coligny (courtesy of the Bibliothèque Nationale, Paris).

compendiums in Europe, used this label, as well as featuring a pronounced Verrazzanian Sea.[51] Other maps, however, referred to the area as "the land of Ayllón"; among these were most of the maps that the Casa de Contratácion relied upon during the 1550s and 1560s.[52]

Guillaume Le Testu's atlas of 1556, dedicated to Coligny, reflects the disagreement among Europeans about the nature of the New World. This Norman map, widely regarded as one of the most beautiful examples of the European cartographic art, reflects the common European uncertainties of longitude regarding North America, and, like most maps prior to the widespread use of Mercator projection, it distorts the relative sizes of different areas. Both Le Testu's maps and text, though they do not reflect the concept of a "Verrazzanian Sea," do depict Florida as lying immediately adjacent to areas explored by Cartier, which may have influenced the admiral's thinking.[53]

While we cannot be certain about which geographical concepts, if any, the admiral accepted as authoritative, there can be little question that

Verrazzano's error contributed to much confusion about the North American continent. As early as 1509, Sebastian Cabot, Pilot Major of Spain's Casa de Contratácion, had explored the Hudson Strait and theorized that it was an arm of the Pacific.[54] Later in the century, English theorists, including John Dee, advocated the exploitation of this possible route for commercial purposes. The younger Cabot, in the service of the king of England after 1548, almost certainly had an influence on such plans. The resultant English effort to find both a Northwest and Northeast passage to China led to the investment of a great deal of time and money, much of it by the English Crown, from the 1540s onward. These culminated during the last two decades of the sixteenth century with the voyages of Martin Frobisher, and they continued into the next century with Henry Hudson, providing a major stimulus to the expansion of English seapower.[55] Early on in this effort, the English were greatly aided by the cartographic and navigational expertise of Norman mariners, whom they persuaded by various means to contribute their services.[56] It is difficult to accept as simply a coincidence that the leader of the French expedition of 1562, the Norman Protestant Jean Ribault, was among the most notable of these individuals who had served the English Crown in search of a passage to the East.[57]

4

The French Intent

Jean Ribault of Dieppe led the first and third Florida expeditions of 1562 and 1565, later becoming the most celebrated victim of the Spanish massacres of 1565. We can find in his career some clues to this mission's character that are frequently overlooked. Born around 1515 into an established Norman family of minor landowning nobility, Ribault followed the traditional family occupation of seafaring in the English Channel, and he was already a veteran pilot when he began to serve in the fleets of the powerful shipowner Jean d'Ango during the 1530s. For the next dozen or so years Ribault took part in Ango's commercial and predatory expeditions against the Spaniards and Portuguese in the eastern Atlantic.[1]

At some point between 1543 and 1546, Ribault followed the example of a number of previous Norman navigators and cartographers by accepting service to the king of England. Henry VIII, involved in various conflicts as an ally of Spain, recognized the need to dramatically improve his kingdom's weak maritime capacity. One of his most fruitful early strategies to accomplish this was the recruitment of skilled foreigners, many of whom were Normans, to help the English admiralty formulate maritime strategy and train their navigators.[2] Most of these men served England willingly, attracted by considerable monetary rewards, and their ranks included the geographical theorist Jean Rotz, who arrived in England in 1540 and later became English Royal Hydrographer.

In Ribault's case, it is not clear whether his service to England was initially voluntary or not, nor can we be certain of the year it began.[3] Whatever the reasons for his emigration, by April 1546, Lord Lisle, the Admiral of England, had commissioned him as a captain. We can only surmise what effect this appointment had on Ribault's political allegiances, since during 1546 and 1547 he regularly supplied strategic information about naval movements between England and Scotland to the French ambassador in London, Odet de Selve.[4] In 1547 Ambassador de Selve tried to recruit Ribault for the French naval expedition to Scotland in which Nicolas Villegagnon transported Mary Stuart to France. However, the English authorities prevented Ribault from returning to France for this mission, accusing him of espionage and briefly imprisoning him.[5] Despite several attempts by the French ambassador to have him returned to France, Ribault remained in England until 1555. During this stay, in 1552, the Vice Admiral of England named Ribault as one of his assistants.[6]

For much or all of this time, Ribault worked closely on charts and sailing directions under the supervision of Sebastian Cabot.[7] The latter, former Pilot Major of the Casa de Contratácion at Seville, had re-emigrated to England, his place of birth, in 1548 or 1549. The expertise, charts, and equipment that he brought with him contributed to a dramatic upgrading of English maritime capabilities; almost upon arrival, Cabot was working with English theorists on a variety of ambitious plans regarding voyages of commerce and discovery.[8]

Despite the positions of responsibility that Ribault held while in England, there is some question about his political and religious loyalties during this time. For one thing, it is curious that although he took an active role in planning missions, there is no evidence that he ever physically took part in any English-sponsored voyages. Among the projects initiated by Cabot at this time, but never carried out, was a plan to have Ribault lead a northerly voyage past Iceland to seek Cathay. Ribault may additionally have been involved in some capacity in a planned joint Anglo-French expedition up the Amazon River to attack Spanish Peru. While it is true that a number of the plans he helped develop never materialized, it may also be that his English hosts did not regard him as entirely trustworthy, and this might explain Ribault's apparent lack of actual maritime action even after his release from captivity in 1550. The English may have been concerned about Ribault's familiarity with their maritime plans and operations. There can be little question that Cabot's tutelage exposed Ribault to geographic and navigational knowledge that had been previously unavailable outside of Spain, and he must have been among the first non-Spaniards to have access to this wealth of strategic information.[9] This by itself may have given the English authorities good reason to forbid Ribault from returning to France.

Besides the knowledge that Ribault absorbed during his English service, it also appears that he received a strong exposure to one or more varieties of Protestantism, and it is probable that Ribault converted to Calvinism sometime prior to his return to France in August 1555.[10] While we cannot determine precisely how and when he became a Calvinist, some of the individuals that Ribault had associated with in England were early Puritans, and regular interaction with the English maritime community no doubt exposed him to individuals of various religious persuasions, including other Normans.

While his religion could have given him an additional reason to stay in England during the reign of Edward VI, it may also explain why he left England during the reign of Edward's successor, the Catholic Mary Tudor, though the circumstances of his return to France are also somewhat unclear. In 1555 the French ambassador, Antoine de Noailles, finally negotiated the pilot's freedom, perhaps indicating that, once again, Ribault had been held involuntarily, possibly because of his religious affiliation.[11]

Whatever the case, in August of that year Ribault returned to his home port of Dieppe, and Admiral Coligny immediately pressed him into service during the last part of the so-called Fisherman's War against Flemish shipping in the Channel. In this action Ribault commanded a squadron of a reported twenty-eight vessels that chased the Flemings to the coast of Scotland, where he inflicted significant damage upon them before his own fleet was dispersed in a storm.[12] Shortly afterward, Ambassador Noailles wrote that the English considered Ribault to be "one of the best men of the sea in Christendom."[13]

Thereafter Ribault's reputation as a mariner expanded rapidly in France. After the failure of the Truce of Vaucelles in 1557, he battled Spanish and English shipping in the Bay of Biscay and in the English Channel, including taking part in a naval action connected to the siege of St. Quentin, the catastrophic setback that resulted in Coligny's captivity. Later, in the waters near Calais in early 1558, Ribault was responsible for keeping open the French naval supply line and preventing English reinforcements from arriving. In the same battle a Spanish captain named Pedro Menéndez assumed the main responsibility for supplying the English forces and trying to wrest control of the harbor from the French.[14] Considering the ultimate French victory, it would appear that Ribault, on this occasion, was more successful than Menéndez in carrying out his task. Seven and a half years later these two would meet again, but with a rather different result.

During 1559 Coligny employed Ribault to negotiate with the English concerning French interests in Scotland and also to gather intelligence for a planned French invasion in support of Mary of Guise's regency.[15] However, Ribault's involvement in these affairs is highly ambiguous. In a coded exchange of July 1559 between Sir William Cecil and Nicholas Throckmorton, the English ambassador in France, the former wrote that he "would [like to] know when the French ships will set forth; [I] think that John Rybaut would tell, if well used."[16] Throckmorton, in France, replied that he had

appointed [my] servant to understand whether John Ribawde was to be won or not, whom [my] servant met on the way back from Dieppe. Ribawde said he had little reason to tarry at Dieppe, being frequently appointed by the Court to ride to and fro for the dispatching of ships into Scotland. He sent [me] word to beware of one man who resorted to him. Told Barnaby that for the conveying of men into Scotland no ships of war are prepared, but all hoys and coasters, fit only for passengers, and that all the footmen at this time to be sent into Scotland shall take shipping at Calais and Boulogne and thereabouts. He said that within a few days he would come and talk with [me] himself.[17]

Unfortunately, we have no report on whether such a later meeting actually took place between Throckmorton and Ribault. Strangely enough, though, an intercepted dispatch from Ambassador Noailles of France to Catherine de Medici, six months later, mentioned the possibility of assigning Ribault to lead an attack on English ships in English ports. Noailles's discussion with Ribault, who at that time was in England, had left him with the impression that he "appears to be a man of judgment."[18]

Now that their prize navigator and strategist had returned to his French homeland, the English were understandably concerned about the threat that Ribault posed to them. The esteem they held for his abilities during this period is quite evident from diplomatic correspondence. Between April 1557 and March 1560, English dispatches mention Ribault's name on at least thirteen separate occasions.[19] In most cases, these were messages from Throckmorton to William Cecil and other members of the Royal Council.[20] All of these display a preoccupation—almost an obsession—with Ribault's whereabouts and plans, and they reveal the extent of English fears that Ribault himself was preparing to launch invasions of England or Scotland from France.

While there is a possibility that Ribault was a "double agent" in providing information to the English while serving the French Crown at the same time, the evidence is not conclusive. It is uncertain whether the above communication indicates that he ever did actually cooperate with the English in revealing a planned Guise-led French invasion of Scotland. The English feared such aggression at least until 1561, even after the French had withdrawn their troops from Scotland in accordance with the Treaty of Edinburgh in the summer of 1560. Perhaps Ribault only wanted to give his English contacts the impression that he was sympathetic to their cause, in the hope of gaining their trust, but we cannot be sure of this either. On the other hand, perhaps all that this particular diplomatic exchange means is that the English at least considered him a likely candidate to be an informer against his own homeland. Clearly, Ribault was privy to high-level information in France, and there must have been a regular three-way exchange of information between Throckmorton and Coligny, both in France, and Ribault. Ribault was often in England during this period, although we cannot determine with certainty what business brought him there in December of 1559.[21] We can more confidently conclude that, during the period from 1557 to 1561, people in the highest circles of the English government were quite familiar with Ribault and respected his capabilities.

Given this contradictory evidence, one may rightly speculate on the direction of Ribault's loyalty, which may have had an impact on some of his later actions. In 1559 and 1560, while the Guises and their followers were directing the preparations for a Scottish invasion, tension over the enterprise swept through the growing Norman Protestant maritime communities.[22] If one accepts that Ribault had become a Protestant prior to 1559—and there is no reason to think otherwise—one can legitimately doubt the extent of his enthusiasm for a plan designed to bring the Catholic Mary Stuart, the niece of the Guises, to the Scottish throne. Alternatively, one can only accept with difficulty the idea that Ribault would have been capable of betraying his own king by covertly aiding a foreign monarch, even if Elizabeth was (to some extent in 1559) sympathetic to Protestantism. Thus, even if we cannot clearly discern Ribault's loyalties in 1560 and 1561, we can certainly understand the difficulty of his situation and its potential for a conflict of interest.

It is entirely possible that sometime around 1561, Ribault may have requested that he be relieved from his role in the planned invasion of Scotland. Either instead of or in addition to this possibility, Coligny—whose own enthusiasm for the invasion could not have been very great after 1559—may have sensed the danger in employing Ribault in such a sensitive capacity. It may well have occurred to Coligny that it would be better for all concerned if he could find a different assignment for Ribault that would make better use of the latter's extraordinary maritime skills, without wasting them on diplomatic intrigues for which Ribault could have had little enthusiasm. The point is that for whatever designs Coligny may have had on the New World at that point, he certainly had a qualified man available who would be better suited for a different type of service.

On the whole, the scattered evidence we have regarding Ribault in the period between 1543 and 1561 contains occasional gaps that necessitate some interpolation. We cannot precisely determine many of his actions or intentions, especially in regard to his relations with the English. Yet certain aspects of his career are relevant to the Florida initiative. Not only do they provide a strong link with England, but they provide some indications of what he may have been trying to accomplish in America. There is no doubt that Ribault, in addition to being a widely respected sea captain, had also been involved in intelligence gathering and maritime strategy for many years prior to 1561. These activities had enabled him to establish relations with well-placed and influential individuals in both France and England, including Sebastian Cabot, Admiral Coligny, French diplomats in England, and the English ambassador to France; moreover, by 1562 the monarchs of both kingdoms recognized his name. It is also evident that his connections in both realms held him in high regard for his various abilities.

Some significant points relating to Florida proceed from this evidence. First, we can see that Ribault, in his intelligence activities between 1559 and 1561, had a potential conflict of interest between his allegiance to France and his religious convictions. Unless one concludes that his activities were guided primarily by mercenary concerns, Ribault's situation by the end of 1561 must have been an increasingly difficult one. Secondly, however impressive his maritime qualifications may have been, it appears that he owed his high-level connections to his past roles as an informer and advisor in maritime strategy. It had been his diplomatic service, and not his naval exploits, that had gained him a close working relationship with the Admiral of France, who by 1561 was an influential Protestant leader and must have shared Ribault's doubts concerning the propriety of the Scotland project.[23]

Another interesting aspect of Ribault's background is that, despite his long experience at sea, there is no indication that he had ever been across the Atlantic prior to 1562. Cabot's tutelage had exposed him to some of the most intriguing geographical theories of the era, and it would be surprising had he not eagerly welcomed the chance to make a journey to

America. Furthermore, despite his apparent lack of firsthand experience in this part of the world, it is even possible that Ribault himself, or one of the other geographical theorists working with Cabot, had seriously considered an expedition to Florida prior to 1555.

Admiral Coligny, as one of France's most important figures in both domestic and international politics, had abilities and a background that complemented those of Ribault. After the debacle in Brazil, he turned his sights northward, to the last possible remaining area for French American colonization that might be acceptable to the Spaniards. However, in comparison to Coligny's rather uncertain concept of the geography of the New World, Ribault possessed essential experience and knowledge to carry out the admiral's bold plan. The timing of this would have been quite convenient, since Ribault's English intelligence activities were likely creating a personal dilemma for him similar to that of the admiral, in that they were requiring him to engage in pro-Catholic—and anti-Protestant—activities.

Perhaps Coligny first targeted Florida for a strategic initiative, on the basis of the negotiations over Vaucelles and Cateau-Cambrésis, and then presented the idea to Ribault. Alternatively, it may have worked the other way around, with Ribault seeking and gaining Coligny's support for a voyage of exploration, perhaps one designed to seek the elusive Northwest Passage almost two decades prior to Frobisher's voyage. Likely there was some element of initiative by both of these individuals. However, no matter whose idea it was in the first place, the active participation of both men was required to make such a bold plan a reality.

Since Coligny, as Admiral of France, had the final authority over the plans and preparations, we must return to his situation on the eve of Ribault's first voyage. This gives us a strong indication of his priorities and how the plans for Florida may have fit into them. By the end of 1561, as noted, Coligny had asserted his leadership in the emerging Huguenot party and was practicing Calvinism openly. The connection between the January Edict and Ribault's voyage is only indirect; given that the latter required much planning, it must have already been in an advanced stage of preparation by January 17. However, the forces that had led to the edict and those that had motivated the admiral to proceed with the Florida project were similar. As Coligny made preparations for Ribault's first voyage to America, during the fall and early winter, he maintained his insistence that official toleration of Protestantism was the surest means of preventing civil violence, and there is no reason to believe that he changed his view of the matter between January 17 and February 18.[24]

Probably the only direct impact of this edict on the Florida mission was that its recognition of Calvinism made it possible for acknowledged Calvinists to undertake such a mission openly, but this could not have altered the scope of the expedition very much, if at all. It would have been political suicide, under the circumstances, for Coligny to employ Crown resources for the overt benefit of Calvinists alone. There should be little doubt that the admiral's official duties had to bring some tangible benefit to France as a whole or, at the very least, had to appear to do so. All of the evidence strongly indicates that in 1562, the admiral was not interested in sectarian or divisive measures but only in inclusive ones. To an even greater degree than most French nobles of that era, Coligny seldom permitted his actions to veer from service to the kingdom of France, and there is no credible reason to believe that this Florida expedition was an exception.

*   *   *

Perhaps the most perplexing historical problem regarding the French initiative in Florida has to do with the long-term diplomatic situation that surrounded it. The decade of the 1560s marked the beginning of a new era for Protestant Europe. In particular, the accession of a Protestant queen to the throne of England made that nation uncertain, at best, to continue its Spanish alliance. As well, Elizabeth's often difficult-to-discern goals made the future relations between England and France less than clear. If Coligny could bring Elizabeth closer to the side of France than to Spain, he could help to isolate Spain diplomatically, which could have clear benefits for French external security.

Even by 1560 and 1561, the French variable in international relations had become horribly complicated. The developing internal political and religious factionalism had created the imminent danger, soon to be realized, of armed conflict within the kingdom. Coligny, as the more moderate Huguenot leader, was desperately trying to prevent civil war. Using his influence with Catherine to try to achieve official recognition of the Protestants' right to worship, he consistently argued that toleration would strengthen the realm, while persecution would weaken it by leading to reprisals and a recurring cycle of violence. If he could persuade the queen regent that religious repression was contrary to the interests of the Crown and influence public opinion in the same direction, he might also diminish the power of his Guise rivals and their supporters, with their pro-Spanish leanings.

One has a difficult time believing that Coligny intended the Florida initiative as a direct attack on Spain and that he was trying to provoke them into a war in the New World.[25] Simply put, such an act would have made absolutely no sense under the circumstances. In a regency situation, with the nobility feuding among themselves, and the social fabric threatening to unravel over the issue of religious conformity, the last thing that the kingdom of France needed was a reopening of the conflict against powerful Spain. By 1562 King Philip had consolidated his control of Spain and his other territories and had shown that he would respond decisively when provoked, as the French had found out much to their regret during the two years prior to the Cateau-Cambrésis Treaty.[26] Moreover, at that point, Spain was still formally allied to England, and if a renewal of the Franco-Spanish conflict would not necessarily force Elizabeth to take up arms against France, English neutrality would be the best the French could hope for in such an event. While Coligny still had some optimism about bringing about a rapprochement within France, one can hardly deny that he was also a hard-headed realist, and anybody with the least sense of reality would have believed that more warfare with Spain could result only in a catastrophe for France.

A second, and equally important, reason to doubt the extent of the admiral's aggressive intentions is the status of his relationship with Catherine. The queen regent, during 1561 and for several years thereafter, remained firmly committed to maintaining harmony between her own realm and Spain, which she actively promoted through frequent correspondence with her daughter, who had been married to Philip since 1559. It would make little sense to suppose that Coligny, who relied more upon her support than anyone else's for the attainment of his goal of toleration, would have either overtly or covertly taken an action that jeopardized his queen's sensitive and critical relationship with her son-in-law.

Is it possible, then, that Coligny might have thought that making a French claim to Florida would have had no effect whatsoever on the relations between the two kingdoms? This seems just as unlikely. He did explicitly instruct the colonists to be nonconfrontational; even in 1564, Coligny specifically ordered his commander Laudonnière in no uncertain terms "to do no kind of wrong to the King of Spain's Subjects." Even so, we cannot realistically accept that he imagined that the Spanish authorities would remain ignorant of a French base on the Bahama Channel; having personally conducted diplomatic negotiations over the respective rights of France and Spain in the Americas, he knew full well that the Spanish position on the issue was not likely to change.

This presents a dilemma in trying to explain Coligny's motivations, which remains perhaps the single most baffling issue surrounding this initiative. While on the one hand it is unlikely that he wanted to risk renewing the war with Spain, on the other, it is also unlikely that he believed that Philip would ignore a French claim in Florida. For either of these to be possible, we would have to accept either that Coligny was ignorant and foolhardy, or that he believed the Spanish authorities were, and neither of these alternatives seems very likely, either.

However, there is another possible explanation for Coligny's motives that, while somewhat Machiavellian, does seem feasible. Considering the domestic problems then unfolding in France, Coligny may have seen some potential benefit in diplomatic tension or even colonial conflict—as opposed to outright war in Europe—between France and Spain. If he knew that Spain had not renounced its claim to North America, he also undoubtedly knew that the issue had not been permanently resolved to either side's satisfaction. Spanish diplomats might well complain about a French presence in the New World, but Coligny was also aware that Philip would be unable to claim that the French had directly violated any formal agreement. In other words, though he knew that the French had been granted no explicit right to settle in Florida, he was also aware that the French had not renounced such a possibility, either.

In hindsight, we can see where such a situation might benefit both France as a whole and the Huguenots in particular. N. M. Sutherland argues that a "vendetta" between Coligny and the Guises was a major factor in the internal problems of France during the decade of the 1560s, with roots extending back into the previous decade.[27] Although Stuart Carroll has recently argued that the feud did not begin in earnest until the assassination of François, the Duke of Guise, in February 1563, there can be no question that tensions between the two leaders and their factions—on personal, political, and religious levels—already existed well prior to that event. As Carroll himself points out, tensions in Normandy during the previous three years had significantly polarized the mostly Protestant supporters of the admiral and the mostly Catholic supporters of the Guise family.[28] While the view here is that Coligny was probably not as personally vindictive as Sutherland argues, even by 1561 he certainly had many reasons to want to undermine the power of the Guise family, which threatened his own influence and political position.

If Admiral Coligny had wanted to drive a wedge between Catherine and the Guises, a colonial initiative that annoyed the Spaniards—without provoking them into a full-scale European war—seems like the perfect means to accomplish this. For one thing, the Huguenots, who at that point had few Catholic supporters within France, prized the amity of England, whose queen and council they hoped to enlist as allies, considerably more than they desired the friendship of Spain. From the Huguenots' point of view, tension in Franco-Spanish relations might be an advantage for their cause, since it might force Catherine to seek an accord with Elizabeth; ultimately it might increase the diplomatic isolation of Spain from England as well as France.

This would explain why the admiral was as careful as he was to instruct the leaders of these expeditions to avoid Spanish territories or settlements in the New World. Foreseeing the problems that might arise, he probably recognized the clear long-term relative advantage to a less provocative initial strategy vis-à-vis Spain. The reasoning behind this makes a certain amount of sense: a Spanish attack on a French settlement in the New World would hardly be a disaster for the Huguenot cause, since the Spaniards would appear to be the aggressors. As long as such a conflict did not escalate into more European warfare—which the admiral knew both sides wanted to avoid—this would actually benefit the Huguenot situation. This would give them a perfect opportunity to demonstrate to the queen mother that, despite their religious nonconformity, they could serve her and France as loyally as any Catholics could. In the long run, Spanish aggression could distance the ultra-Catholic party in France from the moderate Catholics, strengthen the Huguenots' ties to the Crown, and lessen religious persecution in the kingdom—all of which were Coligny's most evident concerns in the months leading up to the first War of Religion.

Thus it is possible to see this bold initiative as a proactive attempt to ameliorate a deteriorating religious and political situation in France. Ultimately, it was most important to avert religious persecution at home. The best way to do this was to convince the queen regent and public opinion that the Guises' stated intentions—to stamp out French Calvinism, possibly with Spanish help—were contrary to French national interests. To isolate the Guises, ideally by creating the public impression that they were in league with the enemy, would be suitable revenge for the humiliations and loss of influence that Coligny had had to endure over the previous five years.

As a long-term possibility, Florida might indeed provide a safe refuge for persecuted Protestants, depending on what happened in France. This could hardly have been envisioned as an immediate goal, however. For one thing, by the time Ribault set sail, Coligny had by no means given up hope of a peaceful conciliation of religious factions; after all, the Edict of January had been in effect for less than a month. For another thing, surely he must have realized that it would take years to create a viable civilian community in America, considering not only the diplomatic uncertainties but also his experience of the Brazil debacle. It may well have been that there were many Calvinists in 1561 and 1562 who felt persecuted enough to seek a refuge, but how many of these would be willing to cross the ocean to an unknown land is debatable.[29] Even by 1564 and 1565, when England and the Low Countries were becoming less attractive as places of religious asylum, it required much active encouragement to persuade French Protestants to emigrate to America, as Nicolas Le Challeux's account testifies.[30] To prepare a place of refuge for any but an insignificant number of oppressed Protestants was obviously a project that would take many decades. Of the solutions that Coligny may have considered to end the persecution of his coreligionists, wholesale emigration to Florida was not among the most feasible in the early 1560s.

Coligny did have some other legitimate incentives to initiate and/or support this mission. Using his office of Admiral of France, he could promote two important goals that, to his mind, were closely related. A successful colonization of Florida would promote the welfare of France in a number of ways, to the benefit of both the Crown and individuals alike. Meanwhile, he could advance the fortunes of the French Protestants, an equally important goal of his at that time. As consistent with his non-confrontational policies, he could accomplish this without encouraging domestic divisiveness; instead, perhaps he could help the cause of domestic tranquillity by winning the Protestants a measure of respect in France and, with that, toleration and recognition.

None of these outcomes, of course, were certain. If he did anticipate something similar to this scenario, he also was well aware that this enterprise entailed a great deal of risk and was unlikely to escape detection by Spain in the long run, which could provoke a reaction. Yet to do nothing to avert an impending civil war was even more risky.

*   *   *

The admiral himself would have admitted to his almost complete lack of personal experience at sea, and the extent of his knowledge of American geography, or of the extent of the Spanish American empire, is questionable. No doubt he had heard much from French seamen concerning their activities in American waters and the previous attempts to establish settlements in "New France." Yet it is a legitimate question how *Terra Florida* fit into Coligny's geographic conception of America, in its relation to either New France or the Spanish Indies. In light of the failure of the colony in Brazil and the circumstances surrounding the Treaty of Cateau-Cambrésis, the only remaining opening for French American claims was to the north of the tropic of Cancer, that is, above the southernmost tip of Florida. On the basis of the less than definitive diplomatic discussions of the matter in 1559 and 1560, Coligny and Catherine may have believed that Spain had given them a brief window of opportunity to stake a claim north of the Spanish settlements in the Indies. While this window was open, they had to take advantage of it.

We must resist the temptation to ascribe a single goal to this French mission to Florida. The relative importance of different intentions varied over time, and the individuals involved had different agendas. Yet we can identify a number of significant motivations that added together gave this venture extreme importance to Crown and individuals alike. Admiral Coligny himself could hardly have been unaware of the potential benefits, although we can be less certain of how aware he may have been of the potential liabilities.

While there can be no doubt that Florida's geographic location was unrivalled as a launching pad for raids against the Spanish silver fleet, how this affected the admiral's plans is not so clear. Certainly the establishment of a permanent base astride the Bahama Channel would have gotten the attention of the Norman maritime community. Raids on Europe-bound Spanish ships had been a lucrative occupation of French corsairs since the 1550s; for example, Sores had undertaken his 1555 raid on Havana for the specific purpose of intercepting the imperial treasure. Additionally, the cabin boy Guillaume Rouffin's testimony to his Spanish captors indicates that, though not beyond a doubt, many of the participants in the initial voyage of 1562 were interested in pursuing such endeavors. On this basis, it is possible that Coligny felt that the location chosen would help attract participants. However, such a location so near to Spanish territories would have made little sense as a haven for fleeing Protestants.

Despite these circumstances, it still seems doubtful that the admiral intended to sponsor such aggression actively and directly. For one thing, there is no indication that he had ever previously shown much interest in such activities. Despite his close ties to the Norman community prior to

1561, the admiral had had no verifiable participation in any of their activities in the Caribbean region that could be construed as aggressive to Spanish interests. Although such attacks continued regardless of the official state of affairs between France and Spain, the only Crown-supported corsair activity against the Spanish colonies that we know of took place during the admiral's captivity.[31] In addition to the lack of a precedent, by the 1560s he had even less reason to get involved in such activity, since, as mentioned above, he would have had to undermine his own position with the queen mother by jeopardizing relations with Spain. Thus, though it is conceivable that Florida's location along the route of the returning Spanish silver fleet may have helped Coligny attract skilled mariners, and possibly financial support, there is no real reason to believe that he intended to establish a corsair base in Florida, and later events support this conclusion.

Coligny's experience in overseas projects had been limited exclusively to Brazil, with disappointing results. Yet despite (and perhaps even because of) the Treaty of Cateau-Cambrésis, the long-standing French designs on the New World were alive and well as a new decade opened. By the fall of 1560, Coligny had learned of the failure of his first attempt to establish an American settlement. Instead of becoming discouraged, it is likely that he had learned some valuable lessons from the Brazil experience that could be applied to a different sort of venture. An initial voyage would make a careful reconnaissance and stake a formal claim to the area chosen. The timing and nature of a follow-up mission would depend on both the domestic and international situations; it remained to be seen whether royal support would be possible or even advisable. Compared to Brazil, Florida represented a different sort of project, both in terms of what Coligny expected to gain and in the problems that it presented to him.

As to potential benefits, the most obvious was the French Crown's desire to lay a formal claim to a part of the New World. The opportunities that might arise from this were not essentially different from what they had always been during the sixteenth century. The Crown was eager to share in the discovery and exploitation of valuable commodities, especially precious metals, as the Spanish had been doing. This remained the primary attraction of the New World, but there were other factors as well. Some geographic theorists, notably the English, hoped to find a Northwest Passage to open a profitable trading relationship with China or Japan; Ribault himself was involved with such ideas earlier in his career. Finally, the proclamation of an empire of "New France" would enhance the prestige for the French Crown, which was hardly a negligible incentive.[32] None of these benefits were by any means certain, of course, but it would be preferable to find out for oneself than to let Spain take advantage of any remaining unexploited opportunities in America.

Coligny was fully aware that little good would come out of starting a war with Spain, which, as we have seen, cannot realistically have been among his goals. He was most concerned with extending France's influence into the New World, and if this required annoying Philip, so be it. If Spanish forces attacked the settlement, Coligny could portray them as the aggressors in the matter. In such a case, perhaps he might be able to sway French foreign policy in a less pro-Spanish direction, and even this "worst-case" scenario might have some benefits. Obviously, though, he preferred that the Spaniards would not initiate hostilities against a French outpost. If this mission was carried out in a nonconfrontational manner or, even better, without the knowledge of Spanish authorities, perhaps the French might eventually achieve formal recognition of their claim to Florida on the basis of effective settlement.

It must be pointed out that both Ribault and Laudonnière explicitly expressed such motives in their histories of the first mission.[33] While neither of these men had previously been to America, they specifically and repeatedly referred to Florida as part of the territory of New France, and they both made it a point to insist that Verrazzano had originally discovered and claimed the entire coastline for France in 1524. Their accounts may reflect either Coligny's position, or official policy, or both; their perspectives are certainly similar to the argument presented to Spanish diplomats by Catherine after the French defeat.[34] Whether they realized that Verrazzano had begun his northward reconnaissance along the coast of present-day North Carolina is a question we cannot answer; perhaps this is just another indication of the French uncertainty regarding North America's geography and previous explorations. The benefits to be derived from gaining diplomatic acknowledgment of such a claim were of course unknown but were potentially immense.

Instead of creating an obstacle, the irresolution of the colonial problem during and after the Cateau-Cambrésis negotiations may have appeared to Coligny as an opportunity to settle this difficult issue. He may have seen the establishment of a well-defended French settlement on the Bahama Channel as a means of forcing the Spanish Crown back to the negotiating table until both parties had satisfactorily resolved the situation. Realistically, Coligny must have known that Philip was unlikely to acknowledge a French claim upon the entire east coast of North America from Florida to the St. Lawrence. Yet such a claim, based upon the principle of effective occupation, might result in some diplomatic advantage for France. Philip, if presented with a secure French colony in Florida—especially one that threatened his shipping lanes—may have been willing to make some territorial or trade concessions in order to increase the security of Spanish settlements and fleets, instead of choosing to remove the French by force. In other words, Coligny could have believed that a strong presence in Florida would give French negotiators more leverage in diplomatic discussions; even if Philip ultimately forced Catherine to agree to abandon an established settlement, the French might get something in return—a right to trade, or even an acknowledgment of their claim to territories farther north.

Admittedly, we have no way of determining whether the admiral actually had these goals in mind for the Florida expeditions. Yet there is even less indication that he intended to provoke Spain into war, establish a base to raid their silver fleet, or use Florida primarily as some sort of religious refuge, since each of these possibilities seems inconsistent with Coligny's evident priorities in 1561 and 1562. It makes much more sense to conclude that, while this initiative could indeed be described as aggressive, it was diplomatically aggressive and not militarily aggressive. Perhaps Coligny saw this Florida project as an attempt to take advantage of a diplomatic "loophole"—one that may have been closing in light of the failure of negotiations—that could have great potential benefits to France in the long run.

If Coligny did have such hopes, he had to ensure that he could indeed claim "effective occupation," and to do so, he would have to develop the Florida project carefully. First and foremost, he had to try to ensure that Spanish authorities were unaware of a French presence in Florida for as long as possible, or at least until such a settlement was in a position to defend itself; among other things, this would explain why Coligny's direct orders to the leaders of this expedition were to avoid conflict with Spain. If this was indeed the intention, the purpose of Ribault's mission of 1562 becomes clearer. We can regard this first mission as the first stage of a process that would require the completion of a number of additional stages, all of which, hopefully, would be completed by the time that Spain raised any objections about the project. Ideally, of course, the initial Spanish response would be diplomatic, and an armed defense would not be necessary.

The French Crown's desire for an American colony was the most obvious motive for a Florida project, and this seems clear enough. By itself, it probably provided adequate reason to undertake it. Yet the admiral himself, and other organizers and backers of the expedition, may have had another reason. As Admiral of France, there were not many specific initiatives Coligny could undertake that would advance his ultimate goal of promoting religious toleration within the kingdom. This Florida venture could give French Protestants a chance to display their loyalty to the Crown, as an answer to the orthodox forces who were then attacking them as traitors. Numerous navigators and sailors in Normandy and elsewhere on the Atlantic coast, already devoted to Coligny's leadership, had obvious desires for material gain that could be combined with their quest for recognition of their newly found religious affiliations.

As to the respective designs of France and Spain on Florida, it is evident that neither side was willing to acknowledge those of the other, never mind accede to them. Although it is almost inconceivable that Admiral Coligny was ignorant of Spain's past attempts to settle Florida, the recent diplomatic negotiations over France's restrictions from the Indies had given him the impression that France could indeed make a legitimate claim to this area. If possession of Florida was not beyond all possible dispute, at least this territory had been less directly circumscribed than points south of the tropic of Cancer. In a context of the French tradition of exploration, trade, fishing, and attempted colonization in points farther north along the North American coast, the amorphous land of Florida was envisioned as lying in the undefined borderlands between New France and the Spanish Indies. Before making a claim to any part of this territory, Coligny had to first make effective occupation, in order to justify them, and he felt that he had to do this quickly to prevent any possible Spanish "incursions" into the "southern part" of New France. If the French had been aware of the Luna expedition—not mentioned by Ribault or Laudonnière—this may have added urgency to their own mission. If Spain was able to claim and settle Florida first, this would minimize the effect of any future French claims to the Americas.

When these strategic and geographical factors are taken into consideration, it is clear that, for Coligny, there was a great deal more behind this venture than simply the carving out of a religious refuge. Coligny and Ribault—both men of war, and both Protestant—were not motivated by religious idealism. Instead, each saw in the Florida venture a chance to serve the Crown during a period when the meaning of the phrase "service to the Crown" had become increasingly unclear to individuals of their religious persuasions.

*   *   *

In reconstructing the fate of the 1562 expedition, we can rely to a large extent upon the accounts of Jean Ribault and René Goulaine de Laudonnière, which are largely consistent and complementary sources. Neither author appears to have had a significant motive to present less than the truth concerning their experiences. In Ribault's description of the mission, one can discern the elements of an official report as well as an advertisement of Florida's potential for settlement; he is trying to explain his own actions—including the reason for leaving a garrison behind—while also attracting further support for a follow-up venture. Neither concern has apparently provoked Ribault into fabrication or extreme exaggeration, with the possible exception of his insistence on Florida's charms.

René Laudonnière was Ribault's second-in-command on the voyage, and he composed his detailed history of the settlement in part to answer criticism of his actions as the commander of Fort Caroline. A nobleman from Dieppe with some experience in maritime affairs, he may have been a distant relative of Admiral Coligny's.[35] Like Ribault, Laudonnière emphasizes the exploratory and nonconfrontational qualities of this first expedition, and he also expresses, in even more detail, his amazement at the wonders of this strange land. The major difference between his and Ribault's versions is that Laudonnière does not hesitate to criticize the actions of individual members of the expedition. In his stated intention of providing a factual, narrative history of this venture, for the most part he has succeeded.

The narrative chronologies of these two leaders seldom conflict, and neither account contains serious internal inconsistencies. Moreover, a third source of a very different type reinforces the essential accuracy of these first two. Guillaume Rouffin, a fifteen-year-old cabin boy, had been among those left at Charlesfort in 1562. Unlike the other Frenchmen, he remained in the vicinity of Port Royal during the next two years until Spanish soldiers captured him. Once they had thoroughly interrogated Rouffin, they recorded his answers and forwarded them to the governor of Cuba.[36] Since these Spaniards wanted first and foremost to know the details of the planning and history of the French mission to Florida, the result is that we have direct answers to many of the precise questions that we are asking here, at least as far as Rouffin's knowledge permitted. In addition to generally confirming the accuracy of Laudonnière's and Ribault's accounts—which in turn confirm much of Rouffin's information—this last source provides us with certain helpful details that the other two omitted.

Ribault's account begins with the following explanation:

> Whereas in the yeare 1562 it pleased God to move your Grace [Coligny] to choose and appoint us to discover and view a certain long coast of the West Indea, from the head of the land called la Florida, drawing towards the north part until the head of Britons distant from the said head of la Florida 900 leagues, or thereabout, to the end that we might certify you and make true report of the temperature, the fertility, ports, havens, rivers, and generally of all the commodities that might be found and seen in that land, and also to learn what people were there dwelling, which thing [a] long time ago you have desired, being stirred unto by this zeal, that France might one day through new discoveries have knowledge of strange countries, and also thereof to receive (by means of continual traffic) rich and inestimable commodities as other nations have done by taking in hand such far navigations, both to the honor and prowess of their kings and princes, and also to the increase of great profit and use to their commonwealths, countries, and dominions. . . . It seems well that we have been stirred hereunto even of God above, and led to it by the hope and desire you have that a number of brutish people and ignorant of Jesus Christ, may by his grace come to some knowledge of his holy laws and ordinances.[37]

As a declaration of intent, we can certainly recognize a clear combination of purposes, the most important being discovery and the exploitation of "commodities," as well as the spread of Christianity. Following this initial passage, he recounts the previous visitors to the coast of North America, and it is no doubt significant that he mentions not a single Spaniard. While he asserts that John Cabot, Giovanni da Verrazzano, and even Jacques Cartier were the first explorers of Florida, he ignores Gomes, Ayllón, and Ponce de León, among others. One must conclude that Ribault, with his close firsthand knowledge of Spanish geographical ideas, intentionally omitted the contributions of these earlier explorers.

Laudonnière almost certainly first began his histories shortly after his return to France in late 1565 or early 1566, which is apparent from his introduction:

> As within these few days past the French have proved to my great grief, being able by no means possible to withstand the same

[a surprise attack], considering that the elements, men, and all the favors which might be hoped for of a faithful and Christian alliance fought against us, which thing I propose to discover in this present history with so evident truth, that the King's Majesty my sovereign prince shall in part be satisfied of the diligence which I have used in his service, and mine adversaries shall find themselves so discovered in their false reports, that they shall have no place of refuge.[38]

Laudonnière also emphasizes that Florida was part of the area of "New France." According to him, Verrazzano, in service to François I in 1524,

discovered all of the coast that is from the Tropic of Cancer, to wit, from the eight and twentieth unto the fiftieth degree, and farther unto the North. He planted in this country the Ensigns and Arms of the King of France: so that the Spaniards themselves which were there afterwards, have named this country Terra Francesca. . . . the second part of America is called newe Spaine. It extends from the Tropic of Cancer in twenty-three degrees and a half, unto the ninth degree. . . . The third part of America is called Peru, it is very great and extends itself in latitude from the tenth degree unto the three and fiftieth beyond the equator . . . unto the strait of Magellan. . . . In one part of this lande Villegagnon planted right under the Tropic of Capricorn, and he called it France Antarctic, because it draws toward the Pole Antarctic, as our France [that is, "New France"] does towards the Arctic.[39]

In summary, Laudonnière wrote that

New France is almost as great as all our Europe. Howbeit the most known and inhabited part thereof is Florida, whither many Frenchmen have made diverse voyages at sundry times, insomuch that now it is the best known country which is in all this part of New France.[40]

In these introductory passages, Ribault makes the only mention to any religious purpose to this voyage, crediting Coligny with a desire to convert those "ignorant of Jesus Christ." Neither he nor Laudonnière is ever specific about the religious composition of this group, and neither indicates that this was intended to be an explicitly "Protestant" settlement. It is only indirect references later in these accounts that allow us to conclude that if this mission's participants were not entirely Protestant, they were largely so. This makes a great deal of sense under the circumstances. Although almost certainly Coligny would not have wanted to advertise this as a sectarian undertaking, especially in his dealings with the Crown, he probably expected that both the leadership and the personnel for this project would largely come from Norman Protestants. Compared to other regions of France, this community had a strong relationship with the admiral, the necessary maritime expertise, the most to gain, and perhaps even the least to lose. The events as recounted by the participants reinforce this conclusion. Although we can probably accept Rouffin's report that almost all of the Frenchmen were Protestant and that there was a preacher, it is difficult to identify any further Calvinist flavor to this reconnaissance.[41]

The extent of their hostile intention is another good question. Obviously, the vulnerability of their *flotas* as they made their way through the Bahama Channel was a constant Spanish worry in the early 1560s, yet Laudonnière and Ribault emphasize that they had no desire to provoke Spain while carrying out this mission. Not only does their explanation conflict with what Spanish authorities immediately assumed when they finally received solid knowledge of the French presence, but it also is contrary to what Rouffin told his captors. According to the cabin boy, not only were the French familiar with the return route of the silver fleet, but as far as he understood, the intention of this voyage was "to settle on the point and river of St. Helena, and to discover whether it was a good location for going out into the Bahama Channel to capture the fleets from the Indies. This he knows because he has heard it said by everyone and it was common knowledge."[42]

Thus, Rouffin, though he confirms the primarily exploratory nature of the 1562 mission, reveals a more sinister long-term purpose behind this project, directly contradicting what both of the expedition's leaders later wrote. There are a number of possible explanations for this discrepancy. First, though Laudonnière and Ribault may have had somewhat different motivations in composing their accounts, both also had good reason to justify this voyage as a peaceful and legitimate one. Certainly, the admission of a hostile intention would not have helped the situations of either Ribault in 1563 or Laudonnière in the late 1560s. Second, and equally likely, is the difficulty in accepting Rouffin's testimony on this point at face value. For one thing, his captors were specifically trying to force from him a confession of hostile intent, of which they wanted proof. To achieve such an admission, they no doubt placed him under some duress and possibly even tortured him.

While it may be that both of these explanations have some legitimacy, there is also a more likely third possibility—one that helps to explain why this initiative ultimately failed. This is that, even if many of the participants in the expedition were indeed interested in plunder, Rouffin among them, plunder was not necessarily among the goals of the mission's planners. As we will see, a conflict of interest between participants and leaders was one of the fatal weaknesses of this initiative, resulting in insubordination and outright mutiny at Fort Caroline in 1564 and 1565. One sees little reason to believe that Rouffin or many of the other sailors and adventurers who participated were even aware of Coligny's long-term strategy, never mind sympathetic to it. Thus, Rouffin's answer to Spanish interrogation—so unlike Ribault's and Laudonnière's statements of intent—may have been truthful in a sense: it may have been what he and many others had thought and hoped, without being aware of the larger and more important strategic and diplomatic goals.[43] On their part, as we will see, Spanish planners were correct in assuming that plunder would be a likely result, whether or not the French planners intended it. One must wonder, however, why Coligny, Ribault, and Laudonnière took few precautions to prevent such a possibility.

In summary, this first voyage in 1562 had both religious and secular objectives. These included exploring the coast, laying a claim to some stretch of it, and determining the site of a future settlement. If this succeeded, both France as a whole and the Huguenots in particular would reap benefits. While neither Coligny, Laudonnière, nor Ribault could have had illusions that a French presence in Florida would please the Spanish Crown, we have to conclude that they desired this project to be nonconfrontational if at all possible. If it could not be, however, they would be prepared to defend themselves by whatever means necessary.

The perspective in Spain could hardly have been more at odds with the French point of view. Never had Philip, or any of his predecessors, renounced either the Papal Donation or the Treaty of Tordesillas. Nor had they ever altered their insistence, held since the days of Columbus, that Florida was as much a part of their realm as any other. Although they had indeed failed to establish a permanent settlers' colony, they had made the first attempts, which in their view was important. Furthermore, the strategic importance of Florida to the overall welfare of the Spanish empire had never been more apparent. The signing of the Treaty of Cateau-Cambrésis had only minimally affected the actions of predatory French corsairs, who were still attacking fleets that carried ever more valuable cargo. It was completely natural that Philip and his officials should interpret a French establishment astride the Bahama Channel as an aggressive act. That such a clear menace to the welfare of Spain was being carried out by heretical corsairs, under Coligny's direction, could only have confirmed their worst suspicions.

5

Charlesfort

Contemporary writers who described the missions dispatched to Florida by Coligny, including Jean Ribault and René Laudonnière, often referred to the French ships that sailed to Florida as "galleasses" (Sp. *galeazas*). In the sixteenth century, this term was used to refer to a heavy oceangoing ship that had both oars and sails but was most notable for firepower. Typically, galleasses had a carrying capacity of more than a hundred tons during this era, and they carried thirty or more mounted cannon, often of considerable size.[1] In shape, they often resembled galleons, with whom they were sometimes mistaken but which did not have oars. In addition, galleasses were usually vessels of relatively shallow draft, which may be why the French found them appropriate for exploration in unknown waters. Galleasses should not be confused with "galleys," from which both galleasses and galleons evolved during the early sixteenth century. Galleys, though they could be enormous and often possessed sails, were primarily oar-driven and had crews of slaves or convicts to row them. Such ships were rare in the Atlantic, because of the much rougher conditions there compared to the Mediterranean.[2]

It is not impossible that the French ships that made these voyages had no oars at all, and that they might have been more properly called "galleons."[3] For one thing, the accounts dealing with this venture make no references to any of these ships ever being powered by oars, only by sail, and it is virtually certain that there were no galley slaves on board to row them. Additionally, the Spanish commander Pedro Menéndez, who had probably the most extensive maritime experience of anyone associated with these events, referred to the French ships he encountered only as "galleons."[4] In any case, we can be reasonably sure that the French ships that voyaged to Florida were not galleys and that their numbers included some large, heavily armed warships designed for sailing the rough North Atlantic.

The literature surrounding these missions most commonly refers to the vessels involved in explorations, river voyages, and trips to shore as "ship's boats," "barks," or most often, "pinnaces"—all of these terms being used seemingly interchangeably and sometimes referring to the same ships. These latter vessels, all of which were significantly smaller than galleasses, varied in size and style. Barks and pinnaces most often had sails but were also usually powered by oars. The presence of these smaller ships on the different French expeditions to Florida probably explains the occasional contradictions of how many ships composed each fleet, since pinnaces and barks may not have been counted, even if they had separate crews and sailed under their own power, as opposed to ship's boats, which were towed.

On February 18, 1562, Ribault and Laudonnière led two French royal ships, described as galleasses, out of the Norman port of Le Havre and headed them southwest along the English Channel. Laudonnière reported that these ships were "well furnished with Gentlemen (of whose number I myself was one) and with old soldiers, that he [Ribault] had means to achieve some notable thing and worthy of eternal memory."[5]

Rouffin is an invaluable source regarding this mission, especially since both of the published sources neglect important details about the nature of these ships and who was on board. Rouffin told his interrogators that the two French ships were galleasses of 160 and 60 tons, respectively. According to Rouffin, the larger vessel carried twenty-five sailors and seventy-five soldiers; the second ship carried a total of fifty men and twenty-five *arquebuses,* the latter possibly corresponding to the number of soldiers.[6] Probably "the Gentlemen" referred to by both Laudonnière and Ribault were military officers. Assuming that Rouffin's details were truthful, we can conclude that this heavily armed undertaking was prepared to defend itself if attacked, but there is little indication from anyone besides Rouffin that an offensive strike was among its objectives.

Rouffin's report also included the interesting information that the voyage was "sent out at the command and expense of the Queen Mother of France, the Admiral, and Monsieur de Vendôme, and that each gave one thousand ducats to equip the expedition."[7] He added that Ribault employed two Spanish pilots from Seville and that almost all of the Frenchmen were *Luteranos,* including one preacher "of the doctrine of Luther."[8] Nicolas Barré, a man of considerable American experience,

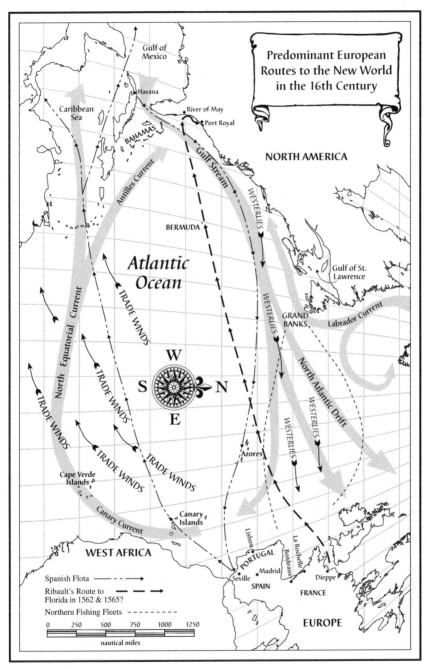

Predominant European
Routes to the New World
in the 16th Century

Gulf of
Mexico

Havana

Caribbean
Sea

River of May

Port Royal

BAHAMAS

Antilles Current

Gulf Stream

NORTH AMERICA

WESTERLIES

BERMUDA

Atlantic
Ocean

WESTERLIES

Gulf of St.
Lawrence

North Equatorial Current

TRADE WINDS

GRAND
BANKS

Labrador Current

WESTERLIES

TRADE WINDS

W

S

N

North Atlantic Drift

TRADE WINDS

E

WESTERLIES

WESTERLIES

TRADE WINDS

TRADE WINDS

Azores

Cape Verde
Islands

TRADE WINDS

Canary
Islands

Canary Current

Lisbon

La Rochelle

Bordeaux

WEST AFRICA

PORTUGAL

Madrid

Seville

Dieppe

SPAIN

FRANCE

Spanish Flota

Ribault's Route to
Florida in 1562 & 1565?

Northern Fishing Fleets

EUROPE

0   250   500   750   1000   1250

nautical miles

Map prepared by Topaz Maps, Inc.

who had been Villegagnon's lieutenant in Brazil, also sailed with this mission.

According to Ribault, his ships initially encountered unfavorable winds, forcing them into a harborage at Brest. After a brief refitting, Ribault "determined with all diligence to prove a new course which has not been yet attempted, traversing the seas of the ocean 1800 leagues at the least which indeed is the true and short course that hereafter must be kept."[9]

To put this voyage in perspective, a slight digression is in order. The Norman ports lie at roughly the same latitude as the St. Lawrence basin, at approximately 50° N. In comparison, Long Island is at 40° N and Florida, Ribault's destination, at 30° N. As Ribault noted, such a direct crossing of the North Atlantic had not been attempted prior to this time, because of the circular flow of prevailing currents and winds. Even by the mid-sixteenth century, only two routes were principally employed by European mariners, which reflected the common European conception of two quite different American zones.[10]

The first of these zones was the northern region, referred to by the French as "Land of the Bretons" but frequented by ships from many parts of Europe. This area was considered useful mostly for commercial fishing and whaling and occasionally for limited trade with the Indians. To sail to this part of America, European fleets relied upon the variable winds to the north of the Gulf Stream, initially sailing toward the northwest before altering course to approach their destinations from the northeast, with the aid of the south-flowing Labrador Current west of Greenland. Although the conditions encountered while traveling to these lands could be unpredictable, from Europe's west coast the total distance to the St. Lawrence was considerably shorter than it was to the Caribbean, and sailors could accomplish the return journey relatively quickly and directly by employing the more consistent tailwinds and Gulf Stream currents to be found in the latitudes between 40° and 50°. To reach the Caribbean from the St. Lawrence region, however, was very difficult, since it necessitated sailing directly against the Gulf Stream that flowed northward along the east coast of North America. Approaching Florida from the north along the east coast of North America could never have been a serious option for Ribault; it would have required constant tacking to fight headwinds, as he followed a largely uncharted coast that contained unknown hazards.

To sail to the Spanish Indies or points farther south, areas deemed more suitable for European habitation, sixteenth-century European sail-

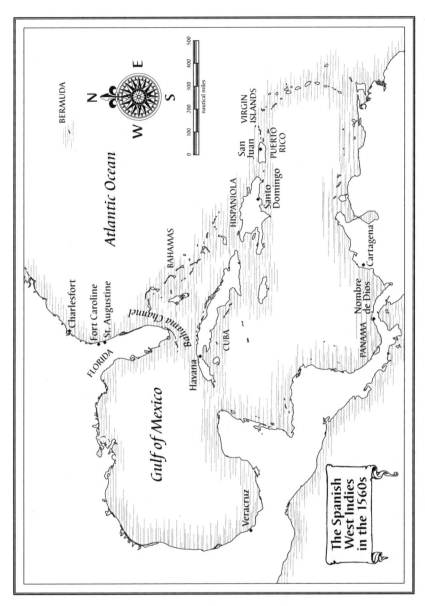

The Spanish
West Indies
in the 1560s

Map prepared by Topaz Maps, Inc.

ors normally relied upon the circular flow of the trade winds. To reach America, both French corsairs and the Iberian powers traveled a busy "ocean highway." As Columbus had proven in 1492, one enjoyed an easterly tailwind from the Canary Islands, which lie at 27°. Thus fleets from Europe invariably set out toward the south, usually calling at the Canaries to resupply before continuing due west. Their return journey from America used the backing westerly trade winds that begin to appear in the latitude of Bermuda, around 33°, and to reach them it required an initial detour north from the Caribbean through the Bahama Channel. Even the Portuguese fleets returning from Brazil and Africa detoured to the north to return home, calling at the Azores (38°) to resupply.

In 1562 Ribault pioneered an entirely new route. We can gather from his narrative that he sailed a slightly diagonal path across the Atlantic on a west-southwest heading, descending from about 45° N to approximately 30° N by the time he touched at Florida. He must have sailed well north of the Canaries, probably by around a thousand miles, and quite possibly he even passed north of the Azores. This route initially put him north of the outgoing trade wind lanes and probably required him, in mid-Atlantic, to cut across the middle of the circular flow of currents. Traditional maritime wisdom held that this was dangerous, since it entailed an unacceptable risk of being becalmed. It is in light of this that Ribault's accomplishment can best be appreciated. Although he had no previous experience in American waters, he had rejected traditional practice and, astonishingly, succeeded in making the crossing in ten weeks even with relatively slow ships. Despite strong contrary winds from the west at the beginning of the voyage, Ribault's perseverance was rewarded by what he termed a "metelye favorable wynde" that enabled him to improvise and strike out to the west.

To make his route even more treacherous, he planned to land in a part of America whose coast and islands were largely uncharted:

> Therefore was it commonly said both in France and in Spain and also among us that it was impossible to come and safely arrive thither where the Lord did conduct us, all which proceeded but of ignorance and lack of attempting that which we have not been afraid to give the adventure to prove, albeit that in all marine charts, they set forth the coast with shipwrecks, without ports or rivers, which we have found otherwise as it follows. . . . Men might not pass nor go in this navigation without the sight and touching of the Antilles and Lucayes [Bahamas] and there to sojourn and take fresh

water and other necessaries . . . foreseeing also that it was not expedient for us to pass through their islands, as well to shun many inconveniences that happen in passing that ways, whereof there spring innumerable quarrels, pleadings, confusion and breach of all worthy enterprises and goodly navigations, with infinite complaints between the king and his friends and allies and also to the end that they [the Spaniards] might understand that in time to come . . . we would not have to do with their islands and other lands, which for that they first discovered them, they keep with much jealousy, trusting that if God will suffer the King, through your persuasion, to cause some parts of this incomparable country to be peopled with such a number of his poorer subjects as you shall think good, there never happened in the memory of man so great good and commodity to France as this.[11]

The clearly stated advantage of such a route was that Ribault could avoid any potential problems in Spanish territories. It did not require calling at either the Canary Islands or the Spanish Indies for supplies, which minimized the likelihood of conflicts, diplomatic or otherwise, that often occurred when French ships called at Spanish American ports. The route taken, which Ribault clearly intended be taken thereafter, could help to accomplish settlement without provocation, while his account emphasizes that he had no intention at that time of trying to challenge or otherwise provoke Spain. Additionally, and perhaps of even more importance, it might enable the French to approach Florida without detection by Spanish authorities.

We cannot know with certainty where or when Ribault came up with such an initiative. His written account appears to indicate that he chose this route spontaneously, given, at least momentarily, favorable winds to attempt it. Alternatively, it may have been an idea that he had developed long before while working with Sebastian Cabot. In any case, whether by luck or by skill, by design or by impulse, Ribault succeeded spectacularly, and his own satisfaction is hard to conceal: no longer would the French have to trespass in Spanish waters in order to reach the part of New France named Florida.

On April 30 the ships made a landfall at twenty-nine and a half degrees, according to Ribault's estimate, that is, just south of present-day St. Augustine.[12] From there the ships proceeded north until they arrived at a great river, where a shore party was met by the local inhabitants, members of a faction of the sizable Indian nation known as the Timucuans, who dominated in the northern part of the Florida peninsula.[13] As Ribault reported, "the next day in the morning we returned to land again, accompanied with the captains, gentlemen, soldiers and others of our small troop, carrying with us a pillar or column of hard stone, our king's arms graven therein, to plant and set at the entry of the port in some high place where it might be easily seen."[14]

They did this for the purpose of establishing a formal claim to the territory, on the banks of what they named the River May, since it was May 1. As well, the French and Timucuans exchanged goods, with the hungry French receiving vast quantities of fish, corn, and berries, the staple foods of the Timucuans. Ribault inquired specifically about the location of a place known as "Sevola," "whereof some have written not to be far from thence, and to be situated within the land and toward the south sea," adding that he understood that this place possessed "great abundance of gold and silver, precious stones and other great riches."[15]

From there, the expedition headed north to explore further along the coast, both on ships' boats and on foot. They came in contact with other small groups of Indians, probably other Timucuans, with whom they traded various items in exchange for food and made further inquiries about the land and its resources. After asking why many of the Indians were wearing silver and copper jewelry, Ribault was made to understand that certain villages five or six days north of the River May possessed great reserves of copper.[16]

By May 17 they had reached and named Port Royal Sound, an area which possessed a good harbor at the confluence of what they believed to be two great rivers. At this point, the local Indians, members of an indeterminate group or groups, received them warmly. Five days later, the Frenchmen placed another engraved column upon the coast, near what they named the Libourne River, establishing the northern extent of their exploration.[17] What he learned about this area, from observation and from its inhabitants, convinced Ribault that he had located "the land of Chicore, whereof some have written, and which many have gone about to find, for the great riches they perceived by some Indians to be found there."[18] The land of Florida had already greatly impressed both Ribault and Laudonnière, and they recounted its positive aspects in superlatives. The inhabitants, the weather, the plants and animals, and the great beauty of the land all gave them reason for comment.

This initial positive reaction of the Frenchmen to the land of Florida appears to have been unanimous.[19] Certainly Ribault and Laudonnière show little hesitation in their praise, and this enthusiasm seems to have made Ribault decide to leave a small garrison behind. Ribault's own report indicates that perhaps he took this step on his own initiative, not because it was part of the original instructions given him. As he felt necessary to explain to Admiral Coligny, "Wherefore (my lord) trusting you will not think it amiss, considering the great good and commodities that may be brought thence unto France, if we leave a number of men there that may fortify and so provide themselves of things necessary, for in all new discoveries it is the chief and best thing that may be done at the beginning, to fortify and people the country which is the true and chief possession."[20]

Laudonnière's account also supports the conclusion that the establishment of a garrison was Ribault's idea. He recounted that: "Captaine Ribault therefore knowing the singular fairness of this river, desired by all means to encourage some of his men to dwell there, well foreseeing that this thing might be of great importance for the King's service, and the relief of the Common wealth of France."[21]

Laudonnière further describes how a speech made by Ribault persuaded many to stay: "He had scarcely ended his Oration, but the greater part of our soldiers replied: that a greater pleasure could never betide them, perceiving well the acceptable service which by this means they should do unto their prince: besides that this thing should be for the increase of their honors."[22] As a result, twenty-six individuals were left behind, apparently in complete confidence that they would be safe, secure, and even prosperous while awaiting further supplies from France.[23]

There is a similar pattern between this initiative and the previous American outpost established in Brazil, where the first stage in the process was a reconnaissance and exploration to find a suitable location for a settlement. The evidence indicates that Ribault's 1562 mission paralleled that undertaken by Guillaume Le Testu in 1551 and 1552, who explored and mapped the coast of Brazil under royal command.[24] Le Testu's mission, intended to select a likely site or sites for future settlement, was followed three years later by Villegagnon's expedition of construction and settlement, which more closely corresponds to the 1564 expedition of Laudonnière. In both cases, the follow-up mission saw a group of soldiers and civilians, supplemented by a detachment of prisoners, assuming responsibility for fortress construction. In both cases, moreover, there appear to have been a number of purposes behind the creation of these outposts, including some expectation of hostilities.

Ribault led the ships back to France, departing on June 11. He noted in his account that they were all aware of the hazards of the season, which probably explains why he and the main part of his company remained at Port Royal for less than a month. As Ribault concludes in his account, it was necessary to depart at that time since "your grace should with diligence be advertised of that which we had done and discovered, which is of great consequence, we concluded through the help of God to return into France to make relation unto you of the effect of our navigation. Praying to God that it may please him to keep you in long health and prosperity and give unto you the grace to cause this fair discovery of this Newe France to be continued and diligently followed."[25]

On the return voyage, the French ships sailed as far north as 40° latitude—beyond the Chesapeake—before striking out to the east toward France. This part of the navigation was no innovation; the ships returned more or less by the usual route taken by the Spanish *flotas*.

* * *

For the fate of the Charlesfort garrison, we must rely primarily on Laudonnière. The very last section of his *1562* is the only source that describes the horrific return of most of these individuals to Europe. Even though he must have compiled it on the basis of others' testimony, there is no obvious reason to question his accuracy or integrity.[26] On the whole, with the exception of just a few points, most of them minor, we have little difficulty in reconstructing a general outline of the history of this initial settlement.

The twenty-six individuals left at Charlesfort used local timber to construct a small fort, which they christened Charlesfort, in a location that gave them both protection and access to the harbor.[27] After doing this, the group waited anxiously for fourteen months for Ribault to return with reinforcements and supplies. During this time innumerable problems beset the small garrison. Initial relations with the Indians had been positive, but they soon deteriorated; the French reliance upon them for food, and French involvement in intertribal conflicts, eventually created resentment. A fire that destroyed their stockpiled food forced the Frenchmen to further impose upon their putative "hosts," jeopardizing both their safety and their ability to procure additional supplies. However, the worst problem, according to Laudonnière, was the harsh command of the individual Ribault had appointed as commander, a certain Captain Albert. His execution of one of the soldiers and his banishment of another for a minor offense caused the men to mutiny against him, leading to Albert's execution. In his place, the men elected as their new leader the pilot Nicolas Barré, "a man worthy of commendation," apparently by unanimous consent.

Barré recognized the difficulty of their position, and his first order of business was ordering the construction of a boat in which the remaining men could depart. Using locally available materials, they built an open boat with help from the Indians, who, understandably, were only too glad to see their guests leave. Even though "there was not a man among them with any skill" in shipbuilding, the Frenchmen used pine for lumber, moss for caulking, and their own shirts for sails, while gathering or bartering for what little food they could.[28] Abandoning the hope of resupply, which was well overdue, they set sail in August on what would be a gruesome return voyage to Europe. As Laudonnière recounted, "being drunken with too excellent joy, which they had conceived for their returning to France, or rather deprived of all foresight and consideration, without regarding the inconstancy of the winds, which change in a moment, they put themselves to sea, and with so slender victuals, that the end of their enterprise became unlucky and unfortunate."[29]

*   *   *

In conducting this reconnaissance, Ribault, as the captain of the fleet, had completed his given assignment. He had reconnoitred a sizable stretch of coast, north of the zone specifically prohibited by the Vaucelles negotiations, while making careful observations and establishing positive initial relations with the Indians. To mark the northern and southern extremities of his exploration, he had planted two columns, one at the River May and the other at the Libourne, laying formal French claim to approximately two hundred miles of North American shoreline.

He had also established a new route to Florida, one that had immense potential advantage for the French. He had demonstrated that it was no longer necessary for the French to call at Spanish ports along the way, risking controversy about their presence. Spanish diplomats had long insisted, with little success, that French navigators stay away from "their Indies"; now Ribault had shown that it was actually logistically possible to do so. The French could come and go to Florida as they pleased, with the Spanish authorities, hopefully, none the wiser as to their movements or intentions.

Finally, in what may have been a moment of impulse, Ribault had left behind a small garrison, perhaps to further legitimize the French claim to Florida and to prepare for the arrival of a larger settlement mission. Having been overwhelmed by the apparently entirely positive aspects of the land he had explored, he left his men behind in full confidence that they would prosper while he and Laudonnière prepared the second expedition. Clearly, Ribault had not foreseen the outbreak of war in France, and he would regret his decision to leave men in Florida. This would be only the first of a series of questionable decisions that Ribault would make that together would severely jeopardize whatever hope of success this venture enjoyed.

In mid-June 1562 Ribault sailed back to Normandy triumphantly, eager to report his discovery of the "marvelous pleasant" land that he had explored and claimed for his king. Having promised those he had left behind that he would return with more colonists and supplies, he looked forward to reporting his success to the admiral.

The situation he found upon his arrival demolished any such optimistic plans. By the summer of 1562, a bloody civil war—the first War of Religion—was tearing France apart. Moreover, Normandy was one of the prime areas of conflict, while Coligny had emerged as a leader of the Protestant faction against the French Crown.[30] Fortunately for Ribault and Laudonnière, they arrived at the port of strongly Protestant Dieppe, which had not yet been attacked by royalist forces. They landed on July 20, after a return voyage of a mere five weeks.[31] An English observer noted the following day that "the captain Jehan Rybaute is coming to Dieppe from his voyage, who has found a new land called anciently La Floryda, which he says was never mentioned before. . . . The Captain left thirty Frenchmen there in a fort that he made."[32]

Under the circumstances, it was impossible for Ribault to act upon his discovery, since his most pressing immediate concern had to have been his own safety. Still, he also must have realized that the men he had left behind would be in serious peril if they did not receive reinforcement within a reasonable amount of time. In this context we can understand both his need to explain his actions to Coligny, and also why he felt it necessary to seek English support for a return voyage to Florida, which were the evident motives behind the account he wrote. He did not feel it would be possible for him to wait an indeterminate period for an opportunity to reinforce his lonely American outpost.

The precipitating cause of the outbreak of civil war had been the Vassy massacre of March 1562, which had occurred shortly after Ribault had set sail for Florida. Over the next year, insurrections against royal authority in Norman maritime communities, including Dieppe, alternated between open warfare and smoldering resentment. The Duke of Aumale,

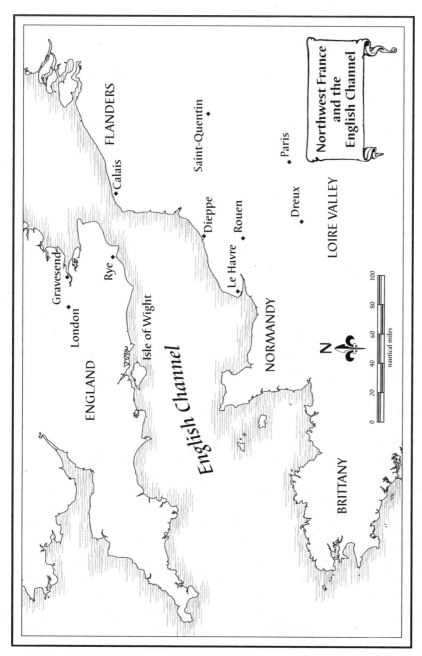

Northwest France and the English Channel

FLANDERS

Saint-Quentin

Paris

Calais

Dieppe

Rouen

Dreux

LOIRE VALLEY

Le Havre

Gravesend

Rye

London

Isle of Wight

ENGLAND

English Channel

NORMANDY

N

nautical miles

0   20   40   60   80   100

BRITTANY

Map prepared by Topaz Maps, Inc.

the brother of the Duke of Guise, besieged Rouen, and his royalist/ Catholic forces quickly seized a military advantage in most of the province, except for a few of the Protestant northern ports, including Dieppe and Le Havre.

In the first few months of the war, things went badly for the Huguenots. Coligny and the Prince of Condé, their two main leaders, found their armies outnumbered and underprepared, and they could not effectively prevent the march of royalist forces through the Loire Valley and into Normandy to recover control of the towns that had revolted. Needing an ally, they appealed to the English for help and found a sympathetic ear: Queen Elizabeth was still stung by the blow to English pride caused by the loss of Calais, captured by the Duke of Guise four years earlier. Influenced by Ambassador Throckmorton, she was persuaded to use the perilous situation of the Huguenots to get Calais back, and she responded to Coligny's impassioned and desperate appeal.[33] On August 18 an English fleet led by Admiral William Woodhouse sailed into Dieppe's deep harbor, intending to contest a planned royalist naval blockade. Jean Ribault was among those who personally welcomed Woodhouse's arrival.[34]

The result of this Huguenot diplomatic initiative was the controversial Treaty of Hampton Court on September 20, 1562. This agreement linked English assistance to the Huguenots with the earlier Treaty of Cateau-Cambrésis. The latter agreement had promised the return of Calais to the English by 1567 unless they acquired other territories in France in the meantime. In the summer of 1562, the Huguenots were in no position to barter. Coligny offered to permit the English to occupy Le Havre—which was still in Protestant hands—in return for direct military support. The terms of the final draft of the Hampton Court agreement stipulated that Le Havre could be held by the English as security until 1567 or sooner, whenever the French Crown returned Calais to the English. Elizabeth apparently was unconcerned whether or not Coligny had the formal authority to make such a deal.[35]

By mid-October, more than three thousand English troops had landed in Dieppe; from there, they intended to join Huguenot forces in the relief of Rouen. However, before the combined forces had a chance to march south, Aumale's forces quickly moved to Dieppe and laid siege, trapping most of the English troops inside the city walls. Within a few days the royalists had tightly encircled Dieppe, and their artillery began to blast gaping holes in the city's defenses. Their situation clearly unwinnable, the besieged English and Huguenot troops were forced to submit on October 30, as Ribault played a role in the discussions over the surrender.[36] Negotiating from a position of strength, the victorious Aumale refused the Dieppois request for freedom of worship in the city, though he offered the English troops a chance to return peacefully across the Channel before his troops marched into the city. As most of the English departed, they were joined by several notable French Protestants, including Ribault.[37]

However, this still left as many as eight thousand English troops in France, mostly in Normandy. After the fall of Rouen, they fled to the relative safety of Le Havre, which they still held. There the English reorganized their defenses, gaining a respite as royalist efforts were redirected against the Huguenot armies that Condé and Coligny commanded in the Loire Valley. In November, Coligny left the vicinity of Orléans for the first time since April, directing a Huguenot march toward Paris.[38] A larger royalist army intercepted his forces, and the resultant Huguenot defeat at Dreux the next month led eventually to the Peace of Amboise on March 19, 1563, which ended the first War of Religion.

Catherine had been enraged when she had learned of the Treaty of Hampton Court, with its stipulation that the English could hold Le Havre as an insurance against the return of Calais. Her anger at both the Huguenots and the English was evident even by November 10, in the wake of the capture of Dieppe, when she demanded that Elizabeth "deliver up those rebels who have taken refuge in England."[39] This marked an important turning point for Catherine's sympathies; because of this perceived Huguenot treachery, she would never be able to fully trust them again.[40]

Jean Ribault was among these "rebels" whose return Catherine demanded. While he had been in France, it is unlikely that he had ever had the chance to meet personally with Coligny to discuss the matter of Charlesfort. While Ribault had been occupied with the defense of Dieppe, Coligny had been in the Loire Valley until after Ribault had departed for England. While it is certainly possible, even likely, that these two had communicated in some way since Ribault's return in July, a French relief mission to Florida had become a relatively minor consideration, and even had either or both of them wanted to do something it would have been impossible. During the summer and early fall of 1562, most Norman ports were being menaced by the forces of one side or the other, and the Protestant maritime community was literally fighting for its survival. In these difficult circumstances, Ribault took a crucial step that—unintentionally—would change the direction of the Florida project. He chose to seek English help in resupplying Charlesfort, another decision that would have disastrous consequences.

Ribault landed at Rye on November 2 and headed directly to London to try to get the English court interested in exploiting Florida's possibilities.[41] Shortly thereafter, he managed to join up with a near-bankrupt adventurer named Thomas Stucley, a Catholic who had served King Henri II of France during the previous decade.[42] Ribault apparently had little trouble persuading Stucley that Florida was a land of promising opportunities. The latter, who was eager to repay numerous creditors, then used his personal connections with Sir Robert Dudley to gain support from the queen. As the Spanish ambassador would later recount Stucley's version of events, "Ribaut, a French captain, being here in the year '63, the queen summoned him [Stucley] and told him that Ribaut assured her that Florida was a very rich and important country, and since he had ships and means he could undertake the voyage thither, although she would not help him with money, or in any other way for the present, so that if Your Majesty should complain she should be able to swear that the voyage had not been made by her orders."[43]

Elizabeth had to think carefully about any venture that might damage her delicate alliance with Spain, which in 1562 was still felt to be essential for the security of England. However, she finally did provide a limited measure of support for Stucley and Ribault, and by mid-May, a fleet of "five ships and a pinnace" was being prepared, with direct aid from the English Crown, to sail out of the Thames.[44]

The involvement of Stucley in the project was regrettable, since as early as February, Stucley had covertly initiated contact with Bishop Quadra, the Spanish ambassador in England. Visiting him secretly on several occasions, Ribault's supposed partner kept the Spaniards informed of their preparations, though even the ambassador himself was not entirely clear what Stucley intended to do. On May 1 Quadra wrote to Philip II that

> Five vessels are being outfitted here by private individuals, the principal of whom is a young gentleman named Thomas Stukeley who is going in command. The talk is that they are going on a voyage of discovery to Florida, where a certain Jean Ribault of Dieppe went to some months ago, who now accompanies Stukeley. Out of

the five ships one belongs to the queen, two to Stukeley, one to Ribault, and one is chartered. They take 300 men and a great quantity of materials and artificers as well as plenty of artillery. Many people think that their object is to attack some of Your Majesty's ships on their voyage from the Indies. Some days since Stukeley sent to me to say that these people were sending him on a bad and knavish business, but that he would be with me and show me how to play them a trick that would make a noise in the world. I sent to seek him several times but he left London without telling me anything. . . . I am endeavouring to find out what is the truth about this business, although I expect really that they are bound for Florida, and that Stukeley's idea was to mutiny with the ships and to magnify his importance by telling me that they had commissioned him to do something prejudicial to Your Majesty's interests. . . . he is quite capable of doing this, and so far as his position is concerned, a good deal more, but is not much to be trusted.[45]

In addition to Stucley's traitorous actions, other ominous developments emerged that threatened this venture. Ribault published his *Whole and True Discouerye of Terra Florida* in London on May 30, which further damaged the relationship between the two principals. Stucley apparently resented the publication of this account, since by then he may have wanted to exclude Ribault entirely from the expedition, and he saw that the publicity would make it difficult to replace the Frenchman. Relations between the two men had never been particularly good, and it appears that they deteriorated further during June.[46]

Relations between England and France were also rapidly deteriorating over the situation at Le Havre. During the first War of Religion, Philip had provided military assistance to the French royalist forces, at Catherine's request, but only under the condition that she not require Spanish troops to fight against the English, who were technically Spanish allies.[47] Because thousands of English troops held this critical Norman port, Catherine was unable to engage the Spaniards against them and had to change her strategy to deal with what she considered to be a "great treason" by the English.[48] Even before the Peace of Amboise had been signed, she had encouraged a union of the French royalist forces with the Huguenots for the purpose of retaking Le Havre. In May 1563, she declared the Hampton Court agreement to be invalid, and she boldly demanded that Elizabeth immediately return Le Havre to French possession. The English refused, insisting that the French would first have to return Calais in exchange for Le Havre, as they believed that the agreement stipulated.

The standoff between the two queens set off an escalation of military preparations.[49] Elizabeth's perceived intransigence helped Catherine to unite her factions, and by the beginning of the summer, the French moved an army that included both Catholics and Huguenots into position for an attack. On her part, Elizabeth readied a fleet of more than a dozen English warships to sail to the aid of her beleaguered garrison at Le Havre, which was being steadily diminished by disease. By August, conflict between France and England seemed to have become inevitable, while Spanish observers followed the developments with great interest.

Stucley's involvement had already jeopardized Ribault's plans to relieve Charlesfort, both through his resentment of Ribault's leading role and because of his own communications with Spanish diplomats. With the breakdown of amicable relations between England and France, and Catherine's bold strategy to unite her warring factions, whatever hope remained of relieving the Charlesfort garrison with English help evaporated. Perhaps worst of all, Ribault's situation in England had suddenly become untenable: he could not consider himself a loyal servant of the French Crown while undertaking a mission for Elizabeth, who was now an enemy. Unfortunately, he had succeeded in arousing English interest in Florida, which was difficult to undo. Stucley, with or without Ribault, was continuing the preparations and readying the fleet.

Ribault's options were limited. If joining forces with Stucley was now out of the question, perhaps he might return home to reestablish contact with Coligny. With the Peace of Amboise in effect, the Huguenot and royalist leaderships were at least temporarily united, and in a situation of domestic peace, perhaps it would be possible to raise a French fleet and get to Florida ahead of Stucley.[50] If he needed any other incentive to leave England besides a desire to relieve Charlesfort, his personal safety was now an issue. Considering his familiarity with both French and English naval planning and capabilities, he could provide valuable knowledge to either side. Under the circumstances, sometime in the late spring of 1563, Ribault was forced to abandon the collaboration with Stucley, and he tried to return home.

However, the English were also aware that Ribault might be tempted to flee. Acting on intelligence provided by informants, in early June of 1563, English authorities intercepted Ribault and four other Frenchmen, including two of his Florida pilots, in the port of Gravesend as they attempted to find passage back to France. They were quickly arrested and placed in the Tower of London. Shortly thereafter, Stucley took advantage of this situation. He posted bond on the pilots (but not on Ribault), while promising the royal authorities to return the two to custody after he got back from his announced American expedition. On June 18, Stucley's five ships left the Thames, ostensibly for Florida, but the fleet ran into adverse winds and Stucley abandoned his original goal. Instead, he embarked upon a series of predatory voyages in the Bay of Biscay that lasted until the following winter.[51]

There is reason to doubt that Stucley ever seriously intended to relieve Charlesfort, or even to sail to Florida at all. Perhaps his talk of Florida was intended only to attract financial support from the Crown or from private investors, and his covert contacts with Quadra designed to allay any Spanish fears. Certainly, the dispatches by the Spanish ambassadors in England reveal Stucley as an individual whose evident motives were limited to self-gain. On June 19, the day after Stucley departed, Quadra wrote that "he is quite ruined here [England] and without estate. . . . My own opinion is that Stukely is bent rather on committing some great robbery than discovering new lands. I cannot say that he is instructed to do so, but I can only believe that his voyage is in consequence of the admiral of France in conjunction with the people who govern here [England] to harass your Majesty's shipping, and conquer on the ocean where they aim at being the strongest, and of course take steps to make themselves so."[52]

Quadra's understanding of Stucley's intentions, if not necessarily of Coligny's, appears to have been correct. With Ribault conveniently under guard in the Tower, Stucley continued his machinations with Spanish agents into the winter. Between raids on Spanish merchant fleets, he offered Philip various services through his contacts with Spanish diplomats.[53]

At the end of October, while he was stalking the shipping lanes between England and Brittany, Stucley went to the rescue of a ship floundering adrift. By a bizarre coincidence, it held the twenty or so barely living survivors of the Charlesfort garrison, who had been forced into cannibalism to survive their three-month voyage. According to Laudonnière's account, "a small English bark boarded the vessel, in which there was a Frenchman who had been in the first voyage into Florida, who easily knew them, and spake unto them, and afterward gave them meat and drink. Incontinently they recovered their natural courages, and declared unto him at large all their navigation. The Englishmen consulted a long while what were best to be done, and in fine they resolved to put on land those who were most feeble, and to carry the rest unto the Queen of England, which purposed at that time to send into Florida."[54]

It is not surprising that Laudonnière's account does not specifically mention Stucley as the rescuer of these survivors. There seems no reason why it would have; Laudonnière's history had to have been based upon the later testimony of some of the Charlesfort survivors, but only after they had been returned to France. Thus when Laudonnière wrote this account it is unlikely that he could have been aware of Stucley's earlier involvement with Ribault, and he probably had never even heard of Stucley. Incredible as it may seem, Laudonnière's mention of the French pilot who had been to Florida makes it virtually certain that it was indeed Stucley, or at least one of the ships of his fleet, who rescued these survivors.[55]

In any case, English authorities took most of the Frenchmen into custody in England and held them there as prisoners. Some or all of them remained there until at least March 1564, despite negotiations for their freedom made by French authorities that began immediately after their rescue.[56] Apparently the English retained Nicolas Barré longer than the others; French representatives in England petitioned for his release for more than a year, describing him alternately as Ribault's "servant" and "companion."[57] The English also were unwilling to part with Ribault. French diplomats tried persistently between the end of 1563 and the summer of 1564 to gain the freedom of Ribault and other French "hostages," which included others kept as a surety for the return of Calais by the Treaty of Hampton Court. In one diplomatic exchange, in December 1563, English Ambassador Smith proposed the exchange of Ambassador Throckmorton—then detained by French authorities on unstated charges—in exchange for four French hostages. Ironically, one of the four was none other than Throckmorton's friend Ribault.[58]

Ribault's attempt to organize a rescue mission with English help had accomplished nothing positive. He himself had landed in the Tower of London, helpless to either aid his country in the conflict with England or to relieve the tiny outpost he had left at Charlesfort. Perhaps worse, his erstwhile associate Thomas Stucley had demolished any French hopes of quietly establishing a permanent presence in Florida. First, Stucley had attracted the attention of the English in the possibilities of North

America, an idea that would soon arouse the curiosity of his more accomplished compatriot, John Hawkins. In 1565 the latter would employ one of the French pilots ransomed by Stucley to lead him to the French fort that was by then established on the River May.[59]

Second, and much more seriously, Stucley had set off a series of alarms in Spain regarding foreign intervention in Florida. One important result of this affair was that for the first time, Spanish authorities had gotten reliable information concerning Ribault's 1562 mission. French incursions into Florida were no longer mere rumors; by the middle of February 1563, Quadra had informed Philip that an actual base had been established.[60] Stucley's betrayals and misadventures had put the Spaniards on guard about foreign aggression against their New World possessions, especially Florida, at a time when they were beginning to appreciate the strategic importance of the Bahama Channel.

Despite the warnings received in Spain during 1563, Philip was unable to determine immediately the precise nature of this threat. The information coming into Spain about foreign maritime activity was unclear and often contradictory, and his responses to this threat were at first uncertain and ineffective. On January 9, 1563, just prior to the Peace of Amboise that ended the first War of Religion, Philip's ambassador in France had already reported a French expedition to Florida readying at Le Havre. His agents had heard this from a Portuguese navigator who supposedly had just returned from Florida; it is possible that he had been a companion of Ribault's, though no Portuguese are mentioned as taking part in the 1562 mission.[61] Nine days later, Ambassador Chantonnay enlarged upon his earlier report, stating that the corsair Le Clerc was leading an expedition of between six and seven hundred Frenchmen.[62] We cannot be sure what truth, if any, there may have been in this later report, or where the ambassador got his information on that occasion. Yet in light of the existing apprehension over French incursions, having Le Clerc's name attached to such a large undertaking must have caused serious consternation throughout the Spanish court.

Quadra's reports about Stucley, which were coming in at the same time, finally provoked Philip into action. Whether Le Clerc headed a French fleet, or Stucley led an English one, or perhaps even both, the Spanish territory of Florida certainly seemed to be in great danger. As early as the end of April, Philip decided to grant an *asiento* to Lucas Vásquez de Ayllón, whose father had held a grant for Florida forty years before. This agreement stipulated that Ayllón was to lead a major expedition of settlement, bringing families and livestock into the Santa Eleña area—that is, the vicinity of Charlesfort—with the aim of establishing Spanish towns.[63] In doing so, he hoped to prevent either the English or French from claiming that they were bound for unoccupied territories. In addition, the king sent a dispatch to his most reliable naval commander, Pedro Menéndez de Avilés, who was then in the Indies accompanying the silver fleet. The king ordered Menéndez to check the Florida coast while returning from Havana, to determine the nature of any foreign presence that may have been established there.

Philip's responses during 1563 and early 1564 accomplished little. By the time the royal order arrived in Havana, Menéndez had already departed, having become impatient with the storms delaying the New Spain fleet in Veracruz. Leaving that fleet to return by itself, he traveled to Havana, where he took command of the Tierra Firma fleet and led it home according to the original schedule, arriving back in Spain in May. Meanwhile, financial and logistical difficulties postponed Ayllón's expedition, which was still making preparations at the end of the year. By then, in December 1563, Philip had received yet another diplomatic dispatch that reported a French expedition of five or six ships departing for Florida.[64]

Spanish knowledge of French intentions remained confused. The missed communiqué to Menéndez had cost the authorities a chance to seek out the French along the Florida coast, and in the meantime, the status of Ayllón's expedition had become questionable. In May 1564, shortly after Menéndez's departure, the governor of Cuba dispatched the navigator Manrique de Rojas to carry out a coastal reconnaissance of Florida in a single small ship. While carefully examining the coast and interrogating the Indians about the French, Rojas succeeded in locating and seizing Guillaume Rouffin, who by then had been in Florida for two years. Using the young cabin boy as a guide, Rojas located the site of Charlesfort in Port Royal Sound. He burned what little remained of the French fort and removed the stone marker that Ribault had planted on the Libourne River. Confident that he had learned all there was to know, Rojas headed back to Havana, arriving in mid-June. He immediately forwarded to Spain his official report, which included Rouffin's account of the 1562 mission, and which indicated that the small French settlement was no longer a threat.[65]

On June 22, René Laudonnière's expedition of three ships, which had left France two months before, reached the coast of Florida. Unlike Ribault in 1562, Laudonnière had followed a more conventional southerly route across the Atlantic, following the trade winds toward the Caribbean. Before reaching Puerto Rico, the easternmost point of Spanish settlement, his ships veered northwest from the vicinity of the Virgin Islands. In doing so, Laudonnière approached the coast of Florida by sailing east and north of the Bahamas. At almost exactly the same time, Rojas was on his way back to Havana by tacking south through the Bahama Channel.[66] A few days later, just as a dispatch boat was speeding toward Spain with the report that the French had abandoned Charlesfort, Laudonnière was starting to build a new French outpost in Florida, one that posed a considerably greater threat to Spanish interests.

6

Fort Caroline

Jean Ribault's captivity did not change the apparent fact that the men at Charlesfort still awaited reinforcement, and once the first War of Religion ended in the spring of 1563, Coligny was finally able to organize such a venture, which he placed under the command of René Goulaine de Laudonnière. The latter's narrative, composed in 1586, is probably our most valuable tool in reconstructing the history of Fort Caroline, even though it has some weaknesses. In particular, Laudonnière provides few details of the events leading up to this second French voyage to Florida, and he is somewhat vague concerning the mission's intentions. We can, however, fill in some of the particulars from two other sources. The first is Jacques Le Moyne de Morgues, who accompanied the mission as a mapmaker and artist, and whose account was eventually published after the author's death in 1591. We can also examine later reports that the Spaniards compiled from their interrogations of French prisoners. These, like Guillaume Rouffin's testimony about Charlesfort, provide us with direct answers to direct questions and are of great value, although they are of uneven reliability.[1]

The beginning of Laudonnière's *1564* relates that

> After our arrival at Diepe, at our coming home, from our first voyage (which was the twentieth of July 1562) we found the civil wars begun, which was in part the cause why our men were not succoured, as Captaine John Ribault had promised them; whereof it followed that Captaine Albert was killed by his soldiers, and the country abandoned, as heretofore we have sufficiently discoursed, and as it may more at large be understood by those men which were there in person. After the peace was made in France, my Lord Admiral De Chastillon showed unto the king, that he heard no news at

all of the men that Captaine John Ribault had left in Florida, & that it were pity to suffer them to perish. In which respect, the king was content he should cause three ships to be furnished, the one of six score tunnes, the other of 100, and the third of 60, to seek them out and to succour them.[2]

We cannot determine with certainty when the French Crown approved Coligny's intention to send a second mission to Florida, since none of the sources is specific about this. Certainly it must have been after March 1563, when the Peace of Amboise ended the first War of Religion. It also must have been prior to November of the same year, when the French began to request that the English return Nicolas Barré, since by that time the news of the abandonment of Charlesfort had reached France from England. As the passage cited above indicates, Coligny had originally planned this second expedition as a reinforcement mission, and he had started to prepare for it before he had received the news that there was no longer an outpost to be relieved. Obviously, if he had known that the French volunteers had already returned to Europe, it would have been pointless for him to send Laudonnière to "seek them out and to succour them."

We can estimate that the planning for the new French initiative began at around the time of Ribault's attempted return to France in June, and it is even possible that a report of a French relief mission in the formative stage may have prompted Ribault's flight. Unfortunately, we have no indication when or how the plans were altered in response to the news that the Charlesfort survivors had returned.

No doubt because Ribault was unavailable and his return uncertain, Coligny entrusted Laudonnière with the command of the expedition. Le Moyne wrote that

the Admiral recommended that a nobleman to the King, René de Laudonnière, a friend of his family and without doubt a man of many accomplishments, yet not so experienced in military theory and practice as he was in naval matters. . . . The Admiral, who was endowed with innumerable fine qualities and was outstanding for his sense of Christian duty, with the King's business to be faithfully administered. He apprised Laudonnière of his commission and charged him to be entirely faithful in carrying out his duty. Above all he must choose suitable and God-fearing men as companions on his expedition since he professed the Christian [Protestant] religion. He told him moreover to collect as many men of unusual ac-

complishment in all the crafts as possible and so that he might accomplish this more easily he was given a letter bearing the king's
seal.[3]

Laudonnière recounted that

> My Lord Admiral therefore being well informed of the faithful ser-
> vice I had done, as well unto his Majesty as to his predecessors
> kings of France, advertised the king how I was able to do him ser-
> vice in this voyage, which was the cause that he made me chief
> captain over these 3 ships and charged me to depart with diligence
> to perform his commandment, which for mine own part I would
> not gainsay, but rather thinking myself happy to have been chosen
> out among such an infinite number of others. . . . I embarked myself
> at New Haven [Le Havre] the 22 of April 1564.[4]

These passages leave little doubt about the direct involvement of both
Charles IX and Coligny. Two documents from the *Tabellionage* of Rouen
also indicate royal involvement, respectively listing tools and munitions
granted just prior to this expedition's departure.[5] This Crown support
indicates that the young king considered the mission to have some value
to the kingdom as a whole. Under the circumstances, he could hardly
have thrown his active support behind an exclusively "Protestant" undertaking, since it took place at a time when he and his mother were both
desperately trying to promote national unity. Coligny's own political
and personal situation was also problematic, since just prior to the battle
of Dreux a Protestant had assassinated the Duke of Guise and under
torture had implicated the admiral as having ordered the deed.[6] After
this event, and the Le Havre fiasco, Coligny had to be especially careful
to avoid any suspicions about his loyalty.

Although neither Laudonnière nor Le Moyne reveals the specific
number of participants involved, other sources enable us to estimate that
there were probably around three hundred men who departed Le Havre
in April 1564. The prisoner Robert Meleneche told his Spanish interrogators that there were "110 sailors, 120 experienced soldiers, and the rest of
them officers of various ranks," while Stefano Rojamonte, another prisoner, specifically said three hundred.[7] John Sparkes, the chronicler of
John Hawkins's second voyage that visited Fort Caroline in August 1565,
wrote that the French settlers told him that there had been "two hundred
men at their first coming"; perhaps he was referring to the number who
remained in Florida, not including the ships' crews.[8] Le Moyne reported
that this mission included not only "men of unusual accomplishment in

Laudibus intactus num Laudionerus abibo ?
Florida regnorum comprendit America quæ nunc
haud minimum cuius Francis virtute subactum.
Perfida quem si non sociorum turpiter hosti
Factio prodisset (cuius tamen, omnibus vlcis,
Elapsus manibus) quæ, qualia, quanta patrassem !

4. René Goulaine de Laudonnière (plate 137b in *The Works of Jacques LeMoyne de Morgues*, "Portrait Engraving of Laudonnière," by Crispin de Passe the Elder, courtesy of the British Library).

all the crafts" but also "a great many noblemen and youths of established families . . . , prompted simply by some urge to explore far-off lands, [who] undertook the voyage at their own expense and without pay."[9] There was also a single woman who sailed to Florida, described by Laudonnière as "a poor chambermaid, which I had taken up at an Inn, to oversee my household business."[10] Her presence was later a cause for complaint against the settlement's commander by some of the sailors who had returned to France in September 1564.

Once again, it is instructive to place this mission in a context of the French political environment during the spring of 1563. During the war, the Duke of Aumale had organized peasant leagues to fight against Huguenot armies and civilians, which left lingering hatreds that destroyed social and economic cohesion.[11] The peace treaty itself contributed to the problem. Neither Coligny nor many of his fellow Calvinists found the terms of this treaty to be entirely satisfactory, and for them, the religious situation in France was by no means resolved.[12] Among other chafing restrictions, the new agreement, in contrast to the January Edict, prohibited public Calvinist worship and instead restricted it to certain towns, hardly satisfying the Huguenots' desire to be able to practice their faith openly.[13] Many Huguenot leaders regarded the Peace of Amboise as a pro-Catholic settlement, or at least one that benefited only the Protestant nobility, while some even suspected that the Prince of Condé had signed it to gain his freedom after being captured at the battle of Dreux.[14]

The largely Protestant population of Normandy especially resented this "peace treaty." Within a few months, the Peace of Amboise provoked Calvinist civil disobedience in the province's towns and cities, and outbreaks of violence by both Catholics and Protestants continued well into 1564.[15] Moreover, the devastation that had been wrought in the areas of heavy fighting during the first War of Religion had been considerable. The war and its constant plundering had ravaged countryside and town alike, which caused sizable numbers of Norman refugees to seek safety in urban areas such as Dieppe and Rouen. A particular problem was that German mercenaries from both sides continued to pillage the Norman countryside even after the formal suspension of military hostilities, as they remained unpaid and were forced to live off the land throughout 1563.[16] Although it is difficult to ascertain the direct impact of the dire situation in Normandy upon the 1564 expedition, it is reasonable to speculate that such circumstances must have aided the admiral's recruitment of civilian volunteers.

The breakdown of amicable relations between the English and French Crowns during 1563 may have been another important factor in the preparation of this reinforcement mission. Since Elizabeth had taken the throne in 1558, various continental Protestants had considered England to be a welcoming refuge from persecution at home. Many were French Calvinists who had fled during the first War of Religion.[17] Despite Elizabeth's wish to support continental Protestantism, and her desire to encourage people with needed skills to immigrate, these refugees had been unable to secure a solid legal standing that protected their property and exempted them from double taxation. Technically, the Protestant newcomers remained classified as "foreigners," rather than "denizens" who enjoyed most of the same privileges as native subjects. From 1558 to 1562, this presented little problem for newly arrived French Protestants, despite lingering resentment in England over the loss of Calais. However, public and official opinion in both kingdoms rapidly shifted during the hostilities surrounding Le Havre; even the former Huguenot "allies" such as Coligny and Condé gave their support to the French Crown against England. In England, one result of this was the legal seizure of much "foreign" property that belonged to recently arrived Huguenots.[18] On the whole, the summer of 1563 was hardly an ideal time for French Huguenots to emigrate across the Channel. Meanwhile, the Netherlands, under increasingly restrictive Spanish rule, could not have been a much better choice.

In such a religious and political environment, it is not surprising that hundreds of Norman Calvinists—persecuted, homeless, or penniless—responded to Coligny's recruitment efforts. Le Moyne's narrative indicates that the Protestant participation in this second mission was considerable, and even that Laudonnière specifically recruited Calvinists. Thus, with this 1564 initiative, we probably see the first manifestation of the concept of America as a "Protestant refuge." In the following year, the civilian component of Ribault's expedition may have had an even more pronounced Calvinist composition.

Unlike Ribault two years earlier, Laudonnière followed the more usual European route to Florida. He initially headed south, stopping both at the Canary Islands and on the north coast of Hispaniola. The passage between the Canaries and the Antilles took an efficient fifteen days with favorable winds, and Laudonnière reported no encounters of any sort with Spaniards before heading north to the coast of Florida, where he landed on June 22. Since this had ceased to be a rescue mission prior to departure from France, there was no immediate reason for the fleet to sail north to Port Royal. Instead, the French reached land near the River May and reestablished relations with the Timucuans, who had warmly greeted them two years earlier.

This time, Laudonnière assented to the Timucuan request that his group remain in that area; he quickly called a council to decide where to "make choice to plant our habitation." In rejecting the site of the Charlesfort garrison, Laudonnière explained that

If we passed further to the North to seek out Port Royall it would be neither very profitable nor convenient: at the least if we should give report of them which remained there a long time, although the Haven were one of the fairest of the West Indies: but that in this case the question was not so much the beauty of the place, as of things necessary to sustain life. And that for our inhabiting it was much more needful for us to plant in places plentiful of victual, then in goodly havens, fair, deep, and pleasant to the view. In consideration whereof that I was of opinion, if it seemed good unto them, to seat ourselves around the River of May: seeing also that in our first voyage we found the same only among all the rest to abound in Maize and corn, besides the Gold and Silver that was found there: a thing that put me in hope of some happy discovery in time to come.[19]

Thus he decided to choose the place that would be able to supply their need for food, instead of the better harbor. Laudonnière's account indicates that he counted on amicable relations with the Timucuans, whom he referred to as the "Paracoussy," in order to have access to the abundant "Maize and corn" of the area.

Though they did not know it at the time, the French had arrived in this area during an unstable period of intertribal relations. The Timucuans,

5. Jacques Le Moyne de Morgues's rendering of the greeting that Laudonnière and the French received at the River May in the late spring of 1564; note the column planted by Ribault in 1562, at center (plate 100 in *The Work of Jacques LeMoyne de Morgues*, courtesy of the British Library).

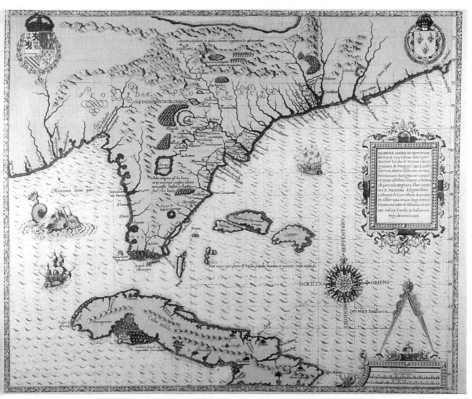

6. Le Moyne's map of North America, based in large part on the explorations conducted from Fort Caroline during 1564 and 1565 (plate 92 in *The Work of Jacques LeMoyne de Morgues*, courtesy of the British Library).

whose territories stretched from the Atlantic coast across the northern part of the Florida peninsula and the southern part of present-day Georgia, were subdivided into various chiefdoms in a decentralized state. Unified by culture and trade, the political relations between these chiefdoms ordinarily shifted a great deal and were frequently warlike. The easternmost part of the River May (today's St. Johns River) was among the poorest Timucuan land in terms of resources and hence was characterized by sparse population density and a looser political structure.[20] In the few years prior to the French arrival, some of the scattered small villages in this area had begun to assert their independence from the major inland chief Outina, confederating under the rebel leader whom the French called Saturioua.[21] Unaware of this situation, the French colonists assumed that the Timucuans around them were peaceful and had abundant resources to share with them. As it turned out, both of these assumptions were mistaken, which would have deadly consequences.

Largely as a result of their confidence that the Timucuans of the River May region would take care of their material needs, Fort Caroline's inhabitants never made any serious effort, during the entire life of the colony, to become agriculturally self-sufficient. Initially, they counted upon being able to procure food merely in exchange for promises of protection against Spanish cruelty. There can be little doubt the French had arrived with the intention of staying, and the proximity of a friendly group of natives with plentiful food supplies was the major factor in their decision as to where to plant their settlement. On July 28, Laudonnière, apparently satisfied with the fort's prospects, ordered his ships to return to France.[22]

During their first month in Florida, most of the colonists, of all ranks, were employed in the construction of Fort Caroline, on the south bank of the present-day St. Johns River, a short distance inland from the sea.[23] Some of the local Timucuans had informed the French that they were in the territory of a powerful and warlike chief named Saturioua, to whom they themselves were subject, and they warned that his main village was nearby. As a result, as Le Moyne put it, "we reckoned that the construction of our fort should be speeded up."[24] Shortly afterward, Laudonnière and his lieutenants received this chief, who was accompanied by eight hundred warriors, and they exchanged gifts and assurances of peace. In fact, Saturioua generously contributed some eighty young men to help the French with fortress construction, and for the rest of the month, "all of us put our hands to the task, nobles, soldiers, craftsmen, sailors, and others, in order to fortify ourselves against the enemy and protect ourselves against the weather."[25] It remains unclear which enemy Le Moyne referred to in this passage, whether Indian or Spaniard. One soldier, in a letter printed in France the following year, apologized that the reason for not writing a longer letter was "that we work every day on our fort, which is now defending us."[26] The writer included a diagram of Fort Caroline, which shows that its exterior walls had been completed by the end of July.

Aside from fortress construction, the colonists' other main occupation was the exploration of the immediate vicinity, undertaken mostly by soldiers. Early on, the French had begun construction of two small barks to enable exploration by ocean and river.[27] During the summer, Laudonnière assigned subordinate officers to lead groups of soldiers on frequent explorations inland to the west and along the River May. According to both Laudonnière and Le Moyne, one purpose of these explorations was to identify and locate the sources of the gold and silver they had occasionally glimpsed among the Indians.

In this regard, the expeditions soon proved disappointing. Two Spaniards who had been marooned on the coast fifteen years earlier revealed to the settlers how some of the Timucuans came to be wearing gold jewelry: they had salvaged the treasure from the cargo of the Spanish shipwreck. Although these castaways indicated that "a great store of gold and silver" could be found in a village they knew of well to the north, the colonists at Fort Caroline were told that there were no natural reserves of the metals in the immediate vicinity.[28]

As a result of this, explorations launched from Fort Caroline went farther afield.[29] In January Laudonnière dispatched a party north to the Charlesfort area in search of Rouffin. In addition to learning that he had been captured by the Spaniards, the searchers brought back news of rich mines in the mountains of "Apalatci," an area the French had first heard of in 1562. This caused Laudonnière to reconsider their prospects. As he wrote, "[since] the mountain was not past five or six days' journey from our fort, I determined as soon as our supply should come out of France to remove our habitation unto some river more toward the north, that I might be nearer thereunto."[30]

However, Laudonnière had limited opportunity to follow up on this idea, because of problems that had begun to appear after this first relatively productive summer. The most serious of these was a breakdown of the colony's discipline. Not surprisingly, most colonists preferred searching for gold to working on the fort, and by the late summer, some of them had begun to launch independent explorations inland and to the north. In particular, the colony's "gentlemen" began to complain that their experience in Florida was not living up to the recruitment promises they had been given before departure from France.

This situation may have been worsened by the style of Laudonnière's command. As Le Moyne commented, "Laudonnière was too easygoing and was clearly under the influence of three or four parasites; and he despised the soldiers, especially those whom he ought to have valued. What is worse, many of these people, who professed that they wanted to live in accordance with the more genuine teaching of the Gospel, were very displeased with him because they were deprived of a minister of the Holy Word."[31]

On September 4, a certain Captain Bourdet cast anchor at Fort Caroline with an unspecified number of ships and men, but whose arrival from France appears to have been expected.[32] One of his soldiers, named Giles de Pysière, dispatched a letter home that described a conspiracy against Laudonnière's command, including a failed assassination attempt.[33] Interestingly, Pysière's letter indicates that Coligny had sent these men to Florida for the specific purpose of helping with the construction of the fort, which continued through the fall. Pysière added that some or most of those who had arrived with him were criminals or "foreigners whom we had taken as prisoners," which may indicate that these most recent French arrivals had captured Spaniards while en route to Florida. However, the presence of these new arrivals contributed to a further weakening of the sick Laudonnière's already shaky command. When Bourdet departed in November, he removed "some six or seven soldiers" from the original contingent for insubordination. However, this did not solve the discipline problem, since those whom Bourdet had brought and left behind seem to have been even worse.

A few weeks after Bourdet left for France, in mid-December, the most damaging revolt against Laudonnière's authority occurred. Some "threescore and six" soldiers whom Laudonnière had impressed into fortress construction mutinied and raided the company's weapons storehouse. Seizing the ill Laudonnière, who was bedridden with fever, they forced him to provide them with a written statement that they could present to Spanish authorities, which attested that they were sailing under his command to trade for food.[34] With this "passport" in hand, they commandeered the two barks that were nearing completion in the river and headed out to sea. Laudonnière's testimony reveals why this was of particular worry to him: "For I feared greatly, that under the pretext of searching for victuals, they would enterprise somewhat against the King of Spaines subjects, which in time might justly be laid to my charge, considering that at our departure out of France, the Queen had charged me very expressly to do no kind of wrong to the King's subjects, nor any thing whereof he might conceive any jealousy."[35]

His fears were justified. The mutineers sailed to the south, attacking Spanish ships and towns around Hispaniola and Cuba in a spree of violent pillage. After several hostile encounters, Spanish authorities managed to deceive one group of French raiders and seize them for interrogation.[36] As for the other Frenchmen who had avoided capture, most of them apparently fell to arguing among themselves. In late March, after becoming drunk on a captured shipment of wine, they unwittingly permitted the French pilot they held prisoner to lead them back to the vicinity of Fort Caroline. Alerted to their presence by the Timucuans, Lau-

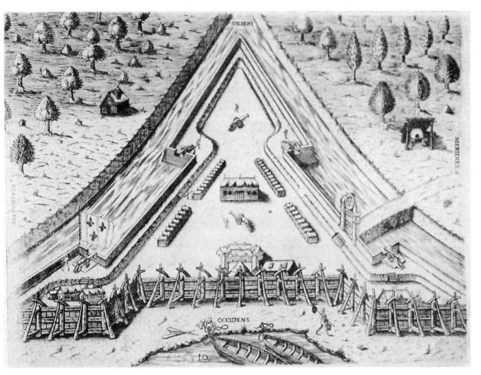

7. The completed Fort Caroline, as pictured by Le Moyne (plate 102 in *The Work of Jacques LeMoyne de Morgues*, courtesy of the British Library).

donnière's men ambushed the mutineers and took them into custody.[37] Though the commander ordered the executions of four of the leaders, the damage had already been done: the corsairs' predations had reawakened the Spanish authorities to the French threat. In response to the news of these raids, the Spanish Crown altered the scope of the expedition that they were already preparing to send to Florida.

Meanwhile, the Frenchmen's relationship with their neighbors was completely disintegrating. The Timucuans were semi-nomadic, growing a regular corn crop but also moving their villages for hunting, fishing, and gathering wild foods. Throughout the fall, the colonists had become increasingly dependent on them for food, especially when their own food supplies, imported from France, began to run out. In January, however, the Timucuans left the immediate area of the River May in order to hunt in the forests, as was usual for that time of the year, and they thus made themselves unavailable to provide for the needs of Fort Caroline. As a result, some colonists turned to violence to force the few Indians they encountered to give them food. At one point, Laudonnière captured the major Timucuan chief, Outina, who had become their most reliable ally but whom Laudonnière believed had betrayed him. The colonists ultimately freed the chief in exchange for a supply of corn, but only after thoroughly disrupting the course of the power struggle between Saturioua and Outina. During the spring, different groups of Frenchmen increased their interference in local disputes, even bringing their arquebuses to act as mercenaries in intertribal warfare far to the west against another major rival of Outina's.[38]

Without voluntary Timucuan assistance, the colony's very survival was imperiled, since the French had never made much effort to grow their own food or to learn to fish. As their food ran low, the colonists at Fort Caroline waited anxiously for the shipment of supplies that they expected to arrive from France in April or May.[39] Before June, their food was all but exhausted, and Laudonnière, losing hope of reinforcement, began to make plans to return to France. However, it was impossible to leave immediately, since before the colonists could depart, they had to wait for the Indian corn harvest at the end of July to be able to stockpile enough food for the voyage. In the meantime, they began to disassemble Fort Caroline to use its timber to build larger ships for the voyage.

During this period of desperation, the settlers continued to fight both among themselves and with various Indian villages, as the prospect of starvation began to loom as a real possibility. This "hideous famine," as Laudonnière described it, had so severely weakened the Frenchmen even by the end of May that their commander worried that the colony had become completely unable to defend itself.[40] By then virtually all of the Timucuans who initially had been so helpful to them had become their enemies, and the colonists feared to venture outside the fort except in large armed groups. In his history, Laudonnière was blunt in laying the blame for this state of affairs: "In the mean while there was none of us to whom it was not an extreme grief to leave a country, wherein we had endured so great travails and necessities, to discover that which we must foresake through our own countrymen's default. For if we had been succoured in time and place and according to the promise that was made to us, the war which was between us and Utina had not fallen out neither should we have had occasion to offend the Indians."[41]

On August 3, while the Frenchmen were readying their ships for departure, the English corsair John Hawkins arrived at Fort Caroline. Hawkins had left England the previous summer for an unauthorized trading voyage to the Spanish Indies, and he had taken along with him one of Ribault's pilots.[42] On the way back to Europe, the pilot guided the fleet to Fort Caroline, at Hawkins's request. There, the English planned to refresh their water supplies and also to investigate the status of the French settlement.[43]

Upon arrival, Hawkins found the French with only ten days' supply of food. The main reason for this, in the opinion of one of Hawkins's officers, was that "notwithstanding the great want that the Frenchmen had, the ground doth yield victuals sufficient, if they would have taken pains to get the same; but they being soldiers desired to live by the sweat of other men's brows."[44] Hawkins had amply provisioned his fleet for its return journey, and he offered to transport the Frenchmen home. Yet Laudonnière, by his own account, mistrusted Hawkins's assurance that England and France were then at peace, and, to the great displeasure of most of his desperate colonists, he decided to decline the offer. Explaining that "I stood in doubt lest he would attempt somewhat in Florida in the name of his mistress," the French commander instead exchanged most of his artillery for one of the five English ships and a quantity of food, in order to make the return voyage independently.[45] Laudonnière pointedly refused to trade any of the silver and gold they had accumulated, again out of fear of arousing English interest in Florida. Despite his hesitation to put complete trust in the Englishman, he concluded that Hawkins was "a good and charitable man, deserving to be esteemed as much of us all as if he had saved all our lives."[46]

Hawkins's fleet left Florida at the end of the first week of August. The colonists immediately began to load their ships and to make biscuit from the English flour, and by August 15, they had adequate vessels and enough food to support them during their journey. After that date, according to Laudonnière, "we did nothing but stay for good winds to drive us into France."[47]

In slightly more than a year, Laudonnière had, with considerable difficulty, succeeded in building a fort and exploring a sizable inland area, but although he had heard rumors of wealthy cities and mines, he had failed to locate any of them. As the months passed, Fort Caroline's situation had rapidly deteriorated: by the summer of 1565, his colonists were starving and under constant threat of Indian attack, while many of them were openly defying their commander. By the last week in August, promised reinforcements were three or four months overdue, and there had been no contact with France in more than a year. It appears that Laudonnière had few options besides organizing a risky voyage home. The challenge of this task was somewhat mitigated by Hawkins's arrival, but even with English supplies, there seemed little point in remaining in Florida. The "land of milk and honey" had become a living hell.

At almost the last possible moment before departure, seven French ships were sighted on the horizon and sailed into the harbor at Fort Caroline. Jean Ribault had arrived at last, bringing food, settlers, soldiers, and artillery. Miraculously, it appeared that the little colony might survive after all. Yet in addition to the settlers and supplies that Ribault brought with him, he also brought the gravest danger yet faced by the French in Florida. A small Spanish fleet followed almost in Ribault's wake. Its ships were battered, but its commander—Pedro Menéndez, the new *adelantado* of Florida—was an angry and desperate man.

* * *

Like his Norman counterpart Jean Ribault, Pedro Menéndez de Avilés had been educated in the unforgiving maritime school of the North Atlantic. Menéndez too had come from an economically modest but highly respected landowning family, in this case from the Asturian coast around the harbor town of Avilés.[48] The northern provinces of Spain, like Normandy, had long relied upon the sea as the basis of their society and economy, and the sons of families such as Menéndez's naturally gravitated toward maritime careers. During the sixteenth century, this often meant that they joined the growing ranks of the *contra-corsarios*, seaborne vigilantes whose ostensible purpose was the protection of legitimate commerce from predators.[49]

Pedro Menéndez, born in 1519, entered this arena as a teenager, following his older brother Alváro Sánchez into service with the independent but royally approved fleets that battled French and Berber pirates. By 1543 he owned his own ship and had earned a command under Álvaro Bazán, another Biscayan who later became the most illustrious Spanish admiral of the era. Before the end of the decade Menéndez had already received two royal commissions—essentially letters of mark—to pursue French corsairs. The second of these led to his first experience in the Indies, in 1550, as the wars with France re-erupted. Assigned by the Crown to guard Indies commerce from the likes of Le Clerc and Sores, Menéndez was captured by French corsairs near Havana in 1552 and had to be ransomed. Nevertheless, the Crown appointed him, at the age of only thirty-four, as Captain-General of the Armada of the Indies, because of his exceptional service.

This was a royal office, which reflected the king's increasing initiative in Atlantic commerce during the decade of the 1550s. Traditionally, the

Council of the Indies issued the first significant proclamation of royal policy regarding French corsairs. It announced that instead of being returned to Spain for trial, all captured Frenchmen henceforth found to be engaged in piracy were to be summarily punished: the crew to galley duty, and the officers put to death. For the council to involve itself in this problem indicates that it considered French corsairs to be a serious threat to the security of the realm, and not just to the Sevillian merchant interests.[52]

Menéndez spent the following three years defending the flotas. On a return journey to Spain in the summer of 1561, he landed in the midst of controversy once again. Believing that five English ships he encountered in the Azores had already robbed a Spanish ship and were intending to attack the silver fleet, he seized the vessels along with their crews and cargo, an action that caused English Ambassador Thomas Challoner to make a formal protest. By the following February, Spanish authorities had freed the English crews from prison in Seville, and Menéndez, upon order of the king, had restored to them the full value of their cargo of wine and textiles.[53] This diplomatic problem was not the only worrisome result of that tour of duty. Upon his return to Spain, he also found that the Casa had accused him of smuggling contraband silver, though they had filed no formal charges.[54]

After resolving the English problem and deflecting the smuggling charges, Menéndez was reassigned as captain-general of the combined fleets in April 1562. The instructions given him prior to his departure reflected the hardened attitude Philip took against corsairs:

> We are informed that in the Indies sailing routes go some French, English, and Scotch corsair ships, seeking to steal what goes and comes from there. This is a disservice to God our Lord, to us, and is against the peace agreed upon by us and the princes of those kingdoms. Because these corsairs should, by rights, be hanged as peacebreakers and robbers and violators of the orders of their own lords and rulers, I order you, if you capture any of the said corsairs, to proceed against them and punish them in conformity of justice, executing it then upon the sea with all rigor: in order that you might do this, we give you full powers.[55]

This is an important statement because of what it reveals about the Spanish view of French interlopers. Since they considered such corsairs to be acting against the commands of their own rulers, the authorities in Spain claimed justification to treat them as common outlaws instead of as prisoners of war. In conjunction with the 1558 Council of the Indies policy statement, Menéndez could have had little doubt that acting with less than absolute decisiveness in dealing with trespassers would be equivalent to disobeying a direct order. It is worth considering that the respective sources of these statements, the council and Philip himself, had consistently supported Menéndez in his legal battles against the Casa. From this point on, Menéndez had direct orders, and not merely legal justification, to impose a swift justice on any French corsairs he encountered in the Indies. It would have been very unwise, to say the least, for him to disregard the specific instructions of his only powerful defenders.

By this time, the disappointing results of the Luna expedition had reached Spain, which caused King Philip to make a proclamation that would have important ramifications for Spanish-French relations in the Indies. He announced that any further attempts to settle Florida would have to be undertaken directly from Spain and concentrated upon the area north of Punta de Santa Eleña.[56] We can interpret this as evidence of the Crown's increasing frustration with the problems of settling Florida, as well as their determination to prevent any foreign encroachments upon lands that they claimed.

Menéndez's next Indies duty had far-reaching ramifications for both his career and his personal situation. During the spring of 1562, he led the combined convoy to the Indies, and from Puerto Rico he accompanied the New Spain fleet west to Veracruz. There he waited for it to take on its cargo, while the other detachment, the Tierra Firme fleet, did the same in Panama. However, weather problems delayed the New Spain ships, causing them to miss the appointed rendezvous at Havana the following spring. Menéndez, apparently disobeying an order to stay with the New Spain fleet, left for Havana and led the Tierra Firme fleet on its return journey as scheduled in April.[57] In his stead, he assigned his son Juan to lead the remainder of the New Spain ships back when they were ready.

Upon arrival in Spain in May 1563, Menéndez found that he had missed the communication that had been directed to him in Havana, which had instructed him to investigate the French settlement in Punta de Santa Eleña. As we recall, Thomas Stucley had mentioned this settlement to Bishop Quadra in February, and the bishop had immediately relayed this information to the king. Philip, upon hearing this, had decided to have Menéndez investigate the truth of this report on his return voyage home. For whatever reason, Menéndez's independent decision to leave with the earlier fleet cost him an opportunity to undertake the search himself, and, ultimately, authorities appointed Vásquez de Ayllón and then Manrique de Rojas to lead their respective expeditions.

The following months were among the darkest of Menéndez's career. Yet again, the Casa accused him of carrying contraband, but before they could carry out their order to arrest him, he fled to the king's protection in the new capital of Madrid and began to organize a legal defense. Although he had posted bond, by August Casa officials took him into custody while he awaited a formal trial.[58] In the meantime, bad news had arrived from the Indies. First, one of Menéndez's own ships in the New Spain fleet, carrying a valuable cargo of mercury, had struck a reef near Cuba and was believed lost. Even worse, in November he learned that his son, leading the remaining New Spain ships home from Havana, had been shipwrecked by a storm somewhere off the coast of Florida.

By winter, the Casa found the captain-general guilty of smuggling charges and imposed a heavy fine, although an appeal to the Crown resulted in a partial vindication. Menéndez then initiated a counteraction against the Casa, charging that they had refused to adequately compensate him for the personal expenses of his last voyage. Throughout the spring and into the summer of 1564, his case was debated and shuttled from one court to another, becoming a hopeless morass of suits and countersuits. This situation presented Menéndez with a terrible dilemma. Although ultimate victory in the legal case appeared possible, while the authorities settled the issues, he was prevented from launching a search party for Juan. Not only was Menéndez still in custody, but he had been unable to settle accounts from his last voyage and thus lacked the financial means to outfit any such expedition. Soon, however, the news of a renewed French threat to Florida provided him with a golden opportunity.

7

The Race to Florida

Lucas Vásquez de Ayllón's expedition, assigned to make yet another attempt to establish a permanent Spanish presence at Punta de Santa Eleña, remained in the harbor of Santo Domingo throughout the summer of 1564. Delayed by problems of jurisdiction and supplies, many of the prospective settlers deserted the effort; ultimately, after Ayllón's death, the fleet's leaders chose a new destination and headed for Peru.[1] Meanwhile, by midsummer, Manrique de Rojas's report had reached Spanish authorities on both sides of the Atlantic: not only did they now have confirmation of a French base at Charlesfort but they also knew of its recent abandonment.

The Spaniards had little time to relax their vigilance, since they soon learned other disturbing news from the Indies. In August, a source reported to the English ambassador in Spain that there was a rumor in Seville that "the Queen has delivered certain ships to Mr. Stukely, and he is bound to Florida."[2] This rumor may not have seemed particularly surprising to Spanish authorities, considering Quadra's earlier reports, but they probably received an official communiqué dispatched from Santo Domingo, at around the same time, with more concern. This one warned them that a noted Portuguese corsair, known as El Mimoso, had already led a squadron of five French ships to Punta de Santa Eleña, of which three had landed and the other two were still at large. Various other rumors of foreign threats to Florida, perhaps less reliable, also reached authorities in Spain during that fall.[3]

These somewhat contradictory reports had an effect that reached the highest circles of power, and we can only surmise the state of alarm and confusion they must have caused. While it certainly appeared that someone was threatening the vulnerable Bahama Channel, it was unclear exactly who they were and what they had in mind. By October, perhaps in response, the Crown had issued a new and more detailed set of regulations for the organization of Indies shipping and had made provisions for a regular dispatch of royal ships as protection.[4]

It is in this context that King Philip ordered Pedro Menéndez, who was still entangled in frustrating litigation, to prepare a report concerning the problems of Florida. Prior to March 15 Menéndez completed a "Memorial" which included both his own interpretation of the threats to this area and his recommendations of what steps might be taken to prevent "foreign powers" from encroaching on Spanish territory.[5] He compiled this evaluation of the situation largely on the basis of firsthand reports he had gotten in Asturian harbors after his return from the Indies. Essentially, he concluded that the two reports of the previous summer were probably true. First, he reported that the corsair El Mimoso had definitely been sighted in the Canary Islands in May 1564, where "they chased four ships of the armada and said they were to go to settle on the coast of Florida." Second, Menéndez told the king that five "very large and heavily armed" English ships had attacked ports in Galicia in December; while doing so their crews had declared that they were bound for "the coast of Florida to settle on it and to await the ships of the Indies." Though Menéndez did not mention Thomas Stucley by name, Philip may well have logically concluded that the latter, perhaps aided by Jean Ribault and French pilots, was bound for Florida to reestablish the abandoned French settlement there. The raid on Galicia had shown that the Englishman's intentions were hostile to Spanish interests; given a chance, he might be more destructive in the relatively undefended Indies.

In addition, Menéndez's "Memorial" warned that

If the above are true and the aforementioned French or English or any other nation so disposed should seek to go make a settlement in Florida, it would be a great harm to these kingdoms, because on the other coast of Florida, astride the Bahama Channel, in some port or ports they would be able to establish a site and fortifications that would enable them to have galleys and other ships of war, to take the *flotas* and any other ships which should come from the Indies and come through there, and it would bring great danger to all of these of being captured.[6]

While this by itself was a matter of grave concern, Menéndez described other threats as well. He warned Philip of the possibility that foreign interlopers might lead slave revolts against Spanish rule in the

Caribbean Islands; he relayed a rumor that French corsairs had found a route from Newfoundland to the South Sea that would enable them to threaten the silver mines in northern Mexico; and finally, he speculated that the trespassers might infect the Indians with heretical ideas. In short, the scenarios outlined in the "Memorial" were catastrophic, if not, in hindsight, entirely realistic. Conceivably, Menéndez may have overdramatized the dangers in order to get Philip to expedite his legal problems, so that the king might assign him to lead a mission to Florida where he could search for his lost son.

In order to prevent any of these unthinkable possibilities from occurring, Menéndez proposed a detailed plan. He recommended that the king should immediately dispatch an armed force of five hundred men to Santa Elena. From there, they should conduct seaborne explorations northward along the American coast and establish a series of armed outposts in all of the best harbors, in order to prevent any foreign encroachments in these territories. He also added, "In the case that there are Frenchmen upon the land, and they have a fleet upon the sea waiting for the flota and ships of the Indies, it is necessary that at the least, what I recommended above should be increased, with four large galleons, with a thousand sailors and soldiers, and these will take the coast."[7]

King Philip responded to this "Memorial" much as if it had been an application to lead such an expedition. On March 20, 1565, he issued Menéndez an *asiento*, or contract, naming him *adelantado* of Florida. In doing so he approved most of what his captain had recommended. The major difference was that while Menéndez had suggested that the Crown undertake most of the expense, Philip followed the standard practice of the asiento contract, requiring Menéndez to raise most of the financial backing privately. The asiento included the following provisions:

and to you Pedro Menendez, Knight of the Order of Santiago, have I offered and do offer, because of the desire you have for the service of God Our Lord, and for the increase to the Royal Crown of these kingdoms, that during the coming month of May of this year, you shall hold ready and prepare to sail six shallops and four zabras, with their oars, arms and munitions, laden with supplies and fully prepared for war, and that you shall take five hundred men, one hundred of them farmers and one hundred of them sailors, and the rest of them naval and military men and officials, others professional stonecutters, carpenters, sawyers, smiths, barbers, locksmiths, all of them with their arms, arquebuses and crossbows, and helmets and bucklers, and the other offensive and defensive weapons which you may see fit and which may be suitable for the said voyage; and two priests.[8]

Philip made the purpose of this assignment quite clear:

You shall go with the said shallops and zabras and the said five hundred men, supplied and prepared for war as has been said, to the coast of Florida, where you pledge yourself to test and reconnoitre the best and most convenient places of the said coast, as it seems to you; coasting along by sea and searching and investigating on land where a harbor and place for settlement can best be found; and you will try to obtain information as to whether there are on the said coast any settlers who are corsairs, or of any other nations who are not subject to us, and you shall endeavor to cast them out by the best means that seem to you possible.[9]

He further instructed Menéndez to explore as far north as "Terranova," that is, between fifty and sixty degrees north latitude, and to map the entire coast.

Such an arrangement—known as an *adelantamiento*—was standard sixteenth-century Spanish procedure for the exploration and settlement of new lands. Designed to save the Crown the expense of the undertaking, it was essentially a royally granted lease for a colonizing venture, and it required that the holder finance the expedition independently. Thus, Menéndez was required to use his own financial means and whatever further private support he needed from his friends and relatives.

Menéndez then owned a galleon of great size and firepower, the *San Pelayo*, which had a cargo capacity of nearly a thousand tons. He and his relatives also had access to a number of smaller ships that would provide the basis of a strong fleet and that would enable them to transport a sizable contingent of settlers, along with necessary armaments and supplies. In return, he expected that once he had carried out the immediate goals of the mission by securing the Florida coast, Menéndez and his backers could enjoy extensive trade privileges as their reward. Compared to previous asientos granted for the colonization of Florida, the trade privileges granted to Menéndez were quite generous.[10] As an additional incentive, the agreement added that "We wish and deem it well that everything you may capture from corsairs with the said galleons, galleasses and patches during the term of the said six years shall be your property and that of your heirs and successors, and the same may apply to whatever prisoners you may take or seize from them."[11]

In essence, Philip had granted Menéndez a potentially lucrative contract to settle Florida, along with explicit orders to remove any foreign threat he encountered there; at the same time, this arrangement would also enable him to search for his missing son as he scoured the east coast. Seizing this opportunity, Menéndez began rounding up volunteers and financial backing for the most important mission of his life.

However, only six days after the king issued this adelantamiento, the circumstances suddenly changed again: the first news of the corsair raids undertaken by the Fort Caroline mutineers arrived in Seville. In mid-January, Spanish authorities in Santo Domingo had interrogated several of the captured Frenchmen about the settlement at Fort Caroline. They sent the resultant depositions and various witnesses' reports by express boat to Spain, where they arrived on March 26.[12] Not only did this give Philip his first certain news of the new French settlement in Florida, but the reports also included statements that the French were expecting a reinforcement of five hundred men, reportedly due to arrive in Florida in May.[13] Upon receipt of this information, the king decided to expand the scope of the operation by giving Menéndez what he had recommended in the last part of his "Memorial." The captain general would now command additional warships and twice as many soldiers and sailors. Little time could be lost.

* * *

At the same time that Menéndez was putting together his armada, Jean Ribault was in Dieppe outfitting his own voyage to Florida. Nicolas Le Challeux, a Norman carpenter who accompanied this expedition, related that

> The King and several princes and lords of his council, due to the troubles and tumults of the civil war that had arisen in the realm, had interrupted the sending of a good number of men with several ships into one of the countries of the Indies named Florida, newly known and discovered by the French: with the Edict of Pacification published under the authority of his majesty, the purpose continued: Jean Ribaud, a man of character and wisdom, and well versed in the marine, was summoned to the court and received the commission of the king to equip seven ships, which would carry men, food, and munitions to that place, honoring him with the title of his

lieutenant and leader of the troops which he had been commanded to raise, to the fulfilment of such an enterprise, and he expressly forbade him from making a landfall in any other country or island, especially those which were under the dominion of the King of Spain; going full sail across the great ocean, he should make a direct route to Florida: news of this voyage spread uncontrollably everywhere, and many were persuaded to put themselves under the command of this captain, and under the authority of the king.[14]

If previous transatlantic missions provide any indication of the time required to organize such an expedition, the French should have begun their preparations before January if they expected their fleet to arrive in Florida during the spring. Laudonnière had stated in his history that Fort Caroline had expected a reinforcement by April 1565 at the latest, yet it appears that neither Coligny nor Ribault had made any significant preparations prior to the beginning of that year. Le Challeux also stated that he and the other recruits raised for this mission had assembled in Dieppe four months prior to May 10, meaning that they must have first gathered there after the first of the year.[15] By that date, it would have already been several months since the ships sent back to France from Fort Caroline (at the end of July 1564) had arrived.

It is difficult to be sure of the reasons why Coligny waited so long. Ribault's absence cannot have been the main factor; it is almost certain that he had returned to France from England by early fall.[16] Thus by the end of September this reinforcement mission would have had both its leader and a report on the establishment of the new colony, so the lack of either of these cannot explain the delay. We cannot escape the conclusion that Coligny and Ribault were late in getting started for one or more other reasons.

One reason for the delay is that it may have taken an unexpectedly long time to recruit volunteers during the last months of the year. Aside from what we can gather from Le Challeux's account, we have little knowledge of the recruitment process. Though there was a fragile peace in France after the spring of 1563, there was also a significant Norman refugee population, and one might think that it should not have been too difficult for Ribault and the charismatic Coligny to find several hundred potential colonists in Normandy. On the other hand, perhaps Coligny had already recruited these civilians without major problem and had ordered them to assemble in Dieppe in January for a departure soon after. Even if this were so, the question still remains of why the mission did not set sail until May.

It is likely that Coligny's own situation had an influence on the departure date. The queen mother and the king were embarked on a royal tour of the provinces for the entire period between March 1564 and May 1566; meanwhile, the admiral spent almost no time in the presence of the traveling court during this period. Aside from a brief visit to his brother Odet at Beauvais, during the fall of 1564 he was home at Châtillon, on the outskirts of Paris, where his wife, Charlotte, gave birth at the end of November. During this period, the admiral busied himself mostly in treaty negotiations with Swiss Protestant cantons, which he conducted from Châtillon through agents and correspondence.[17] At the end of January 1565, the admiral left Châtillon for Paris, while the court was in the south of France, and he returned home soon afterward, where he remained during the next two months. It further appears that at no time between September 1564 and the following spring did Coligny ever visit Normandy.[18]

The lack of direct contact between the admiral and the king likely had a significant effect upon this expedition. Considering Coligny's movements and activities between September 1564 and April 1565, he could neither have overseen preparations in Normandy nor have personally discussed the mission with the king or the queen mother. One might expect that, since this was a royally sponsored expedition, either or both of these would have been important responsibilities. The planners would have had to procure supplies, arrange officers' commissions, and obtain necessary licenses and orders. Thus, a lack of direct contact with Charles and Catherine may largely explain why the project never got off the drawing board until at least January 1565.

Le Challeux's testimony clearly indicates that these volunteers had expected to leave for Florida soon after gathering in Dieppe and that the four-month period of inactivity caused many of them to abandon the mission. It is likely that another delay during the early spring was the cause of this development. Le Challeux reported that it was not until May 10 that the royal authorities had promised the civilian volunteers that they would receive six months' pay in advance, and it could well be that a disagreement over pay was one reason for the long wait.[19]

The surviving documentation also suggests another, more significant, cause of the delay. This is that sometime after early April, the scope of the expedition itself changed, which required additional outfitting. Between March 19 and April 2, Coligny issued a series of royal commissions, appointing Ribault and three other individuals as king's officers of the fleet; this is the first indication that we have that preparations were actually under way.[20] By the beginning of April, then, Coligny had set the command and assembled the civilian volunteers; it could well be that by that date, or shortly thereafter, the fleet may have been ready to sail.[21] Had such an expedition left in early April, fewer civilian volunteers would have deserted, and perhaps five hundred or more would indeed have arrived in Florida in early June. Yet the fleet did not actually leave Dieppe for another six weeks, that is, not until mid-May. This could not possibly have been the original timetable. The terribly late start must have been due to factors besides delays prior to January, or a pay disagreement.

The most likely explanation for the delay is that Coligny and Ribault altered the intent of their expedition because of reports they had received from Spain. On April 3, the day after the last officer's commission, the French ambassador in Spain informed Charles IX that Menéndez was bound to Florida "with a good fleet of 600 men to fight the French and put them to the sword."[22] As far as we can determine, this led to the first French knowledge of Menéndez's expedition, and it is logical to conclude that this had a significant impact on the entire scope of the French reinforcement plans. Other evidence also supports this interpretation. The Inventories of Artillery for Ribault's mission, which tell us a great deal about the ships and their armaments, were all dated between the end of April and mid-May, indicating that the orders for this equipment were placed only after the king and admiral had received the alarming information about Menéndez.[23] Additionally, an ambassador's report arriving in Madrid on April 11 reported five, not seven, French ships preparing to go to Florida.[24] This may actually have been accurate at the time. Originally, five ships may have been all that Coligny had considered necessary to transport the civilian contingent, and they may indeed have been preparing to depart on that date, which would have allowed them to reach Fort Caroline sometime in May or early June—which would have gotten them there approximately at the time Laudonnière was expecting them.

In light of these circumstances, we can deduce that the diplomatic report of April 3 not only caused a delay but altered the purpose of Ribault's relief mission. The knowledge of a planned Spanish strike in force against Fort Caroline required that the French more heavily arm their fleet and reinforce it with additional soldiers. This would have necessitated additional ships, as well as more time for outfitting, which could explain why the fleet was not ready to leave Dieppe until May 22. Further, it is perfectly logical that Le Challeux would not have mentioned such a development in his account of the preparations, because he himself probably would have been unaware of it. There would have been no reason for the planners to have notified him or the other civilian volunteers of a change of plan, especially since informing them that a Spanish force planned to attack them upon arrival in Florida might have caused massive desertions.

Rather than leaving in mid-April, then, Coligny and Ribault took another month to ready the fleet, planning instead to depart on May 10. However, yet another even less avoidable obstacle presented itself: contrary winds, the perpetual nemesis of Channel sailors. The French ships could not get out of Dieppe's harbor until May 22, and even then, winds forced them almost immediately into anchorage a short way down the coast at Le Havre. On a second attempt to gain the open ocean, on May 28, they got only as far as the Isle of Wight, where they had to remain for more than two weeks. On June 14, a full two months after Laudonnière had expected them at Fort Caroline, Ribault led the vessels on a direct ocean crossing similar to the route of his 1562 voyage.[25]

*   *   *

On June 3, Spanish authorities in Madrid received a communiqué from a Spanish intelligence agent in Normandy, Dr. Gabriel Enveja. The report contained detailed observations of the fleet while it had been at anchorage in Dieppe between May 17 and 19.[26] In most regards the information Enveja forwarded agrees with the Inventory of Artillery in terms of the ships and their armaments, and it is also more specific about the personnel embarking. Among this account, the artillery inventory, and Le Challeux's testimony, we can gather a very accurate idea of the final composition of Ribault's fleet. It is difficult to conclude on the basis of this evidence that, by the time the French sailed, this was merely a civilian reinforcement intended to augment the workforce in Florida and establish "effective settlement." Whatever the composition of this fleet had been originally, by May it had become a heavily armed mission of war, intent upon defending Fort Caroline from an anticipated Spanish attack.

As such, this mission included two somewhat separate groups of participants: civilians and military personnel. According to Enveja, between seven hundred and a thousand persons were readying for departure. At least five hundred of these were French soldiers, while the civilian contingent included a considerable variety of occupations, especially skilled craftsmen.[27] Among these civilians were a hundred farmers, who brought livestock including pigs and chickens. There were also family groups, although it is difficult to determine the total of women and children. Additionally, Enveja's report also noted the presence of "seven or eight ministers" as well as several German officers. Perhaps most significantly, he further asserted that all the members of this expedition were Protestants (*todos Luteranos*), even the soldiers and sailors, though the French sources do not specifically confirm this. While there is no good reason to doubt the veracity of Enveja's claim, later events make clear the extent to which this information, even if not true, alarmed Menéndez and the Spanish authorities and added urgency to their own planning.

If we accept that after the first week of April the French planners augmented their expedition with additional military supplies and soldiers, we can conclude that this first group of somewhere around three hundred civilians, though diminished by desertions, had been the original nucleus of the expedition. Initially—that is, prior to April 3—the main goal was to reinforce Fort Caroline with skilled individuals, according to the original plan as described by Laudonnière. Presumably, by the time this reinforcement arrived, the original colonists, supplemented by Bourdet's earlier relief fleet, would have completed the construction of Fort Caroline. With the main fortification finished, this larger expedition of 1565 would now make "effective settlement" to establish a permanent claim to this part of "New France" by bringing families, farmers, and even livestock.

What the French planners had told these civilian volunteers, according to Le Challeux, was that they were going to "a country among the most fertile and rich on the globe," where they would find "only great pleasure and singular delight."[28] While admitting that the promise of adventure or gold had attracted some of the French civilians, he emphasized that the overwhelming incentive for most was the lure of a "promised land." To those whose farms and houses had been destroyed during the heavy fighting in Normandy during the first War of Religion, or to those who continued to resent the religious restrictions imposed by the Peace of Amboise, this no doubt appeared to be an attractive proposition. If Le Challeux's case is any indication, these French civilians held no expectations of impending hostilities upon arrival. Finally, as had been the case with the two earlier missions, Le Challeux noted that this group had been expressly forbidden "from making a landfall in any other country or island, especially those which were under the dominion of the King of Spain."[29]

It further appears that this group was either entirely Protestant or at least overwhelmingly so. As Enveja reported, he had been told "the intention of the group collected is to conquer the land, populate it and fortify it, and to plant there, as they say, the gospel. They permit no other books to be brought except Lutheran ones."[30] There is little reason to question Enveja's accuracy, and it is for this, the final attempt at French settlement in Florida, that the concept of a "Huguenot refuge" probably has the most validity for any of the overseas missions engineered by Coligny. Though no French source explicitly says so, not even Le Challeux, it is reasonable to conclude that at least on an individual level the promise of religious freedom was a significant factor in the decision to emigrate. Together with the wondrous descriptions of the charms of Florida, many Norman Calvinists must have considered the prospect of religious liberty a strong incentive to leave their war-torn and repressive homeland.

But if Coligny and Ribault had initially planned this as a nonconfrontative reinforcement of Fort Caroline, the addition of a heavier component of soldiers and armaments in April indicates how they had adjusted the purpose of the mission. By the time of departure from Dieppe, some five hundred soldiers had joined the three hundred or fewer remaining civilians, and the entire group now sailed on seven heavily armed ships of war, "galleasses" (or more probably galleons), four of which were more than a hundred tons. When Menéndez received this information, no doubt he felt that his worst fears were being realized: it would certainly have been logical for him to conclude that Ribault's fleet intended to attack Spanish shipping and towns. In this situation, he could have had few illusions about the proper response required of him as adelantado.

Whatever Menéndez may have assumed about the type of threat to Florida posed by this French expedition, the nature of the French weapons provides us with a truer indication of the French intentions. Both the Inventories of Artillery and Enveja's report confirm that many, and probably most, of the armaments carried by the fleet were land weapons. There were literally hundreds of arquebuses, pikes and lances, and various small artillery pieces on board.[31] What we can learn about the military personnel from these sources also supports this idea. Although in this era there may have been no clear distinction between the duties between soldiers and sailors, and thus the respective complements of five hundred and one hundred are not as significant as they might appear, one must wonder what the purpose would have been of having such a heavy proportion of infantry, as well as a small contingent of cavalry. This evidence leads one to believe that the defense of Fort Caroline, rather than launching offensive seaborne operations, was Ribault's main priority. This explanation also makes the most sense under the circumstances, since we know that by April the French were anticipating a virtually certain Spanish attack upon arrival. Not surprisingly, Le Challeux gives no indication that he or the rest of the civilians were aware that such an attack was likely, although the size of the military contingent may have caused them to wonder.

Certainly the ships themselves carried enough weapons of different types to launch a seaborne offensive, had they decided that such a move was needed. For example, Ribault's ship *La Trinité* carried thirty-two heavy mounted cannon, making it almost the equal of the *San Pelayo* in firepower if not in size.[32] Yet we have no positive indication that Ribault planned to launch corsair raids or attack Spanish shipping. Naval strength could be just as valuable in deterring a Spanish attack from the sea; perhaps the admiral had learned a valuable lesson from the fate of the Brazil colony, which, without ships at its disposal, had found itself unable to respond to a merciless Portuguese bombardment five years before.

In sum, the fleet that departed Dieppe in mid-May still had the same primary intention as it had had in January: to reinforce Laudonnière's nascent colony in populating and settling Florida. The fleet had been a bit tardy in getting organized in the first place, but by January Coligny had gathered several hundred civilian volunteers in Dieppe. As he and Ribault completed the outfitting of a predominantly civilian undertaking, the disturbing news of Menéndez's expedition forced them to add a heavier military component, which required an additional delay. By the middle of May, the French ships carried, in addition to the civilians, hundreds of soldiers and a great quantity of munitions. Finally, another delay, caused by weather, resulted in an even later departure. Ribault's ships did not begin to make the crossing until late June, and it was early September—hurricane season in the Caribbean—by the time the French fleet finally arrived in Florida.

*   *   *

The Spaniards, too, had needed to alter their plans on the basis of information received about the French. In response to the disturbing rumors concerning Stucley and Mimoso that Menéndez had cited in his "Memorial," Philip issued his royal asiento on March 20. By that date, Spanish authorities still had no definite news of Fort Caroline's existence, and the expedition as originally planned followed Menéndez's primary recommendations in his report, that is, exploration, settlement, and defense. As

Menéndez's brother-in-law, Gonzalo Solís de Merás, later wrote, the two original primary intentions of Menéndez's mission, as ordered by the king, were closely related. First, he was to "navigate along the whole coast of Florida, in order to discover the inlets, harbors and shoals that were there, so as to record them with exactness and set them down on marine charts; because, on account of this not having been done, many ships had been lost which went to and from the Indies, with much treasure and many people on board." As part of the same expedition Menéndez agreed to undertake "the conquest and settlement of that land" to keep it out of the hands of foreign trespassers.[33] These goals reflected the most pressing concerns of the Spanish Crown in regard to Florida, and Menéndez himself had stressed these, especially the second, in his report.

These goals coincided with Menéndez's personal interests, especially his overwhelming desire to mount a search for his shipwrecked son, a task he could not even contemplate without royal intervention in resolving his legal and financial difficulties. Solís de Merás also emphasizes another powerful motive. In light of his recent difficulties, Menéndez "desired to regain his reputation, which he had obtained through such hardships and dangers, at the cost of his property, and the loss and death of his son, brothers, kinsmen, and friends."[34]

Thus the original contract originally worked out was, either by design or happenstance, a quid pro quo—the king would intervene in Menéndez's legal and financial problems with the Casa, and in return, Menéndez agreed to put his experience and abilities to use in conducting the mission as adelantado of Florida. As the spring progressed, though, Menéndez altered the scope and purpose of his expedition in response to the intelligence received about French activities, much as the French plans were changing during the same period with news of Spanish preparations.

News that arrived in Spain on March 26 caused the first change of plans, when Philip and Menéndez learned of the predations of the Fort Caroline mutineers. Aside from confirming the fort's existence, these reports gave Philip and Menéndez two additional impressions. First, this intelligence indicated to them that Fort Caroline's purpose was to support French corsair activity, which of course had been a constant Spanish worry. Second, this information told them that French reinforcements were expected in Florida sometime in the spring. To the authorities in Spain, who included Menéndez, these reports served as an alarming proof of French hostility.

This news made it necessary for them to change their original plans and to adopt the contingency option Menéndez had added to the end of his "Memorial." To accomplish this, the Crown became directly involved by increasing the number of ships and troops taking part in the mission, which required that preparations proceed more covertly. On March 30, the king ordered Menéndez to depart no later than May 1 and to keep his destination a secret; apparently, Philip did not want news of what was now considered to be at least partly a punitive expedition to jeopardize the upcoming meeting between the Duke of Alva and Princess Elizabeth with Catherine de Medici and Charles IX, planned for mid-June in Bayonne.[35] However, it proved impossible to keep the outfitting of either fleet a secret, and in early April each side had received a report about the other. First, the dispatch describing Menéndez's preparations reached French authorities shortly after they had begun, on April 3. In response, Ribault's fleet increased its own military component. On April 11, the Spaniards had their first direct report of Ribault's involvement, through the diplomatic dispatch mentioned earlier that described five ships being prepared.

On May 1, Philip received a more alarming report from Menéndez himself. The captain relayed what he had heard from his contacts on the northern coast of Spain: that sixteen French ships and two thousand soldiers were readying in Normandy for a mission to Florida.[36] Within days the Council of the Indies ordered that the Spanish fleet be reinforced with royal support, "because as the port of the French is in the Channel of Bahama, which is the passage of the Indies, it is of great importance to the service of Your Majesty to drive that people out from there."[37] Yet Spanish Ambassador Alava y Beaumont, in Paris at the time, believed that Menéndez had exaggerated the size of the French expedition, and that the expedition reported arming in Normandy was a smaller independent corsair fleet.[38] To determine which, if either, interpretation was correct, Philip dispatched his own agent, Dr. Enveja, to Normandy. The resultant report arrived during the first week of June, containing the definitive proof of the French initiative and its clearly military nature. In the meantime, despite the risks to diplomatic relations that both Coligny and Philip recognized, each fleet continued to escalate its military capabilities in anticipation of what appeared to be an inevitable showdown in Florida.

In addition to the verifiable reports referred to above, it is possible that the Spaniards received other intelligence from within France. In particular, it has been written that the admiral's political enemies, including the

Duke of Guise, had informed Spanish agents about Ribault's voyage.[39] While it is certainly possible that such communications had been made, this could not have had much real impact on Spanish planning. Menéndez had adopted his contingency plan in response to the news received from the Indies about the Fort Caroline mutineers, on March 26, and not, quite clearly, upon any firm and definite news of Ribault's expedition.[40] Moreover, the subsequent changes in the fleet's preparations—specifically the increase in direct royal involvement during April and May—had come about because of the arrival of the diplomatic dispatches mentioned above. By June, Spanish authorities had received Enveja's full report on the French fleet, which made any previous reports superfluous. In any case, Enveja's source was not the Guises, who were unlikely to have been privy to the very specific facts that were collected. Instead, Enveja wrote that he had spoken directly to Jean Ribault himself, who had for some unknown reason answered him quite openly about both the nature and intent of his force. Thus it is safe to conclude that even if the Guises or any other French Catholics had revealed French plans to go to Florida, the impact was insignificant and in no way jeopardized this expedition; the plans were already known in Spain from other sources.

From April to June, Menéndez hurriedly traveled back and forth between Seville, Madrid, and the Asturian coast, trying simultaneously to settle his legal problems, raise money and volunteers, and oversee the outfitting of an adequate fleet. During this period he was able to take advantage of the king's obvious desire for haste and his own need for a resolution of his legal and financial problems with the Casa.[41] He benefited greatly from royal involvement in his problems. Philip reduced the fines imposed by the Casa, which Menéndez argued was essential for the outfitting of his fleet. With royal help, Menéndez also achieved the restoration of his confiscated property, pending a final settlement of the case. Additionally, the Crown furnished Menéndez with royal ships and promised that upon his arrival in the Indies, the governor of Santo Domingo would provide him with soldiers. With his son still missing, it is questionable whether Menéndez actually went so far as to delay his departure to get a more advantageous settlement, but it is clear that the main reason for the delay of the Spanish fleet was Menéndez's dissatisfaction with the resources he had at his disposal, resulting in his continued petitions to the Crown and to the Casa for more money.

In this way, by the end of June, two separate Spanish fleets had been assembled for departure. Menéndez himself commanded the larger, which sailed from Cadiz on June 29, and which included a number of individual merchant ships that had joined the convoy for protection. A slightly smaller squadron on the Asturian coast was to sail independently to the Canary Islands with the intention of meeting the southern group there.[42] This northern force was dominated by a heavily Asturian leadership largely drawn from Menéndez's relatives, in-laws, and friends; many of these individuals, summoned by ties of personal loyalty, were risking everything that they owned on this venture.[43]

As early as April, with the meeting at Bayonne approaching, Philip had ordered the Duke of Alva to prepare a presentation to Catherine that would ask her to acknowledge the Spanish claim to Florida. If Ribault had not yet departed by the time they met at Bayonne, Alva was to try to persuade her to prevent the French fleet from setting out.[44] Enveja's report had apparently removed all doubt about Ribault's intentions, leading Philip to write to Chantonnay in Paris:

> I have learned that a French fleet is intending to leave Dieppe for a destination in Florida. If up to now I have made no remonstrance to the queen mother on the subject of vessels that have already departed for Florida, it was because I was thinking that it was without orders and solely for pillaging and I had commanded that they be brought to justice; but today I learned that these preparations are made by her orders and those of Admiral Coligny to go to a province which belongs to me, if the queen does not prevent the departure of this fleet, I will take measures according to the interest of my realm. If this fleet has left, leave it to the Duke of Alva the task of dealing with this affair when he sees the queen.[45]

By June 8 authorities in Spain believed that Ribault's fleet, now known to have had royal backing, had already sailed. Philip thus decided that it was pointless for Alva to raise the issue of Florida at Bayonne and instead ordered Menéndez to intensify his final preparations in Cadiz and Asturias. Any further discussion of Florida with the French would have to take place pending the outcome of Menéndez's assignment.

As the Bayonne meeting wound to a close at the end of the month, a dispatch from the Spanish ambassador in England, dated June 25, arrived in Madrid. This reported that eight French ships and twelve hundred men had been in Portland on June 13, "bound for Florida." The dispatch added that "considering the weather we have had they must still be off this coast."[46] The Duke of Alva, in Bayonne, must have received this intelligence via Madrid too late for it to make any difference.

Had he known of the problems Ribault had had in getting under way, and that he might still have been within recall before the conference ended on June 29, quite possibly he would have carried out his original instructions from the king, that is, to try to force Catherine to call off the French expedition. While it is questionable whether she would have agreed to such a request, at the very least, a discussion of the issue may have exposed each side to the point of view of the other.

Instead, authorities in both France and Spain made their frantic final preparations to determine the issue by force of arms. After Menéndez received Enveja's report in June, the intention of this new French expedition no doubt seemed obvious to him: the heretical corsair Ribault, with royal assistance, was launching an offensive strike at the Spanish Indies and the silver fleet. This news seemed to reinforce what Menéndez had suspected all along, aside from the particularly aggravating news that the French Crown was involved; under these conditions, it would seem surprising had he entertained any other possibilities about the French intentions. There is no reason to suspect that he realized that the heavy military component of the French expedition had not been added for offensive purposes, but out of the French fear that they would be attacked by Menéndez himself.

Ribault and the French, on their part, had little understanding of why the Spaniards felt it necessary to ready such a well-armed fleet. As far as they were concerned, Fort Caroline posed no immediate threat to Spain, especially since their explicit orders were to avoid Spanish territories entirely. Thus, by the time these two fleets departed, each credited the other with only the worst of intentions. By then, it was already too late for any peaceful resolution of the problem.

8

In the Eye of the Hurricane

The colonists at Fort Caroline, of course, were completely unaware of the preparations being made in Europe. They knew only that, by late June, their reinforcements were more than three months overdue. It would have been impossible for them to know that by then not one, but two, sizable fleets had set out across the Atlantic, each heavily armed and eager for battle.

Menéndez intended to capture Fort Caroline before it could be reinforced, and he expected that if he could arrive ahead of Ribault, his forces would enjoy a crucial element of surprise. It is difficult to say with precision how many ships ultimately departed under his command, or the actual numbers of individuals, both civilians and soldiers, who sailed from Spain that June. It is impossible to accurately determine how many private vessels had attached themselves to the armada, while some of the royal ships left behind schedule. It further appears that earlier in the month a contingent of royal ships had already sailed for the Indies, which Menéndez expected to assume command of upon his arrival.[1]

In any case, it is largely irrelevant how many originally departed, because of the losses suffered by the Spanish fleet during the voyage. Damage from violent storms prevented some ships from getting any farther than the Canary Islands, while a handful of other ships apparently were either lost at sea or turned back. Menéndez, on his thousand-ton *San Pelayo*, left the Canaries on July 8 accompanied by seven other ships, and on this last leg of the journey the fleet encountered their worst storm, fortunately just prior to reaching land. This one was so severe that Menéndez's chaplain, Francisco López de Mendoza Grajales, on the *San Pelayo*, wrote that "all had to make confessions, expecting death momentarily. The wind was so great it tore out the foremast together with sails and rigging. . . . Thinking the ship to be lost and without ability to sail [the officers] let it drift in the waves until God in his mercy brought them to port."[2] (See map 3 in chapter 5.)

This last storm caused the *San Pelayo* to lose contact with another two ships, while others suffered severe mast damage. During the second week of August, well behind schedule, they reached the harbor at San Juan, Puerto Rico.[3] There, Menéndez found that there had been no report of the two royal ships he had expected to meet there, which had departed from the Canaries a week ahead of him. Worse, there was no news at all about the Asturian contingent, which composed almost half of his expected forces. In all, Menéndez's original armada had been diminished by at least two-thirds, while his remaining ships and men were in poor condition. This loss of military capacity narrowed his options considerably.

Menéndez's major concern continued to be time. As he wrote to the king from San Juan, on August 13: "It is chiefly important that I should arrive in Florida before the French, and in all reason, judging from the speed with which I have come thus far, and shall go from here to Florida, I shall arrive before them, and although in doing this, we incur some risk, and undertake great labors, yet it seems to me that we ought not, for these reasons to fail to venture; for if the French should arrive first in Florida, all the force that I have, although it go all together, is too small to attack them."[4]

Only two or three days after reaching San Juan, Menéndez decided to take his four least-damaged ships and a borrowed vessel to Havana, in order to get needed repairs and meet up with reinforcements before sailing north. However, even before leaving Puerto Rico, he received the news (which turned out to be false) that Ribault had captured a Spanish dispatch boat off the Puerto Rican coast two days before. This caused him to worry that a report of his planned attack might reach Fort Caroline ahead of him, and he would lose the crucial element of surprise. Finally, some of the Fort Caroline mutineers that Menéndez had taken on board and interrogated provided disturbing details about the physical setting of Fort Caroline. According to them, sandbars and its shallow harbor gave it superb defense against seaborne attack.[5] On the basis of this information, the *adelantado* abruptly decided to lose no more time by going to Havana—he must attack Florida at once. Solís de Merás wrote that Menéndez

not knowing whether the other [ships] had been lost in the storm, and whether the ships from Asturias and Biscaye would arrive. . . .

Trusting in the Divine Will, he held it to be very proper that they should sail thence for Florida, without waiting for or seeking further aid; for if they succeeded in finding the place where the Lutherans were settled he considered victory to be beyond a doubt, as the French would be taken unawares, and the more so if succor had not reached them; whereas if they should wait for the whole armada at the Windward Islands, there would follow the difficulty of their arrival being made known, and of the enemy to have the opportunity to fortify themselves so as to become invincible.[6]

Menéndez's fleet at that point numbered only five ships, three of them very small and four with unrepaired storm damage, including the *San Pelayo*. In a letter written during the next month, he recounted that his available personnel numbered "800 persons, 500 of them soldiers, who could be landed, with 200 seamen, the other hundred being useless people, married men, women and children and officials."[7] It was hardly the force he had counted on, but with the factor of surprise, it might be sufficient.

Evidently, even with diminished sailing capacity, Menéndez still considered it possible to reach Fort Caroline ahead of Ribault. If he found the French defenses unprepared, he believed that his five hundred soldiers might yet be enough to storm and take the fort. A quick and decisive surprise attack would enable his forces to take the advantageous defensive position by the time Ribault's forces arrived and, with any luck, additional forces might even have joined him by then. None of the other alternatives, which involved using costly time to make repairs and wait for reinforcements which might or might not arrive, seemed likely to accomplish his objective of removing the French. Heading immediately to Fort Caroline appeared to offer the only realistic chance of ensuring that Florida would remain in Spanish hands, that the silver fleet would be safe, and that he himself would reap great rewards and glory from his success.

Conversely, Menéndez's greatest fear as he left San Juan was that Ribault would arrive at Fort Caroline first and that the French would be able to deploy their considerable forces in defending it. In such a case, even with the original full complement of Spanish forces, an attack on the fort would be difficult, while an attack with a smaller force would probably be futile. Recognizing that he might have already lost the race, Menéndez had developed a contingency plan. Should Ribault's armada have already arrived, he would lead his ships on a retreat farther to the south to await reinforcements; if necessary, he could depart Florida altogether and regroup his forces in Havana. There he could await a better opportunity to launch an offensive, perhaps in the spring when there was less danger of turbulent weather. Solís de Merás reported that, en route, Menéndez had told his troops: "In case they should find them fortified and with ample aid, and should not be able to land nearby because of recognizing some great danger, they would turn back their prows towards Hispaniola and Cuba, where they could discuss what had to be done, while being reinforced by the men, supplies, and munitions that would be arriving."[8]

The major unknown factor was how many reinforcements he might get, and when they might arrive. Menéndez was enough of a realist to recognize that he could not count on substantial aid arriving anytime soon. He would have to consider the small force he had as the extent of his resources for the immediate future. Should more support arrive, he could then reevaluate the situation; even if Ribault had already reached Fort Caroline, Menéndez might be able to launch a successful siege, depending on the circumstances. From Puerto Rico, he wrote to the king: "When the cavalry from Santo Domingo should reach us, we should be masters of the campaign, both by land and sea, and should have them surrounded, however strong they might be, and be able to destroy them, without their being able to receive help, either by land or by sea."[9]

Arriving at Fort Caroline first still presented the best chance for success, and Menéndez hoped that his contingency plan would not be necessary. He therefore set his course for Florida. But instead of using the Bahama Channel, which was less direct and where he believed he might encounter Ribault's fleet, he sailed through the middle of the uncharted Bahamas archipelago, risking dangerous reefs and shoals, gambling that by doing so he could save a few days of precious time. Almost miraculously, his limping fleet suffered no further losses. On August 25, the Spaniards sighted land around sixty miles south of their destination and began to make their way up the coast.[10]

*　*　*

Apparently Ribault did not share Menéndez's sense of urgency. The French fleet, by crossing the Atlantic farther to the north, had avoided the adverse weather that had bedeviled Menéndez. By August 14, after a seven-week journey, Ribault had already reached the coast of Florida, landing somewhat more than a hundred miles south of Fort Caroline. After stopping to take on drinking water and to interrogate a shipwrecked Spaniard, his force had proceeded north at an unhurried pace, not arriving at the River May until August 27 or 28.[11] In the conclusion of his third book, Laudonnière wrote, "I will plainly say one thing, That the long delay of Captaine John Ribault used in his embarking, and the 15 days that he spent roving along the coast of Florida, before he came to our fort Caroline, were the cause of the loss that we sustained."[12]

It is hard to disagree with this assessment. Ribault's slow journey up the coast would prove fatal to French interests, and the reason for its slowness remains difficult to adequately explain. It appears from Le Challeux's narrative—the only description we have of the voyage it-self—that Ribault decided to reconnoitre this stretch of shoreline, which had been unexplored by him since it lay farther south than his landfall in 1562. As he headed north, he took the time to send an expedition up a river and to negotiate with the Indians who welcomed their arrival.

Once more, we see Ribault's inability to evaluate the likely conse-quences of his actions. One might conceivably explain Ribault's earlier errors as the result of circumstances largely beyond his control or at-tribute them to plain bad luck. Leaving a garrison at Port Royal had be-come a problem only because of the course of French domestic affairs, which could not have been foreseen. Even trying to get English help in reinforcing Fort Caroline would not have been such a questionable deci-sion except for the rumors about Thomas Stucley, which had so alarmed the Spaniards in early 1565 about foreign incursions in Florida. But in August 1565, with the fate of Laudonnière's little colony in the balance, Ribault seems to have been oblivious to the realities of his situation, and the result was his colossal and inexcusable blunder of not making di-rectly for Fort Caroline with all possible haste.

We can only conclude that, for some reason, Ribault must not have anticipated that Menéndez would try to reach Florida ahead of him, but if so, it is hard to understand his reasoning. There is no question that prior to leaving France, he had learned of Menéndez's fleet and where it was heading.[13] With this in mind, it should have been obvious to him that his prime responsibility lay in getting to Fort Caroline quickly, to rein-force Laudonnière and prepare for a coming attack. Incredible as it seems, these were not his highest priorities. Apparently, he was so confi-dent that Menéndez would not arrive until much later that he felt justi-fied in conducting a reconnaissance of a previously unknown stretch of coast. But even had he been completely unaware of Menéndez's planned attack or had received a report that we are unaware of that Menéndez planned to delay in the Indies, this still would not excuse his actions. By early August Ribault was already at least three months overdue. If for no other reason than to resupply Fort Caroline, he had an obligation to get there as quickly as he possibly could.

Despite Ribault's best efforts to squander it, the advantage remained with the French in late August. Not only had they won the race to Florida, though only barely, their available military forces outnumbered those of Menéndez by a factor of almost two to one. Additionally, having avoided the storms that had beset the Spanish fleet, Ribault also enjoyed a great advantage in sailing ability, although he could not have known it at the time. However, even these factors would not be enough to ensure the success of the French effort, since Ribault still had a couple of more mistakes to make. Together, his lapses in judgment would not only cost him and several hundred of his men their lives, but they would also doom the French design to claim Terra Florida.

*　　*　　*

On the afternoon of August 28, as Menéndez was touching land at the future St. Augustine, Laudonnière's settlers at Fort Caroline had loaded their ships and were preparing to depart. Just that morning, the wind had become favorable; by noon the tide began to go out, and the abandonment of Fort Caroline would become a reality in a matter of hours. Just as Laudonnière and his captains were giving final orders, they sighted the sails of Jean Ribault's relief fleet on the horizon.[14]

Ribault had been authorized to replace Laudonnière as governor of the fort, because of negative reports about the latter's command that had reached Admiral Coligny from the malcontents whom Laudonnière had sent back with Captain Bourdet.[15] According to Laudonnière's history, Ribault's commission from Coligny stated the following:

> Captain Laudonnière, because some of them which are returned from Florida speak indifferently of the Country, the king desireth your presence, to the end, that according to your trial, he may resolve to bestow great cost thereon, or wholly to leave it: and therefore I send Captain Jean Ribault to be Governor there, to whom you shall deliver whatsoever you have in charge, & inform him of all things you have discovered.
>
> [Postscript]
>
> Think not, that whereas I send for you, it is for any evil opinion or mistrust that I have of you, but that it is for your good and for

your credit, and assure yourself that during your life you will find me your good Master.—Chatillon[16]

Apprehensive about the situation at Fort Caroline, Ribault initially held all seven of his ships outside the sandbar at the mouth of the river until he could be certain that things were well. Although Laudonnière had sent a boat to meet him the day he arrived, Ribault took the crew on board without sending word back to the fort. It was only the next day, when Ribault finally released Laudonnière's men after a lengthy interrogation, that the Fort Caroline colonists even learned the identity of the fleet that had arrived. By then their commander had displayed his anxiety by deploying artillery into position to withstand a possible attack; soon afterward, his men returned with the joyous news that their reinforcements had finally arrived.

Though many of Ribault's passengers disembarked on August 29, it was another entire day before the newly arrived ships began to unload their cargo of food, supplies, and artillery. The difficult entrance to the estuary hindered their progress, since the four largest ships had to remain outside the sandbar while small boats ferried their cargo onto land; as a result, the unloading was a tedious process.[17] In the meantime, Ribault officially took command of the fort, persuading Laudonnière to remain in a position of authority after assuring him that he had been convinced the negative reports were false.

Ribault's slowness in unloading his ships, though it was only a matter of a few days, magnified the negative consequences of his slow progress along the Florida coast. Menéndez, advancing north as fast as his ships' limited sailing ability permitted, had learned from Indians that they were within a short distance of the French fort. By the afternoon of September 4, Menéndez sighted four large French vessels in the distance, anchored outside the River May. At the same time, the French caught sight of the Spanish fleet as it approached. The moment of reckoning had arrived.

Having lost the element of surprise, Menéndez would normally have returned to the south to regroup and rendezvous with the rest of his force, and most of the officers favored this course of action during a hastily called conference aboard the *San Pelayo*. However, the fact that the French ships were still outside the sandbar caused Menéndez to reconsider the possibilities in light of what his French prisoners had told him about the harbor. Observing carefully, he could determine a couple of important things. First, he saw that the French had not yet unloaded their cargo, which probably meant that they had just arrived, and he also saw that their ships still had some of their sails unfurled and were in a position to set sail almost immediately. No doubt it occurred to him that if his own damaged fleet retreated, the French ships, ready to sail and in much better condition, could pursue and easily overwhelm him. In other words, a retreat might be the worst possible course of action. However, since he felt that the four larger French ships were momentarily vulnerable, a successful preemptive strike might ensure that "the French would not have an armada sufficient to go out in search of him on the seas," then or at any later time.[18]

This explains why Menéndez felt it necessary to attack, despite his force's inferiority. Before he could carry out this plan, on the night of September 4, a sudden rain squall appeared. This delayed the Spanish approach, and by the time the weather cleared, growing darkness had caused Menéndez to alter his plans once again. Instead, he ordered his vessels to approach the French ships and anchor right next to them. By midnight, his ships were in position, awaiting the dawn light to make a boarding attempt. Through the hours of darkness, shouted communications between the French and Spanish sailors established each others' nationalities, religions, and commanders. As Menéndez wrote to the king, he personally called across to the French that "I, Pedro Menéndez, by command of Your Majesty, had come to this coast to burn and hang the French Lutherans whom I should find there, and that, in the morning I should board their vessels to see if any of that people [Lutherans] were on them, and that, if there were any, I should not fail to execute upon them the justice that Your Majesty commanded."[19]

Shortly before daybreak, the four French ships—with most of their crew on land but much of their cargo, including the valuable artillery, still on board—fired a sudden volley, cut their anchor cables, and headed out to sea under cover of darkness. The Spanish ships pursued and returned fire but gave up the chase soon after because of their sailing difficulties.

This first encounter between the fleets had been inconclusive, with neither side gaining any significant advantage. The French had successfully avoided any damage or losses and were now well aware of their danger. For Menéndez, the problem remained of how to protect his damaged ships from a French counterattack. With daylight, he could see that the French ships he had attacked were some distance away on the horizon, but he also noticed, for the first time, that there were three other French ships within the harbor. Under the circumstances, Menéndez decided to withdraw. As he explained, "It appeared to me there was little reason for wasting time there, as my flag ship [the *San Pelayo*] could not go in there [into the harbor], and the little ones could enter only with great risk, I decided to turn back to the Bahama Channel to look for a harbor where I could land near them, and eight leagues from that harbor by sea and six by land, I found one which I had reconnoitred before, on St. Augustine's Day."[20]

Reaching the relative safety of land, the Spaniards frantically began to build defensive positions from logs and dirt. Three of the French ships had followed them southward, but, perhaps because of lack of personnel, they did not attack as the Spaniards had feared. The French merely observed the location of the Spanish landfall and then returned north to Fort Caroline. By that evening, they had reported the Spanish situation to Ribault, who called for a meeting of "nearly thirty officers, in addition to noblemen, officials, and other administrators."[21]

The French leaders found themselves at odds over their next move. The conservative path, favored by Laudonnière and possibly most of those assembled, was for the forces to regroup at Fort Caroline and prepare their defenses against a future Spanish attack. Ribault, however, after learning where the Spanish forces had gone, disagreed. Le Moyne's account describes this difference of opinion in some detail:

> The more reasonable part of this council was of the opinion that the fort should be rebuilt and fortified as soon as possible and that a large section of the soldiers, under the leadership of Laudonnière, men who knew the routes, should be dispatched to the place where the Spaniards were; and thus it would happen that with God's help the matter would be quickly settled. For that province was not under Spanish jurisdiction, the nearest boundaries of which were three or four hundred miles away. But Ribault realized that everyone was inclining towards this view and said, "Gentlemen, having heard your opinion, I would like to put forward mine as well, but I think that you should be informed that shortly before I left France I received from the admiral a letter, at the foot of which these words were written in his own hand, "Ribault, we have been warned that the Spaniard wants to attack you; see that you yield him nothing and you will be doing right." So I tell you frankly, if we follow your plan, it may happen that the Spaniards do not wait for our attack but will take to flight and board their ships again; and in this way we should be deprived of the chance of ridding ourselves of those

who wish to destroy us. But this seems to me a more effective plan, that I put all our soldiers aboard those four ships we have at anchor, and that we go straightaway and seize their ships which are still anchored at the spot where they have landed. When these are taken we shall go ashore and engage them in battle with so much more confidence.[22]

Laudonnière openly criticized this option, or so he claimed later. His account asserts that he warned Ribault of the hazards of the weather at that time of the year and later, in private, cautioned against leaving Fort Caroline undefended.[23] Since Ribault was technically in command, due to the orders he carried from Coligny, Laudonnière had little choice but to cede authority.

Three days later, on September 8, Ribault led six of the nine ships at Fort Caroline to the south in pursuit of Menéndez.[24] If we can accept Laudonnière's testimony, almost all of the able-bodied French soldiers were on board. It was a bold plan, at least partly motivated by Ribault's conviction that since Menéndez had come to Florida for the express purpose of removing the French, the French had clear justification for taking the offensive.[25] We cannot know what evaluation Ribault had made at that point of the Spanish fighting abilities. Perhaps he correctly sensed their naval weakness and decided that his best chance was to provoke them into a sea battle, though, in hindsight, Menéndez clearly had no intention of accommodating him.

Once again, Ribault did not appreciate the importance of time. It took him three days to ready his pursuing forces, although it seems that contrary winds may also have contributed to the delayed pursuit. As a result, the French ships did not arrive at St. Augustine until the morning of September 10, when they found Menéndez's troops disembarked and still constructing barricades. Meanwhile, the two largest Spanish ships, which included the *San Pelayo*, were nowhere to be seen, since the previous night, Menéndez had sent them to Hispaniola to avoid capture.

The Spaniards were heavily outnumbered by their attackers, they had little food, and in the three days they had been ashore they had not had adequate time to prepare defenses. Chaplain Mendoza Grajales later recounted that the Spaniards had had no tools with which to construct fortifications, and he added that "if the French had attacked at once when they arrived, it would have been a very great capture, because our people were not supplied with arms and were carrying provisions."[26] However, when Ribault arrived he hesitated to order his ships to cross the shallow harbor entrance, and instead he anchored them outside the harbor while he demanded Menéndez's surrender.

No doubt the layout of the coastal landscape around St. Augustine and its barrier islands has changed somewhat during the last four hundred years, due to the cumulative effects of wind and water, and it is difficult to get an accurate sense of the width and depth of the harbor as it was in Ribault's era. Generally, the eastern Florida coast is sheltered from the open ocean by narrow sand islands extending alongside it, while narrow and frequently shallow openings give access to the sea. The geography in the sixteenth century must have presented similar challenges. Menéndez himself had apparently felt that his two largest ships had drafts that were too deep for them to cross the barrier into the harbor, which explains why he had dispatched them to the south, rather than leaving them exposed outside the sand barrier, which apparently had been his sole alternative.

Ribault must have been faced with a similar dilemma: he did not want to risk grounding his ships by approaching the Spaniards, yet he could not unload his troops from outside the barrier. In order to attack, he would have had to ferry his soldiers in small boats, which would not only have taken much time but also would have minimized his advantage in numbers. It is difficult to be certain about what Ribault had in mind, especially since there is some disagreement in the Spanish sources about how long the French waited outside St. Augustine harbor.[27] It may well be that Ribault was awaiting a higher tide to enter the harbor, as Solís de Merás suggested, but if so, this would have delayed him only by a few hours. Alternatively, Le Moyne's account tells us that the primary French intent had been to capture the ships and not to attack the Spaniards on land. Perhaps Ribault hesitated, uncertain as to his next move, once he realized that the two largest Spanish ships were gone and that the other two were inside the harbor.[28] He would have been faced with the choice of pursuing to the south or launching an attack on the Spanish defenses.

Menéndez must have appreciated the difficulty of Ribault's situation, and although his own position was precarious, he refused to yield. He apparently still hoped that reinforcements from the south might arrive, but even if they did not, there was a good chance that the navigational hazards of entering the harbor would prevent the French forces from making a coordinated large-scale assault. For the moment, there appeared to be a stalemate: the Spaniards could not escape, while the French could not, or would not, attack.

As it turned out, the hand of fate favored Menéndez. While the menacing French ships lingered offshore in full view, the calm weather conditions rapidly gave way to terrifying winds and rain. As Menéndez wrote later, "A hurricane and terrible storm came upon them, and it appeared to me that they [the French] could not have returned to their fort, and ran risk of being lost, and that in order for them to come and attack me, as they had done, they must bring a large and better force than they had, and that their fort must have been left weak and that now was the time to go and attack it."[29]

Whether Ribault was waiting for a better moment to attack, or had decided to chase the departing Spanish vessels, or was merely caught by indecision, it is baffling that such an experienced mariner could have failed to notice the signs of an impending storm. Had he done so, he might have reached the relative safety of the open sea, or even launched an attack. Whatever its cause, Ribault's inability to attack Menéndez at St. Augustine cost him his final opportunity to achieve success in his mission.

The hurricane, coming from the south and blowing in from the northeast, changed the situation completely.[30] Until it struck, Menéndez's entire undertaking, as well as his forces, had seemed doomed. Now, a brief opportunity had arisen. Menéndez suddenly ordered that five hundred men—which included all but a hundred of his soldiers—prepare to march overland to attack Fort Caroline. This required crossing unknown swamps, with almost no food, in the middle of a hurricane. To his hungry and exhausted men, this appeared to be sheer lunacy.[31] To Menéndez, it appeared the only way to carry out his original plan of capturing Fort Caroline.

The alternative to an overland attack was to remain at St. Augustine and improve their defenses. As Menéndez was no doubt aware, there were a couple of problems with this course of action. For one thing, the high winds coming from the northeast would further delay or prevent any Spanish reinforcements arriving from the south and perhaps even destroy them. As a result, his forces were now effectively isolated at St. Augustine, lacking food, weapons, and ships. Also, once the hurricane subsided, the presumably regrouped French forces would have a second opportunity to engage the beleaguered Spanish position. For Menéndez's forces to remain where they were would not significantly improve their desperate situation; they would be as helpless as before except perhaps further weakened from lack of food.

It is important to point out that Menéndez clearly could not have known at the time that most of the French ships that had come to attack him were being run aground by the storm even as he readied his troops for the march north. What he did know, or at least must have suspected, was that the attacking French ships carried most of their troops. As long as the weather made it impossible for the French to sail to the north, their fort would be left largely undefended. Helping in Menéndez's decision was his belief, based on Indian reports, that Fort Caroline could be reached by only two days of marching. This may have been true under normal circumstances, as it was less than thirty miles away.[32]

However, after a few days of preparations, it took four days for the Spanish soldiers, guided by a French prisoner they had brought with them from San Juan, to reach their destination on the night of September 19. As described by Solís de Merás:

> as during those four days there had been much rain, they had crossed many marshes and had carried their arms, and knapsacks with food, on their backs, the soldiers arrived very tired and weak, and because the showers that night were so heavy, there was no way to keep the powder and wicks from being all wet, and the little biscuit they had in their knapsacks, and no one wore anything on their body that was not soaked with water: at this point the Adelantado feared greatly to take counsel with the captains . . . because some were beginning to be insolent, and his officers were saying abusive words against him so audibly that he heard many of them.[33]

When the Spanish troops arrived in view of Fort Caroline, on the evening of September 19, they were wet, hungry, tired, without dry gunpowder, and in a near-mutinous state. Although they had been joined by an indeterminate number of Timucuans, there were fewer than four hundred Spaniards, because many had either gotten lost or deserted along the way.

Once more, the weather aided Menéndez. Because of the night's torrential rains, the French had decided that only a token complement of sentries was necessary.[34] As dawn broke, Menéndez's troops and their Indian allies entered the fort virtually unopposed. While Solís de Merás provides us with many dramatic details of the attack that Menéndez does not, the latter merely noted in his letter to the king:

> on the 20th, on the eve of the day of the Blessed Apostle and Evangelist St. Matthew, in the morning when it began to dawn, having prayed to God Our Lord and to his Blessed Mother that they would give us victory over these Lutherans, for we had already deter-

mined to attack it openly with the twenty scaling ladders that we had brought with us, and the Divine Majesty showed us such favor and so directed us that, without losing a man killed, nor wounded, save one, who is well already, we gained the fort and all that it contained. One hundred and thirty men were put to death.[35]

Both Menéndez and his brother-in-law quite definitely stated that the former gave strict orders to spare the women and children found in the fort. Menéndez says that there were "some 50 persons who were either women, infants, and boys of 15 years or under. . . . I have feared that Our Lord would chastise me if I should deal cruelly with them."[36]

Le Challeux had a different recollection of the same events, writing that "The Spaniard, having traversed woods, ponds, and rivers, led by the savage, arrived the twentieth day of September in the morning, with the weather very rainy, and, entering with no resistance into the fort, committed a horrible execution of the rage and fury that they had conceived against our nation, each trying to outdo the other in slaying men, healthy and sick, women and babies, of the sort that it is not possible to dream of a massacre that is equal to this one in cruelty and barbarity."[37]

Le Challeux's memory of this attack emphasizes the terror and confusion of awakening to find Spaniards, along with some Indians, already within the fort. His first impulse, shared by the rest of the French, was to flee and not to resist. The slaughter was so one-sided that he declared "it seemed to me I would not find greater cruelty among wild beasts."[38] He illustrated the Spanish brutality by recounting the fate of some of the Frenchmen with whom he found refuge in the woods. Trusting that they might surrender peacefully to the Spanish victors, these were "treated in the fashion of the others: they thus had their throats slit and were massacred."[39]

Le Challeux was the only eyewitness who claimed that the Spanish executed women and children, an assertion made by neither Laudonnière nor Le Moyne. In Laudonnière's case this may be because his account is preoccupied with his own actions and narrow escape, and it details no specific atrocities of any kind.[40] Although Le Moyne left the details of the massacre to Le Challeux, he did make some relevant observations. According to his narrative, the Spanish attackers first sought out the French soldiers' quarters, in order to kill them first. Le Moyne also describes in graphic detail the dismemberment of his companion Grandchemin, who had tried to surrender.[41] Interestingly, the sole mention of women and children in Le Moyne's account is a brief reference to

Laudonnière's maidservant, who was wounded during the attack and fled to safety with Le Moyne.

To Menéndez's evident annoyance, the three French ships still in the harbor avoided capture by his troops. One of them was sunk, either scuttled by the French themselves to avoid its capture or else sunk by Spanish artillery.[42] The other two vessels, one commanded by Jacques Ribault, set sail and fled to the open sea.[43] Either the next day or a few days later, depending upon the account, the ships returned to rescue fifty to sixty fortunate individuals, including Le Challeux, Le Moyne, and Laudonnière, each of whom had escaped the carnage by fleeing into the woods. In all, perhaps slightly more than a hundred surviving Frenchmen were later able to reach Europe on these two vessels. In doing so they departed from Florida without having learned the fate of Ribault's fleet.

Despite the capture of the French fort, Menéndez's problems were far from over. The one-sided victory had left him in command of four hundred exhausted Spanish soldiers and fifty French women and children. With the storm beginning to clear, he had to prepare for the possible return of the French fleet that had pursued him to St. Augustine. At that point he had to anticipate a possible attack on two targets fifty miles apart, but he had no ships with which to return any of his soldiers to the south. Moreover, it seems that Ribault had not unloaded most of the precious food his ships had carried, so there was little to be had at Fort Caroline. The dilemma faced by the Spanish commander is clear from the address he was reported to have given his troops:

> Now, more than ever, is the time for us . . . to provide all things so that we can defend this place against the French armada when it returns to it. Let us likewise insure the safety of our people, artillery, arms, munitions and supplies we left at St. Augustine . . . it behooves me to return the day after tomorrow with those who must go back, because it is needful that St. Augustine be well-protected; so that while we shall be defending this fort against the French if they come with their armada, they cannot set foot in this country by going to St. Augustine, which has a better harbor.[44]

Since few of his men were then in much condition to undertake another march, Menéndez ordered most of his troops to remain under the command of one of his ablest officers at the captured fort, now rechristened San Mateo. After waiting for the hurricane to die out, he personally led a picked force of thirty-five men back to the south.[45] Despite getting lost, Menéndez and his men reached St. Augustine three days later, on September 27. Immediately after arrival, he dispatched the two small vessels in the harbor back to the north with his artillery and what little food was available, hoping that his reinforcements from the Indies would arrive before another French attack could be launched. He was totally unaware of the fate of Ribault's fleet and could not have realized that, for all intents and purposes, the French had already been defeated.

*　*　*

The day after Menéndez reached St. Augustine, on September 28, local Indians reported to him that a group of shipwrecked Frenchmen were stranded on a sandbar a few miles to the south. Menéndez immediately went in search of them, taking between forty and fifty soldiers on a barge, since he had just dispatched his ships north.[46] Traveling through the night, the next morning they located the French survivors of three ships sunk during the hurricane, who were on the other side of a swiftly moving channel and were unable to reach the mainland. Menéndez related that one Frenchman swam over to the Spanish and explained that they were the only 140 survivors of 400 men, the rest of whom were presumed drowned. They had been without food or fresh water for more than a week and were mostly unarmed, and they initially pleaded that Menéndez provide them transportation back to their fort.

In words that echoed what he had told the French upon their first encounter outside the sandbar at Fort Caroline, as well as his "Memorial" to the king early that year, Menéndez informed them of the true circumstances of the situation:

> I replied that we held their fort, having taken and put to death those who were in it, for having erected it without the leave of Your Majesty, and because they were planting their wicked Lutheran sect in these, Your Majesty's Provinces, and that I made war with fire and blood as Governor and Captain-General of these Provinces upon all who might have come to these parts to settle and to plant this evil Lutheran sect, seeing that I had come by Your Majesty's command to bring the gospel into these parts, to enlighten the natives thereof with that which is told and believed by the Holy Mother Church of Rome, for the salvation of their souls; that therefore I should not give them passage, but on the contrary, should pursue them by sea and by land, until I had their lives.[47]

Menéndez reported that, in response,

There came across to this side, a gentleman, the Lieutenant of Monsieur Ludunier, very crafty, to tempt me; who having discussed some time with me, offered that they would lay down their arms and give themselves up if I would spare their lives. I answered that they might give up their arms and place themselves at my mercy; that I should deal with them as the Lord should command me, and that he had not moved me from this nor could move me, unless God Our Lord should inspire in me something different. And so he departed with this reply, and they came over and laid down their arms, and I caused their hands to be tied behind them, and put them to the knife. Only 16 were left, of whom twelve were Bretton seamen [presumably Catholic] whom they had kidnapped, the other four being carpenters and caulkers of whom I had great need. It seemed to me that to chastise them in this way would serve God Our Lord, as well as Your Majesty, and that we should thus be left more free from this wicked sect to plant the Gospel in these parts and to enlighten the natives, and bring them to allegiance to Your Majesty.[48]

Solís de Merás's version agrees with this account in most essentials. He also added that the French attempted to ransom their lives for fifty thousand ducats, which was immediately refused, and that when Menéndez specifically inquired as to whether there were any Catholics among them, he spared eight who said that they were.[49] Mendoza Grajales recounted that, "after much parley between [the French officer] and our General, the General replied and said that he did not wish to give such word but that they should bring their arms and their persons so that he should do with them as he wished, for if he gave them their lives he wished them to be grateful and if death they should not complain of his broken word."[50]

As to those who were spared, the chaplain's account added "his Lordship [Menéndez] decided to condemn them all to death. I, being a sacerdote and with the bowels of a man, petitioned him to grant me a favor, and it was that those who were found to be Christians [Catholics] should not die. He granted me this, and proceedings were carried out by which we found ten or twelve. These we brought with us. All the rest died for being Lutherans and against our Holy Catholic Faith."[51]

Although there are some differences of detail, especially various numbers involved, all three Spanish accounts agree on the sequence of events and the clear refusal of Menéndez to promise mercy if they surrendered.[52] Ultimately, the Frenchmen decided to surrender, and it is legitimate to inquire why they might have done so had they not been promised clemency. The answer is that the only alternative appears to have been starvation. Without food for over a week, and probably without either fresh water or shelter from the sun, their weakened condition made most of them unable to swim to the mainland. Very likely, it appeared that an excruciating death was a certainty unless they surrendered. Even if they were not definitely promised that they would be spared, at least the Spanish commander had not specifically promised that he would kill them all. In light of their lack of options, it is not entirely surprising that the Frenchmen agreed to be ferried across the channel, ten at a time, in the Spanish boat. After having their hands tied behind them, they were marched in groups of ten across the dunes, out of sight of the other Frenchmen, where Menéndez's troops executed them using swords and knives. The Spaniards then returned to their base at St. Augustine.

As late as October 10, Menéndez evidently believed that Ribault still posed a serious threat, fearing that the French corsair might reappear with salvaged cannon or in the company of hostile Indians. Menéndez's insecurity at that time is underlined by the letter he composed that day to the king, which related what he supposedly learned from French captives taken at Fort Caroline. At this point, Menéndez's understanding of the French intentions in Florida comprised a bizarre mixture of truth, misunderstanding, and paranoia.[53]

So far, Menéndez had accounted for the deaths of perhaps three hundred out of a thousand Frenchmen at Fort Caroline and Matanzas combined, not counting those who had drowned. As far as he knew, there were then several hundred French soldiers at large, led by Ribault, who still had anywhere from two to five ships. Menéndez did not know either where they were or and in what sort of condition they might be. As he told the king, his prime concern following the first Matanzas massacre was to ready his defenses against the regrouped Frenchmen and even possibly against reinforcements from France and/or England. The taking of Fort Caroline and the execution of somewhat more than a hundred Frenchmen in the first massacre were portrayed to the king as merely the first two steps in carrying out his orders to remove the French threat from Florida. As Menéndez makes quite clear in his letter, he considered his task to be still far from complete, and he desperately needed reinforcement to ensure victory. However, before Menéndez had a chance to send this report to Europe, startling news reached him, which he relayed in the letter's last paragraphs as almost a postscript.

Only hours after learning that his northern position at San Mateo had suffered a devastating accidental fire, Menéndez received a report of Frenchmen stranded in virtually the same spot as the first group had been. An expedition of about 150 soldiers was quickly readied to seek them out, as by now there were more forces available at St. Augustine who had arrived by boat from San Mateo. They encountered a reported two hundred survivors of the flagship *Trinité*, which had sunk further south than the first three, possibly around the location of present-day Cape Canaveral, and who had been making their way north to Fort Caroline under Ribault's command. Another fruitless discussion was held as the Frenchmen, unaware that their fort had fallen, pleaded for safe passage north. Presented with apparently identical terms, only seventy of the French surrendered, while the rest fled into the interior.[54]

After the surrender, the sequence of events Menéndez recounts is similar:

> I wished to make sure whether there were any Catholics among them, but found none. I spared the lives of two young gentlemen of about eighteen years old, and three others, drummer, fifer, and trumpeter, but Juan Rivao and the others I caused to be put to the knife, understanding this to be necessary for the service of God Our Lord, and of Your Majesty. I hold it our chief good fortune that he is dead, for with him the King of France could do more with 500 ducats, than with any others with 5,000, and he would do more in one year than many other in ten, for he was the most skillful sailor and corsair that was known, very experienced in this navigation of the Indies and of the coast of Florida and so much a friend to England that he was nominated as Captain-General of all the English fleet against the Catholics of France, in past years when there was war between France and England. . . . I was his enemy and waged war against them with fire and blood, for that they were Lutherans, and because they had come to plant here in these lands of Your Majesty their evil sect.[55]

Certainly the Spanish commander already had adequate reason to deal harshly with his enemies, but this letter gives us yet another reason. It indicates Menéndez's obvious regard for Ribault and the enormous threat he still represented to Spanish interests, even as a prisoner. At that point Menéndez still considered Ribault to be extremely dangerous, and as his letter points out, he felt that Ribault possessed so little honor that he might violate any surrender terms given. In retrospect it appears unlikely that seventy near-starving, unarmed Frenchmen composed much of a threat, but it may not have appeared that way to Menéndez at the time, especially considering Ribault's reputation.

Even with Ribault and his men as prisoners, Menéndez had to worry about many other Frenchmen who were then unaccounted for. These included those who had refused to surrender as well as the soldiers on board any of the six attacking ships that had not sunk, as well as the two ships that had escaped Fort Caroline.[56] Some or all of these might attempt a rescue or launch an attack while Spanish troops were occupied with the French prisoners. Moreover, Menéndez, expecting to be in charge of the colony for the foreseeable future, may have feared that Ribault might return at a later date to exact his revenge, should he eventually be ransomed or otherwise repatriated.

The adelantado's letter asserts definitively, and repeatedly, that he was exterminating heretics as ordered by both God and King. Later French authors, who probably never read this particular account, accuse Menéndez of a virtually identical motivation for these executions, in presenting Menéndez as a paradigm of Catholic intolerance and cruelty. We may also conclude that Menéndez's celebrated actions at Matanzas may have been equally motivated by self-preservation. Though he reminded the king in his letter that he was exterminating heretics upon direct royal orders, he could also have claimed, with equal justification, that he was carrying out his specific instructions to punish corsairs on the spot. The safest choice for Menéndez was clearly to remove as much of this threat as he could, given the opportunity.

One can also understand these executions by looking at Menéndez's likely psychological state at the time. He had experienced a bewildering series of changes of fortune in the previous months. Just since the beginning of the year, his legal and financial troubles had come very close to destroying his career, while his son was missing and presumed lost. Suddenly and unexpectedly, the Crown's concern with the threat to Florida had given him an exceptional opportunity. All at the same time, he could redeem his honor, repay the king's faith in him, search for his son, and even, quite possibly, get rich. However, it required a risk more daunting than he had ever faced. Undertaking this assignment meant investing all of his own resources and many of those of his family and friends. Failure could not be contemplated, since it would not only end his career, but it would mean letting down his supporters, who included the king himself.

The pressure on Menéndez only increased after he departed from Spain, as it may have seemed to him that God, who was ultimately responsible for this opportunity in the first place, was testing his faith with continued trial. The storm encountered during the crossing had damaged and dispersed his fleet; Ribault had arrived first to Florida; and finally, Menéndez and his men had become trapped at St. Augustine, awaiting only the furious onslaught of the French heretics to send them to their doom. As rapidly as a hurricane could arise, Menéndez was presented with another awesome change of fortune. Unexpectedly, he found himself holding a final, desperate chance to not only survive but possibly even to succeed. Against long odds, and the resistance of his own officers, he engineered the march to Fort Caroline and captured the fort. Amazingly, upon return to St. Augustine, he found that fortune had again smiled upon him: the French fleet had not regrouped for an attack, but, instead, the survivors of three sunken ships had been stranded helplessly on a sandbar. It is doubtful that Menéndez interpreted this rapid turn of events as luck; it was no less than Divine Providence taking a hand and rewarding him for his continued faith. It would be cynical for the modern reader to assume that the frequent references to divine assistance that appear throughout Menéndez's letters were anything less than sincere.

The adelantado's lack of personnel and supplies may indeed have had much to do with his choice of what to do with the surrendered Frenchmen. The logistical problem of marching these prisoners back to St. Augustine to put them in custody no doubt appeared daunting. Yet we have no indication that he even considered this possibility. At this point, it may well be that Menéndez did not see these Frenchmen merely as surrendered opponents, as he might have under less trying circumstances. Instead, with a personal zeal sharpened to the breaking point by all that he had experienced in the previous month, he may have regarded them as heretics whose fate had been handed to him as a reward for his faith. Overwhelmed by emotion, pressure, hunger, and fatigue, Menéndez executed them with the only means he had available, to take no chance that victory would elude him.

Menéndez could not afford to relax in the aftermath of this episode. As he pondered the available information, and the likelihood that Ribault was at large and capable of destroying his still-beleaguered forces, he tried to deploy his limited resources to maintain his tenuous hold on Florida. While he composed his letter to the king, a second group of shipwrecked Frenchmen, led by Ribault himself, miraculously appeared. It may have appeared to him that God, pleased with his reaction to the first opportunity, had given him a second. Though only seventy Frenchmen surrendered on this occasion, Menéndez again acceded to the divine will by slaughtering his prisoners.

As Menéndez finished the last part of his letter to Philip, his task was still far from complete, but the purpose of this expedition seems to have been transformed in the period since he had left Seville. His letter reiterates his intentions regarding any additional Frenchmen he should encounter: "because they are Lutherans, and that so wicked a sect should not remain alive in these parts, I shall do everything in my power . . . so that, within five or six months, not one of them shall remain alive."[57] By mid-October, this had ceased to be merely an expedition of conquest and settlement. By then, Menéndez had very personal reasons to see his mission as a religious crusade.

Three weeks after the second massacre, Menéndez had yet another encounter with French shipwreck survivors. Searching for the remainder of the French forces, he led more than two hundred of his troops on a march along the south Florida coast, accompanied by three supply boats. Near present-day Cape Canaveral—an additional eighty miles to the south—he found another group of between seventy and eighty shipwrecked Frenchmen.[58] This time, however, they were not stranded and helpless, and when confronted with a far superior force, the French fled into the woods. For Menéndez to capture them, it was necessary to promise to spare their lives. As he wrote, "Seeing that the country was so thickly wooded that we could not catch any of them, and that it would not be proper that so wicked a sect should remain in the land, I sent a French trumpeter who had been with Juan Rivao, whom I had brought along with me, into the mountains to tell them to surrender, and give up their arms, and that, if they would come to me, I would spare their lives. So they all came, save he whom they had chosen for captain, and three or four others from Navarre and servants of the Prince of Condé."[59]

When these Frenchmen finally surrendered, Menéndez kept his word, although had it not been necessary to promise clemency in order to capture them, perhaps Menéndez might have executed this group as well. Religious zealotry aside, taking so many prisoners presented him with the serious problem of what to do with them. Ultimately, he decided to create a garrison a few miles to the south near an Indian village. He left most of his soldiers there to guard the prisoners, planning to send reinforcements at a later date. Menéndez himself took two of the supply boats and sailed to Havana, along with fifty Spaniards and twenty of the Frenchmen.[60] In any event, it was long past the time that the *San Pelayo* should have returned to St. Augustine, and he was further perplexed by the continued absence of his other reinforcements. As a result, his outposts to the north were pitifully short of supplies, and Menéndez needed to rectify this situation and find the reasons for the delay. Though Menéndez continued to fear French attack, the victory had been won so decisively that no French colonial initiatives in Florida would again be considered for more than a century.

While we can at least see that he certainly had many possible justifications for his actions against the French prisoners, his letters give us little indication that he personally felt it necessary to rationalize them, either before or after the fact. Nothing that he wrote at the time or afterward displays even a tinge of regret. One can argue whether his concerns had been serving God, his king, his backers, or himself, or some combination of these, but one thing is quite clear. At Matanzas, as at every other stage of this torturous Florida expedition, Menéndez did what he felt was necessary both to survive and to justify the faith that had been shown in him.

9

Aftermath

Both her contemporaries and later historians criticized Catherine de Medici for having been indifferent to the outcome of the Florida affair.[1] Certainly her response was weak, as was that of her son King Charles, but there were important reasons why this was so. One was that in the aftermath of the conflict, continuing domestic crises prevented her from placing colonial interests at the top of her agenda. Another contributing factor was a lack of timely and reliable information about her forces' defeat. As a result, Catherine and her diplomats lost any opportunity they might have had to gain strategic or political advantage from this situation.

It was only when Jacques Ribault returned to La Rochelle in mid-December that the French court was able to receive any direct report on the fall of Fort Caroline, but the younger Ribault could not have been aware of the ultimate fate of the French fleet or of his father's death at Matanzas Inlet.[2] Even by the end of the year, Catherine probably did not know the full story, although what she must have known by then was unhappy indeed. She would have heard about Ribault's arrival at Fort Caroline, and also about his pursuit of Menéndez. She also would have learned from Jacques Ribault that Menéndez's troops had easily taken the fort in a savage dawn attack and that they had executed most of its defenders.

However, it would have been impossible for her to know where Ribault's force had gone during the hurricane; none of the Frenchmen who by then had returned to Europe could have answered this. What had happened to the French fleet was not the only area of confusion; it was also unknown what had happened to the main body of Menéndez's fleet. For all Catherine or anyone else in Europe knew, the conflict in Florida had not yet run its full course, and it was even possible that Ribault might have ridden out the storm and recaptured the fort.

Lacking firm knowledge of the final outcome, Catherine was unable to ask the Spaniards for either an explanation or any apology, never mind asking them for compensation. She refused, quite properly, to react to news that she understood only imperfectly through the initial reports of Jacques Ribault and Laudonnière. Instead, she consistently avoided specifics in her direct correspondence with Philip and in her instructions to Fourquevaux, emphasizing only the general French right to be in Florida.[3]

It is not entirely certain who brought the first news to Spain of the final outcome in Florida. Menéndez's report to the king, dispatched from St. Augustine on October 15, did not arrive in Europe until the following spring, since shipwreck and bad weather had delayed this letter.[4] Yet it seems that the Spanish court had some knowledge of Menéndez's victory prior to the return of the defeated French from Fort Caroline. On November 29, during a conversation with French ambassador Fourquevaux, the Duke of Alva had hinted that a French defeat had taken place in Florida, in which the former had argued the legitimacy of French claims in the New World. As Forquevaux recounted, in response to the duke's criticism of French aggression, he had replied that

I had seen for thirty years on ancient marine charts that the coast that you say La Florida is located, is both named the land of the Bretons and is very far from the islands of Hispañola, Cuba, and others of New Spain. In the event that their [Spanish] navigation is interfered with, they [the French] had no royal command, either to attempt anything nor to dispossess [the Spanish] . . . that if the Spanish vessels were required to pass by Florida they could expect to receive all favor and comfort.

The Duke replied to me, Sire, that the Catholic King will employ all his forces to recover his possession, and that whatever may have been said the French there already fare badly due to the arrival of the Spaniards who were sent there last summer.[5]

A fuller report reached the French court in January, and the timing of this news was less than ideal. After the New Year, Catherine held court in Moulins, where she was occupied with attempting to reconcile the Guise and Châtillon factions, a difficult enough task under the best of circumstances. At Catherine's request, Admiral Coligny himself had appeared at Moulins in order to exonerate himself of, among other things, his alleged complicity in the assassination of François de Guise almost three years before.[6] In the midst of the rancorous atmosphere at court,

Catherine received a communication from Fourquevaux that appears to indicate more certain knowledge of the loss of Ribault and his fleet. On January 17, the ambassador reported to her, "If it is true, Madame, that [the Spaniards] did not spare anyone at all in chasing out the French, since they take this affair seriously, and if they have been victorious Your Majesties will hear piteous news from Your subjects, that [the Spaniards] made all of them die cruelly."[7]

This dispatch was followed a few days later by a report of a large Spanish fleet being assembled to go to Florida, to which the ambassador added pessimistically that "the French have lost the fort and abandoned the country."[8] In the meantime, on January 20, Catherine directed Fourquevaux to reiterate that the French intentions had been peaceful:

Well do I know that some of our people have gone to a land known as the *Terre aux Bretons*, a place discovered by subjects of this Crown; in doing this they neither thought to do anything prejudicial to the said peace and friendship [between France and Spain], nor was there any fault on our behalf, since this land we believe to be ours, but if they had in any way infringed upon the affairs of the Catholic King, they had been in this enterprise admonished and commanded to use caution there, and if they departed from these orders my son the King would take their doing so as an offense against himself, which has always been the position we have held in this undertaking.[9]

While it is hard to determine whether she was aware of the completeness of the French defeat when she sent this dispatch, only three days later the English ambassador in France reported with no further detail that he had learned from sources at court that "the Spaniards have slain all the Frenchmen that were in Florida."[10]

Four weeks later, the return of the first Spaniards from Florida made the totality of the French disaster publicly known. On February 18, Fourquevaux sent Catherine the news of the deaths of the shipwrecked Frenchmen, and one of Menéndez's cousins was among his sources.[11] This is the first official report that is known to have reached France with a generally accurate account of the Matanzas massacres. He relayed the information that "this court is rejoicing more than if it had been a victory over the Turk: also they say that Florida is more important to them than Malta. In compensation for the massacre made by Menéndez upon your poor subjects, Florida will be made a marquisate, and [Menéndez] will be made its marquis."[12]

By then, Catherine and Charles knew beyond a doubt that not only had Menéndez captured Fort Caroline, but that he had also destroyed Ribault's armada. Yet before they could react, Spain took the diplomatic offensive. At the same time that Fourquevaux was learning of the later massacres, Spanish diplomats accused the French Crown of directing hostilities against their possessions. In his letter of March 6, Fourquevaux relayed their demand that Catherine punish Admiral Coligny and explain the Crown's involvement in this affair.[13] To support their accusation of French aggression, they claimed that Menéndez, while capturing Fort Caroline, had seized official orders from Coligny to Ribault that contained evidence of a hostile intent by the French Crown.[14]

By doing so, the Spaniards essentially preempted any immediate attempts by the French to exact restitution for this disaster. Ambassador Fourquevaux could only respond defensively by repeating the justification that Catherine had previously expressed: that the French had a legitimate claim to this land and that there had been no aggressive intent. Meanwhile, the queen mother demanded nothing more than an explanation for the massacres from Ambassador Alava y Beaumont. On March 17, she wrote to Fourquevaux that the Spanish ambassador had told her that "Pierre Melendez having found in the land of Florida some Frenchmen admitted and charged with letters from Monsieur l'Admiral, who had in their company some ministers who were planting the new religion, and he punished them according to the commandment of the King his lord. He [Menéndez] even confessed that this had been done a little more rudely and cruelly than his lord had desired, but that he had not even the means to chase them as pirates and as people who were trespassing upon lands belonging to him."[15]

Thus stated, the Spanish position was quite clear, and it changed little in the following months. Their justification was based on two main points that echoed through the subsequent communications on the issue. First, Philip considered the presence of heretics in his possessions, which included Florida, to be an unpardonable offense, far worse than if the trespassers had been Catholic. Second, the king was convinced that Menéndez had carried out his orders the only way possible given his limited means. Clearly and unambiguously, Philip approved of what Menéndez had done. As he explained it, Menéndez had merely been following royal orders to the best of his ability; henceforth, any quarrel that Catherine had was to be addressed to the Spanish Crown. Regarding the second point, Philip wrote to Menéndez in May, "we believe that you have done this with full justification and prudence, and hold ourselves well-served thereby."[16]

The king himself reiterated these positions to Fourquevaux during an April interview in Madrid, which was reported in detail in a letter to the queen shortly afterward. Philip had refused to comment on the ambassador's claim that the French intent was peaceful, and he quickly dismissed the historical argument of French discovery. The king also brushed aside Fourquevaux's complaint that Menéndez had not offered the French a chance to surrender. Only at the end of this disappointing meeting did Philip offer any sort of explanation at all, while he added some more justifications for the slaughter. According to Fourquevaux's report, the Spanish king told him that

> Having known of the departure of a good force of Lutherans of different nations, as many French as others, and their descent on the strait of the Indies, the most important to [Philip's] navigation, be-cause it is necessary that all ships that wish to return to Spain pass in front of that coast and the promontory of Florida, he had no other option but to send men there to dislodge them. This he had to do since he had requested one and several times, both by his ambassa-dor and by the Duke of Alva at Bayonne, that you should call back your subjects who had gone to the land of his [Philip's] ancient conquest.[17]

Again, there is a strong religious justification, which had earlier been emphasized by both the Duke of Alva and Menéndez himself. The claim that there were other nationalities involved besides the French made it easier for the king to respond that he was reacting against a "Lutheran" threat rather than a specifically French one. Philip also revealed his con-viction that the interlopers posed a threat to his shipping, which he could easily justify on the basis of the previous actions of the Fort Caroline mutineers. Philip also added a new reason for his approval of the mas-sacres—though perhaps one with less justification—by claiming the French had been previously warned to stay away from Spain's American possessions.

In regard to this last point, while it is true that both the Spanish and French were aware of the other's preparations well before departure in 1565, there is no evidence that either side had made a formal complaint. The Duke of Alva had indeed prepared to present a Spanish protest to Catherine at Bayonne, but he never did so, since he believed at the time that Ribault had already departed. However, if the Spaniards were guilty of not warning Catherine of Menéndez's intentions, the French were not diplomatically guiltless, either. The apparently undeniable fact that the French Crown had been involved in outfitting a powerful armada—and this under the command of one of their most noted corsairs—certainly gave Philip just suspicions of their claim of peaceful intent.

During the spring and summer of 1566, Fourquevaux's continued requests for compensation seem to have had little effect besides irritating Philip. After July 1566, French diplomatic efforts became less strident, and they concentrated on the repatriation of the hundred or more French prisoners then held by Spanish authorities, with Coligny playing a significant role in persuading the queen to pursue this course.[18] Faced with Philip's firm refusal to admit any wrongdoing, it appears that by that summer Catherine had given up any serious hope of exacting compensation for the French loss, even though there is no reason to believe that she felt her cause was not just.

Realistically, there was little else that she could accomplish regarding this matter besides trying to save those who had been captured. Any further French attempt in Florida was out of the question, especially since it was known that Philip had just sent yet another large Spanish armada to Florida. As far as the French Crown was concerned, the cause was irretrievably lost. Revenge for the massacres would have to be carried out by others.

*　　*　　*

The lack of reliable information available in Europe during the first half of 1566 also affected the reaction of the French public to the Florida defeat. The reports of Jacques Ribault and Laudonnière during the winter, which concerned only the loss of Fort Caroline, were followed in the spring by wild rumors of the Matanzas massacres. Predictably, the French Atlantic ports were the focus of especial outrage, directed against both Catholicism and Spain.[19] The French Crown's perceived indecision in reacting to the Florida defeat strengthened this conviction, leading some to conclude that Catherine valued Spanish amity more than redressing this blow to French honor.[20] This news also seemed to confirm the widely held suspicion among French Protestants that the Bayonne meetings in June had resulted in a secret agreement with Spain, designed to provide for mutual assistance in the protection of religious orthodoxy.[21]

Various inflammatory publications, which had begun to appear in France by the summer of 1566 and purportedly described the French defeat, contributed to this dissatisfaction. Of these, Nicolas Le Challeux's narrative, published in May, was undoubtedly the most influential. Its descriptions of real and imagined Spanish outrages included a graphic description of the supposed murders and mutilations of Ribault's men at Matanzas: "The men, women, and children found inside the aforesaid fort were murdered and maimed by the Spaniards without mercy. On the contrary, they displayed the pierced bodies of the little children held aloft on the point of their pikes, and secondly, they killed the aforesaid Captain Jean Ribaud and all his company of seven to eight hundred men, in spite of the assurance they had given to spare their lives."[22]

Another influential publication that appeared in 1566 was a lengthy list of complaints by French mariners over the failure of the Crown to support them. While also criticizing the lack of a royal response for the destruction of Fort Coligny in Brazil, it described various Spanish horrors committed in Florida, relating that "an abominable massacre, accomplished in the name of good faith, Ribault was burned alive, thirty-five officers were hanged by their private parts, the captains of the marine were nailed by their ears to the masts of the ships, [while] the soldiers and sailors were sown into the sails and thrown into the sea."[23]

Later in the same year, in November, a strongly anti-Catholic work entitled *Traité preparatif à l'apologie pour Herodote* by the Geneva printer Henri Estienne used Le Challeux's account to portray the Florida massacres as a prime example of cruelty and intolerance.[24] This work emphasized the cruelty of the Spaniards in the New World, and it employed many of Le Challeux's precise descriptions of supposed barbarities committed against French women and children during the storming of Fort Caroline.

These and other publications, and the proliferation of rumors upon which they were based, provoked the maritime communities of the French Atlantic coast into taking action for themselves. By summer, the English reported "great preparations" on the French coast, of as many as twenty vessels outfitting for Florida, specifically mentioning St. Malo and Bordeaux as points of departure.[25] These English reports probably refer to an expedition that Pierre-Bertrand Peyrot de Monluc, the second son of Marshal of France Blaise de Monluc, launched during August. He led an expedition of six ships toward West Africa, which were prohibited waters for the French, and perhaps planned on sailing to Florida afterward.[26]

Though Peyrot's fleet never reached any of these destinations, its fate contributed to rising tension on the diplomatic scene. The Portuguese attacked the Frenchmen while the latter were resupplying at Madeira and killed Peyrot. In retribution, Peyrot's soldiers and sailors turned their wrath upon Madeira itself. Since it was then widely believed in France that the Portuguese had played a role in the massacres at Fort Caroline, Peyrot's men later explained the resultant orgy of death and destruction at Madeira as suitable retribution for Fort Caroline and Matanzas.[27] This incident had serious diplomatic repercussions. Not only did the depredations committed at Madeira damage the chances of a projected marriage alliance between the French and Portuguese, but they also hindered the last attempts made by the French Crown to gain reparations for its defeat in Florida.[28]

A more direct reaction against Spain was undertaken the following year, shortly after Menéndez had returned to Spain for the first time since his victory. In the summer of 1567, Dominique de Gourgues, a Gascon nobleman who had escaped from the Spanish galleys a few years before, led a reprisal expedition out of Bordeaux.[29] With the aid of Indians who were hostile to Spanish rule, de Gourgues's force of more than two hundred men destroyed three Spanish forts on Florida's east coast, including San Mateo. The last was burned to the ground, and in direct retaliation for the massacres they hanged some two hundred Spanish prisoners. De Gourgues left their bodies exposed, along with an explanation: "But instead of the writing which Pedro Melendes had hanged over them, importing these words into Spanish, I do not this as unto French men but as unto Lutherans, Gourgues caused to be imprinted with a searing iron in a table of Firewood, I do not this as unto Spaniards, nor as unto Mariners, but as unto Traitors, Robbers, and Murderers."[30]

There remains some question as to de Gourgues's religion. While it is known that he was buried as a Catholic in 1582, Spanish sources, including Solís de Merás, described him as a "heretic."[31] This is difficult to substantiate, since the 1568 account gives little indication of his religious leanings. Instead, this narrative, presumably the work of de Gourgues himself, emphasizes quite plainly that de Gourgues was redressing wrongs committed against France and Frenchmen, as evidenced, for example, by the above epitaph left for the dead Spaniards.

When de Gourgues returned to Bordeaux, a Spanish ransom forced him into hiding, and Philip was angry enough to send a fleet into the Gironde estuary to try to capture him. French authorities, however, never made any serious effort to punish de Gourgues. To the contrary, both Catholics and Protestants in Gascony celebrated the exploits of this "avenger of Matanzas," while powerful individuals of both religions protected him from Philip's fleet and from potential bounty hunters.[32] Although the material gain of de Gourgues's expedition was limited to the recapture of some of the artillery originally taken from the French in 1565, this reprisal gave the French public some sense that their honor had been avenged. Moreover, as early as April of 1568, a narrative of the mission, probably written by de Gourgues himself, appeared in print, which helped further assuage the outrage over the French defeat. Also, the resultant diplomatic furor over Philip's demand that de Gourgues be punished gave King Charles IX the rare opportunity to stand up to the Spanish king, somewhat redeeming himself for his perceived lack of response to the French defeat three years earlier.

*　　*　　*

In contrast to the rapid appearance of French propaganda, especially Le Challeux's influential work, the Spaniards paid considerably less attention to these events. By 1568 two biographies of Menéndez had been written, but they remained unpublished during Menéndez's lifetime, as did Chaplain Mendoza Grajales's memoir.[33] It may well be true that a Spanish reading public used to the dramatic accounts of Cortez's and Pizarro's exploits found the episodes in Florida to be relatively "peripheral events."[34] In any case, the Spanish public did not immediately appreciate the importance of either the victory over the French or the foundation of St. Augustine.

If the Spanish reading public did not consider Florida to be as lucrative or romantic as Mexico and Peru, neither, apparently, did the Spanish Crown. In fact, after Menéndez had removed the French threat, it was exceedingly difficult for him to gain adequate resources to properly follow up on his victory. By the time the testimonies of Solís de Merás and Barrientos were written, Menéndez was already encountering severe obstacles to the development of his *adelantamiento* of Florida.[35] Arriving in Havana from Florida in November 1565, he found that not all of the reinforcements he had expected had reached the Indies after all. Those ships that he found in Havana had just arrived and had as yet been unable to procure supplies, and, worse, Menéndez's own *San Pelayo* was missing.[36] Hindered by a lack of cooperation from various officials and his old nemesis the Casa de Contratácion, he was unable to gather sufficient food for his colonists in Florida, never mind arms and soldiers to solidify the conquest. The first year after the French victory saw the *adelantado* holding only tenuously onto the new Spanish territory, beset by desertions, revolts, and conflicts with the Timucuans and other Indians.

Despite the crippling lack of resources, Menéndez formulated ambitious plans to expand his territory and make it viable. These included a settlement in Chesapeake Bay, which he later abandoned, and the construction of a total of five coastal forts, including St. Augustine and San Mateo, stretching along the Florida coast from Santa Eleña in the north around to the west side of the peninsula. He also tried to reconcile the various Indian states into a confederation under the dominion of Spain, and he continued to search for both a passage to the Pacific and an overland route to New Spain. He succeeded in instituting a regular system of Indies-built galleys to protect Spanish harbors from corsair attacks, and he assumed much of the responsibility for further tightening the regulations required for safer convoy journeys in the Indies.

Menéndez's plans were ambitious but his means were limited. Try as he might to settle, fortify, pacify, convert, and explore the enormous territory he had won, by the time of his death in 1572, only St. Augustine and Santa Eleña survived as Spanish outposts in the Florida territory. However, even though he ultimately had to abandon most of his initiatives, at least he had achieved something in this vexing land that had escaped every single one of his predecessors: he had succeeded in permanently establishing a Spanish presence in Florida.

*　　*　　*

When de Gourgues's account was published in the spring of 1568, the second French War of Religion had already concluded and the third war was imminent. The Duke of Alva had marched his army along the French eastern frontier toward the Netherlands, where he began the anti-rebel campaign known as the "Council of Blood" in August 1567.[37] At this juncture, not only was Philip angry over perceived French contributions to the "sedition" in the Netherlands, but many in France, especially Huguenots, feared Spanish intervention in French affairs.[38] The *Histoire memorable de la reprinse de l'isle de la Floride*, the published account describing the de Gourgues reprisal mission, appeared shortly after the Peace of Longjumeau of March 1568, but before many people had a chance to read it, the third War of Religion started at the end of that summer and lasted for two years. Compared to these more direct European threats, the defeat in Florida and de Gourgues's subsequent raid were probably not major factors in the expanding French hostility toward Spain, although they could have done little to smooth the waters between the two realms.

Catherine continued to avoid a direct confrontation with Philip, and even by 1565, the results of her Bayonne interview with the Duke of Alva had begun to unravel the Peace of Amboise. Many Huguenots, unable to accept that the meeting had been a complete failure, afterward suspected that the Spanish court and Catherine had reached a secret agreement to deal with religious dissenters. Huguenots throughout France continued to suspect her motives, especially after Alva's repression in the Netherlands began in earnest in late 1567.[39]

During 1566 Catherine's attempted reconciliation of her kingdom's noble factions failed. Despite her efforts, that year saw increasing tension both between and among the realm's leading families. Although it briefly seemed to be possible during the summer of 1567 for the French leaders to unite against a common enemy, this was a transitory hope. While the French readied defensive preparations for a possible Spanish attack, disagreements over both military leadership and the employment of foreign mercenaries led to a schism between Constable Montmorency and the Prince of Condé. Admiral Coligny chose to side with the latter; with Montmorency staunchly backing Catherine, this now isolated the admiral and his supporters from the queen mother, as well as giving the factionalism at court a more religiously identifiable form.[40]

After the disaster of Florida, Coligny had urged Catherine to exact reparations from Philip; when that failed, he was somewhat more successful in arranging for the liberty of some of those captured by Menéndez.[41] By 1566 the admiral had already begun to take an aggressive posture toward Spain which was closely related to his own personal struggle against the Guise faction. Initially, he had tried to ingratiate himself with the queen mother as her defender against joint Spanish/Guise perfidy, but she did not share his enthusiasm, and gradually the relations between Coligny and Catherine deteriorated as the second and third Wars of Religion took their violent toll.[42] By September 1567, fears of attempted Spanish interventions into France from the north and west were at their peak. The admiral, mistrusting the purpose for which Catherine had hired Swiss mercenaries, took an active part in the attempted seizure of the court at Meaux that started the second war.[43] For the next three years, until the Peace of St. Germain ended the third war in the summer of 1570, the admiral devoted most of his energy toward leading Huguenot armies, and he had little time, and probably little incentive, to devote his energies to overseas projects.

After 1570 Coligny's influence with Charles rapidly increased, largely as a result of the young king's increasingly anti-Spanish foreign policy, which itself was due to his wish to distance his own policies from those of his mother, which had largely failed.[44] Coligny, the sole surviving Huguenot leader after the death of Condé at Jarnac during the third war, continued to emphasize both religious toleration and national interest at Charles's court, but he could now promote such values as part of a theme of anti-Spanish French unity. He took an instrumental role in arranging the royal marriages in August 1572, which were largely intended to reconcile the Huguenots with the Crown. The occasion of these marriage celebrations in Paris resulted in Coligny's own assassination, providing the spark for the St. Bartholomew's Day massacres and decades of European religious polarization.

Aside from some bothersome independent corsair activity, the next publicized maritime conflict between France and Spain took place in July 1570, shortly after the Peace of St. Germain, when Jacques Sores attacked the Canary Islands. In doing so, he threw forty Jesuit missionaries, bound for Brazil, into the sea to drown. This provoked an interesting letter from Menéndez to the king, in which he described many of Sores's most notable accomplishments; despite Menéndez's typically spare prose, his admiration for the skills of his counterpart is evident.[45] Elsewhere in Catholic Europe, and even among many Frenchmen, the reaction to Sores's aggression was more pronounced, resulting in a number of Catholic diatribes that grossly exaggerated the nature of Sores's cruelty.[46] During the same year, in an apparently unrelated development, René Laudonnière was sent to the Indies at the command of Charles IX, in charge of a war fleet.[47] The royal artillery inventory for this mission indicates neither its exact destination nor its purpose, though it makes clear that its intentions were anything but peaceful. It is uncertain what success, if any, Laudonnière had on this mission, but there is little wonder that his experiences in Florida had made him anxious to avenge himself against Spain.

What may be seen as a final episode in the colonial rivalry between France and Spain involved the navigator and mapmaker Guillaume Le Testu, who had dedicated his 1556 atlas to Coligny. In 1573 along the north coast of Panama, Le Testu and sixty Huguenot corsairs encountered an English squadron under Francis Drake. The two Protestant captains joined forces and improvised an ambitious attempt to capture Spanish silver shipments as mule trains hauled them across the isthmus. Their plans for an ambush went awry, and in the resultant skirmish, Le Testu was killed by a shot from an arquebus.[48] However, Drake and most of his men escaped with a sizable amount of silver and were able to claim a moderate success in this expedition, the first Indies raid that was undertaken under Drake's own command. While the death of Le Testu symbolizes the end of French challenge to Spanish-claimed territories in the

New World, this incident also signaled the beginning of an English colonial initiative, led by Drake, that would be considerably more fruitful and longer lived. While the English succeeded in permanently wresting the eastern seaboard of North America from Spain, the next serious French design on the New World, after a respite of forty years, was directed at points safely north of Florida and the Spanish shipping lanes.

The emergence of English maritime power during the last part of the century was a key ingredient in heightening tensions with Spain, and religious differences played a major role. The English rebuff of the Spanish Armada in 1588, aided by a "Protestant wind," initiated an era of direct military conflict between these two kingdoms. Most of the hostilities took place at sea, especially through the rapid escalation of corsair action throughout the Atlantic and into the Pacific. Even prior to 1588, the English had tried to establish their first American colony along the Virginia coast. Though these early attempts failed, the Treaty of London in 1604 permitted English trade in Spanish possessions, leading ultimately to the English right to found settlements without fear of Spanish reprisal. Jamestown and later Plymouth were among the results of this Anglo-Spanish truce.[49]

Today St. Augustine is the oldest continuous European settlement in the present-day United States. Despite Drake's destruction of the town in 1586, it was rebuilt and continued to guard the path of the *flotas* into the nineteenth century, when Spain finally relinquished control of Florida. By that time, the flow of silver across the Atlantic had slowed to a trickle.

*   *   *

It is impossible to regard this French initiative in Florida without placing it in a context of the crises of the sixteenth century. One cannot argue that this violent episode was primarily the work of a few daring explorers or corsairs seeking glory and gold, or alternatively, of persecuted Protestants seeking a safe haven from the religious struggles in Europe. Nor can one seriously argue that this was merely a hastily conceived and misguided effort to claim New World territories for the French Crown. While each of these elements did play a critical role as the drama unfolded, none by itself provided either necessary or sufficient cause for these events.

The fact that there were so many differing factors, often working at cross purposes, no doubt narrowed the odds of a successful conclusion to this initiative. However well Philip and Menéndez understood or misunderstood the French motives, they responded decisively and consistently to this threat, while French intentions wavered. In light of these circumstances, it remains a good question whether this colonial effort ever had a realistic chance of success.

Yet it is hard to escape the conclusion that problems in execution were of critical importance. As we look at how the venture developed, we can also attribute the French defeat to a series of baffling decisions by their leaders, especially by Ribault. In the late summer of 1565, the French did not exploit decisive advantages in military forces, mobility, and position. French blunders permitted a near-certain military victory to slip from their grasp by granting Menéndez the opportunity to display his impressive capabilities as a military commander. Even so, there was also a critical element of fortune responsible for the Spanish victory. Despite their mistakes and indecision, the French still appeared likely to emerge victorious until a hurricane arose at precisely the wrong moment; indeed, a "Catholic wind" struck the fatal blow and carried the day. The result was a decisive, crushing defeat that effectively ended any French challenges to Spanish America for decades.

There is a temptation to indulge in counterfactual speculation and wonder what might have happened had Ribault defeated Menéndez in 1565. At that time, Philip's military resources were stretched to the limit. In the Mediterranean, his navy was engaged in a desperate conflict with the Turks, and though his forces had won a brief respite by lifting the siege of Malta in October 1565, control of the Mediterranean continued to be his main priority even after his dramatic victory at Lepanto in 1572. Simultaneously, events in the Netherlands required an increasing deployment of Spanish land forces to the north, even as Philip's relations with England deteriorated and French instability continued. By the time of Menéndez's triumph, all of these threats were testing Spain's ability to meet them, both financially and militarily.[50]

In light of these circumstances, it is difficult to imagine how Philip might have responded to a defeat in Florida. Certainly his decision would have been an unenviable one: having to remove the French by diverting significant new Spanish forces across the Atlantic would have seriously hindered his ability to deal with the more immediate European crises. Even with these other priorities, though, it is hard to imagine that Philip would not have responded decisively to recapture his American territory, upon which the financial health of his empire depended. Had the French been able to firmly establish a fortified presence, it would have grown only more difficult with time for Spanish forces to dislodge them. One wonders how this might have affected Philip's aggressive posture in Europe, especially in the Netherlands, during 1566 and 1567.

There can be little doubt that a French victory in 1565 would have greatly affected, or even prevented entirely, later English initiatives in that part of the world. Most likely, if Menéndez had suffered defeat in 1566, this would have spurred Philip to forcefully settle and defend this coast, especially points farther north of St. Augustine, within a few years. Such a situation would no doubt have seriously influenced, in one way or another, the later English initiatives in North America.

It is a more difficult question whether the French could ever have overcome their various problems to "effectively occupy" this area in the long term. Had they been able to make and defend such a claim for a decade or more, this could have restricted any later English designs, since even during the 1570s, Elizabeth was relying upon the goodwill of French moderates and Huguenots to keep France from allying with Spain. Almost certainly, the English would not have been so eager to contest North America's Atlantic coast had it been claimed by France or, alternately, firmly held by Spain. Thus we can conclude that Menéndez's victory over the French had a rather unexpected result: while it was sufficient to discourage any further French settlements, it still left the territory vulnerable to later English designs.

This outcome was neither inevitable nor insignificant, but as events unfolded, French designs were undermined by two major weaknesses. One is that, in the long run, the Spaniards were simply more determined to protect their silver fleets than the French were to establish a colony in Florida. Yet this by itself did not ensure the final result, as the French still came tantalizingly close to a major defeat of Spanish forces. The fatal flaw proved to be in execution. In hindsight, Ribault's mishandling of his considerable opportunities stands in stark contrast to Menéndez's ability to recapture the initiative when fortune bestowed a brief smile upon his beleaguered garrison. Ultimately, the differences between the commanders doomed whatever chances remained for a successful colonization of Florida by the French. Though largely unrecognized by contemporaries, the failure of this effort was a major turning point in the history of Europe's involvement in the New World.

APPENDIX

A Note on the Sources

As indicated in the introductory chapter and elsewhere, the contemporary narrative accounts that describe these events are often contradictory. In using these sources, it is not always possible to discriminate between accurate and complete descriptions and accounts that contain honest misunderstandings, intentional distortions, or complete falsifications. Untangling the sources requires patience, a keen eye for detail, and a certain amount of plain common sense. The contradictory accounts present us with the most problems regarding the weeks immediately following the arrival of the two fleets in Florida in late August 1565. Somewhat paradoxically, this is largely because these events attracted the most attention from contemporary chroniclers, who wanted to publicize them for various political and religious reasons. Even after careful analysis, we are faced with some significant historical problems about this affair, and in all probability we will never know for certain what happened.

In evaluating the reliability of these sources it is important to employ a logical strategy. First, it is essential to regard them comparatively so that inconsistencies can be noted; second, it is necessary to consider each in the context of its publication circumstances. Doing both of these helps to clarify not only what happened in Florida but why it happened.

A comparative perspective reveals that the events that took place in Florida fit into two rough "phases," each with a different historiographical situation. The first phase includes the events between September 4, when Ribault and Menéndez first caught sight of each other's fleets, up to and including the capture of Fort Caroline on September 20. Five known eyewitness accounts describe most of the developments of this period, two Spanish and three French.[1] Though they represent different perspectives, there are remarkably few direct contradictions among them, and one can synthesize them reasonably well without resorting to excessive guesswork. The few points upon which they appear to disagree, which are usually matters of omission, can be explained by the varying experiences and intentions of each writer. We can see some exaggeration and subjectivity, but there is not a single obvious instance where it seems that any of these writers willfully fabricated events, with the possible but important exception of whether Menéndez's troops killed French women and children during their capture of Fort Caroline.

The French accounts authored by Le Challeux, Le Moyne, and Laudonnière are especially problematic, and, as essential as they are, we must be wary in utilizing them. The most obvious problem with the first two is that neither writer distinguished between the occurrences that he observed firsthand and those events he had learned of only indirectly. The firsthand material, unsurprisingly, is much more reliable: not only is it logically consistent, but also other sources corroborate most of the descriptions of events. In contrast, the secondhand material is far more dubious. In particular, both of these accounts include narrative sections that describe events that took place after both authors had left the scene, notably the executions of French prisoners at Matanzas Inlet.

The main theme running through Le Challeux's account, which was first published in 1566, is the extent to which he and his compatriots were innocent victims of Spanish savagery. We can best appreciate his perspective as that of a civilian caught in rapidly unfolding events that he did not understand well. Throughout Le Challeux's first book, which is the only part of the account actually based upon direct observation, the author shows that he had little comprehension of the problems faced by the French commanders. Nevertheless, we can accept his version of events at Fort Caroline with only limited qualification; if the storming of the fort, in particular, did not take place precisely the way he says that it did, we can forgive him, since his recollection was clearly affected by panic and confusion. Le Challeux is most successful at conveying the shock and terror he experienced during the attack, no doubt shared by most of the victims, and one doubts that he had much reason to exaggerate.

The second major French source, Le Moyne's *Brevis Narratio*, was not published until 1591, well after numerous editions of Le Challeux's account had appeared. Though *Brevis Narratio* is similar in many respects to the earlier account, there seems little reason to assume that Le Moyne relied on Le Challeux's book for his information; we may accept Le Moyne's description of the fall of Fort Caroline as a direct eyewitness testimony largely since it is consistent with, yet not identical to, Le Challeux's first section. Le Moyne's account is comparatively briefer, because, as he wrote, "since one of our company, a carpenter called Le Chaleux, has briefly described the disaster, I will say nothing more about it."[2] Still, the first part of *Brevis Narratio* contains valuable details about the period prior to Fort Caroline's capture that are absent from Le Challeux's account. Of particular value is his account of the council called by Ribault to discuss whether or not to pursue the fleeing Menéndez after September 5.[3]

Regarding this first "phase," the third French account, that of the fort's commander, Laudonnière, is less emotionally charged than either of the first two, though it is pervaded by a certain pathos. His too-frequent protestations of his own blamelessness lead to suspicions that he was not reporting the full story; one gets a sense that Laudonnière may have been intentionally vague in some places. His need to absolve himself of any personal responsibility for the fall of the fort may have caused him to emphasize the power of the Spanish onslaught, but most likely he was not intentionally exaggerating in this respect any more than were Le Challeux or Le Moyne. For each of the three French witnesses, the surprise Spanish attack of September 20 must have seemed invincible when it occurred, and one senses that it would have been scarcely possible to exaggerate the extent of its savagery.

Because of their varying publication dates, and since these three French works have similar emphases, one is tempted to believe that each of them built upon what had been published previously; in other words, that Le Challeux was the original source for information that the others reworked at a later date. A close examination is inconclusive, however. First of all, we have no reason to doubt that each of these individuals was in fact present in Florida, and, moreover, that each of their accounts demonstrates a perspective appropriate to the role of its author. For example, Le Moyne's interpretation of Ribault's council varies enough from that of Laudonnière that it is very unlikely he used the latter as his source. These differences lead one to conclude, paradoxically, that they corroborate each other. Le Moyne, the latest of the three French authors, had no personal stake in his description of this council, and his version of it lends support to the idea that, once again, Laudonnière's presentation of these same events puts his own actions in the best possible light, which largely explains their apparent contradictions.

In sum, one can see that all three of these accounts are consistent enough that one cannot dismiss any one of them as completely unreliable. They also are different enough, especially in regard to the relative interpretations of events offered, that one must consider each to be primarily an original work, even if each successive author was probably aware of the work of his predecessor. If we have any reason to doubt the originality of any of these accounts, it is in the relationship between Le Challeux's work of 1566 and Le Moyne's of twenty-five years later, but this is probably more true in regard to the later, that is, non-eyewitness, sections of each work.

Fortunately for the historian, the Spanish accounts of the events between September 4 and September 20 present evidence that largely complements the French sources. The two most valuable of these are Solís de Merás's biography and Menéndez's letters to the king. Both of these, authored by central figures in this drama, emphasize the extent of the Spanish problems and uncertainties during the same phase of the conflict. Solís de Merás's account is considerably more detailed than Menéndez's, and it appears that the former relied on later testimonies from others involved as well as on his own personal observations. It is fairly obvious from the outset that his intention was to present Menéndez's actions in a positive light. He does this mostly by focusing on his subject's individual actions, which is helpful to the historian, instead of by employing positive value judgments. Presented in this fashion, Solís de Merás's portrayal of Menéndez as a decisive and capable commander is convincing; one might conclude that serious distortion of the truth was not needed to make his point, especially since many of the details he presents are also sustained by the French accounts. Solís de Merás may have given us a number of minor exaggerations, though it is more difficult to detect any willful invention.

Menéndez's own letters to the king are entirely different in purpose and perspective, since they served as official reports to the king in describing the expedition's progress. One likely ulterior motive is his insistence upon pointing out how carefully he followed orders, and although this may have affected his choice of what to report, it does not seem to affect his reliability. What is perhaps most surprising about these letters, in stark contrast to Solís de Merás's narrative, is the curious lack of stress upon Menéndez's own accomplishments. One might expect that the *adelantado* would have emphasized his own personal responsibility for the Spanish successes, but he did not do so. This is especially true of his description of the capture of Fort Caroline; in comparing the two Spanish accounts, one even suspects that Menéndez was being self-consciously modest about his role in the action. In general, as to events prior to September 20, Solís de Merás and Menéndez closely substantiate each other's claims. Moreover, both of these accounts are logically consistent and individually credible. When the Spanish perspective is added to that of the French, the events leading up to and including the capture of Fort Caroline emerge reasonably straightforwardly.

The only serious issue of contention among all of these accounts is Le Challeux's assertion that Spanish troops committed barbarities against French women and children. There is good reason to conclude that Le Challeux is mistaken on this point. Most obviously, there is a lack of supporting evidence. Even the other French accounts give no corroborating testimony for this claim, while the Spanish witnesses, Menéndez and Solís de Merás, directly contradict it, though they admittedly had reason to deny it. A second and more compelling reason why this assertion is probably false is that Solís de Merás, later in his narrative, devotes much attention to the complications that arose from having fifty women and children in their custody after the capture of the fort, especially concerning the logistical problems of dispatching them to Santo Domingo.[4] This would seem too elaborate a ruse to be an invention.

It is reasonable to conclude that Menéndez did in fact spare a significant number of women and children by direct order, as he himself claimed. However, it remains possible that individual Spanish soldiers did kill some other women and/or children, either acting against their commander's orders or because they were unaware of them. This is especially possible considering the exhausted and rebellious state of the soldiers. Had there in fact been atrocities committed against these most defenseless members of the French garrison, determining their extent is complicated by the fact that not a single one of our sources gives us an indication of how many women and children had arrived in Florida with Ribault. While we can probably accept that some fifty altogether were spared and taken prisoner, it is impossible to determine whether Le Challeux completely invented such barbarities, although this author, at least, suspects that he did.

Thus we can conclude that, for the first phase of the French defeat, our sources give us a fairly complete version of the capture of Fort Caroline. The bloody conclusion of this conflict, centered on the fates of the shipwrecked survivors of the French fleet, presents us with a different situation in terms of historical evidence. Our first-person testimony is more limited, and there is a sharp conflict between the French and Spanish versions of these events.

The most obvious reason to doubt the veracity of these testimonies is the fact that Le Challeux, Le Moyne, and Laudonnière had departed for Europe a few days after September 21. This means that none of them actually witnessed the fate of Ribault's pursuing armada. Le Challeux's description of the events he personally witnessed appeared in the first section, or "Livre Premier," of his 1566 *Discours de l'histoire de la Floride*. As published, this fairly reliable section appeared with two additional sections of lesser reliability. "Livre Deuxième" describes a horrible massacre of the survivors of Ribault's fleet, while the briefer "Livre Troisième" appeared in the form of a "Request to the King," purportedly by the "widows and orphans of Fort Caroline," which describes additional Spanish atrocities.[5] Le Moyne, in 1591, contributed a largely corroborating version of the later massacre, insisting, as did Le Challeux, that Menéndez had ordered a single massive slaughter of French prisoners.

To say the least, the source of each writer's information is quite suspect. Both Le Challeux's "Livre Deuxième" and Le Moyne's later section are purportedly based upon the testimony of a different individual who had miraculously escaped from the Spaniards. Le Challeux asserted that he was "faithfully repeating" what he had been told by a carpenter who had been spared by Menéndez and shipped to Spain as a prisoner, an individual he identifies as "Christophle le Breton of Havre de Grace, who secretly left Seville to the city of Bordeaux."[6] However, Spanish documents indicate that the French prisoners whom Menéndez captured at various points were all held in the New World at least until the late spring of 1566.[7] This makes it doubtful that the testimony of such a witness could have reached Le Challeux in time to be published in May 1566. As for Le Moyne, he asserts that he gathered his information from an unnamed "sailor of Dieppe," whom Spanish soldiers had left for dead and who eventually returned to France, after many trials, some years later. This source's unlikely odyssey had included periods of hiding in Florida and of Spanish slavery.[8] Strangely enough, according to Le Moyne there were only three Frenchmen whom Menéndez spared. He describes all three, and none even remotely resembles Le Challeux's "Christophle le Breton."[9]

Le Challeux's second and third sections, which appeared in all five editions of 1566, provided the basis for the exaggerations and fabrications that shortly afterward started to appear in France, England, and elsewhere, permanently staining Menéndez's reputation as the "pious butcher of Florida."[10] It requires no great stretch of imagination to determine how and why this flawed history became the standard version of events. There can be no doubt that Le Challeux's first section is a firsthand testimony that is founded upon direct personal observation, though it is understandably biased. Having established a certain amount of credibility, this first part is followed by a version of later events—after the departure from the scene of the primary author—that the publisher and/or Le Challeux himself gathered from a separate source, which possibly was fictional. Moreover, some years after the fact, another eyewitness account, that of Le Moyne, appeared to substantiate Le Challeux's main points. Although the author of the later work admitted his familiarity with the earlier one, his publication added further credibility to the "original version" of these episodes.

Even if we assume that Le Challeux's second section did in fact "faithfully repeat" the testimony of his informant, despite the unlikelihood of this source's very existence, a careful examination of the story as presented reveals serious internal weaknesses, casting even further doubt on its reliability. Le Challeux wrote that his informant told him that Ribault's four ships had been "intent on continuing to defend the coast against the descent of the Spaniards," when they were all run aground within a short distance of each other some "50 leagues below the River of May."[11] With the exception of Captain La Grange, who drowned, all of these Frenchmen—who remain unnumbered in this account—survived the shipwreck and reunited under Ribault's command, whereupon they attempted a journey back to Fort Caroline.[12] After nine days with almost no food, having crossed the River May in a "petite barque" that had miraculously appeared, they viewed the Spanish flag flying at Fort Caroline. In this way they first learned of the fort's capture and began negotiations for their own safety.

In this version of events, Menéndez specifically promised humane treatment to the starving Frenchmen if they surrendered. This they readily agreed to, and as soon as they were disarmed, a Spanish officer identified as "Vallemande" quickly reneged on the promise. After some thirty skilled tradesmen were separated from the others, "the impudence of these mad Spaniards was brought down on these poor Frenchmen, who were bound and garroted."[13] After the French prisoners were all dead, the soldiers took great delight in mutilating and dismembering the corpses, especially that of Ribault.

There are problems with this account that are difficult to adequately explain. First of all, Le Challeux tells us that even though all four ships were broken up (rompus) in the hurricane, only a single man, Captain La Grange, drowned. Considering the nature of the storm as described by even the French sources, this is rather hard to believe. Whether the ships actually sank or were run aground, it would have been extremely fortunate had as many as half of these sailors survived. Yet Le Challeux insisted that this group of presumably hundreds of Frenchmen was able to safely reunite under Ribault's command soon afterward and begin a march to the north. Even if this were so, it is difficult to accept that a group described as suffering from severe hunger could have walked fifty leagues (that is, well over a hundred miles) from their point of shipwreck back to Fort Caroline in merely nine days, while a hurricane stormed down upon them the entire time. Equally unlikely, these hundreds of Frenchmen also must have traveled this entire distance along the coast without being detected by Menéndez's soldiers or their Indian allies, who were actively looking for them. For this account to be accurate, Ribault must have led his men on a trek that makes Menéndez's march on Fort Caroline seem effortless in comparison. A final illogicality is that this massacre is reported to have taken place nine days after the shipwreck, that is, simultaneously with or immediately following the capture of Fort Caroline on September 21.

These weaknesses alone make Le Challeux's account highly suspect. Its credibility becomes even more doubtful when one regards its points of direct contradiction with the Spanish sources. The Spanish and French testimonies about these last events present so much incompatibility that one cannot even attempt a synthesis. In contrast to the French, the three Spanish sources—each an eyewitness to at least some of the events—are quite consistent among themselves. Where they differ, it is usually regarding the numbers of people involved at different stages, and occasionally there are minor differences in times of day and dates. In terms of the sequence of events, and where these events took place, there is no disagreement whatsoever. These reasons alone strongly indicate that the Spanish version of events is much closer to reality than the story presented by the French.

Each of the three Spanish sources—Menéndez, Solís de Méras, and the friar Mendoza Grajales—reports two separate massacres, both occurring in roughly the same location about ten miles south of St. Augustine and more than thirty miles south of Fort Caroline, in a location that was probably the southern extremity of Anastasia Island. Named Matanzas or "Massacres" Inlet by later Spanish settlers, this channel between the mainland and Anastasia still bears the name it earned as a result of these events.

The Spanish witnesses consistently reported these two massacres as having occurred about two weeks apart, on September 28 and October

12. In the first case, approximately 140 Frenchmen in the first group surrendered en masse, and Menéndez's force of no more than fifty Spaniards executed all of them except perhaps a dozen. Two weeks later, 150 Spanish soldiers, personally commanded by Menéndez, confronted a group of as many as 200 Frenchmen. On this occasion, only 70 or so of the latter, including Ribault, surrendered, and these men were executed while the rest fled. The Spanish sources tell us that during these two episodes a total of between 180 and 220 Frenchmen died by Menéndez's order. They also indicate that more than 250 of Ribault's men were believed to have drowned, and that by the end of November, more than 100 other Frenchmen were eventually captured but spared execution. Importantly, none of the three Spanish sources maintains that Menéndez promised to spare the Frenchmen if they surrendered, nor is there anywhere in these accounts a single mention of the mutilation or dismemberment of Ribault's corpse or that of anyone else.

The adelantado's own letter to the king of October 15, which briefly describes both occurrences, remains our most important source of information about the massacres. Most of this lengthy account was composed just prior to October 10, almost two weeks after the first massacre. The purpose of this letter was twofold. First, he was bringing the king up to date on the events that had transpired since his last letter, which had been dispatched September 10 while he awaited the French attack on St. Augustine. The letter's second purpose was to outline the expedition's needs and plans in light of recent events and the perceived continuing threat to his enterprise. However, before he could complete this communication, the occurrence of the second massacre required him to make a hurried addition to it. Thus, Menéndez composed most of this letter—which included his descriptions of the capture of Fort Caroline, the first Matanzas massacre, and his analysis of his situation—prior to the second massacre. Only after this late addition could the Spanish commander dispatch it to Madrid, via Santo Domingo and Seville, as an official report to the king.

Another important aspect to this letter is that Menéndez expected it to be the first news that King Philip received of the conflict.[14] Therefore, at the time of this letter's composition, Menéndez had no need to defend himself against reprimand, official or otherwise. Both the tone and content of the letter suggest that its writer did not anticipate any future criticism; somewhat the opposite appears to have been the case. The details that Menéndez divulges are intended to demonstrate the success of his mission up until that point, even though he de-emphasizes his own personal contribution to this success.[15] Instead, he makes a point of how precisely he had carried out his instructions: he credits the wisdom of his orders, as well as divine intervention, for his victory. At the same time, he stresses his dire situation and need for continued support. The result is curious—his account of the massacres is largely matter-of-fact and emotionless. If Menéndez is trying to hide anything in this letter, it is certainly not apparent from either his circumstances or his tone.

The adelantado's brother-in-law, Solís de Merás, reports on both incidents in greater detail than does Menéndez, generally supporting the latter's report. While we can determine that he was almost certainly not present at the first massacre, he probably witnessed the second one and may even have played a major role in it.[16] It may well be that he exaggerated some of the details, especially the respective numbers of Frenchmen and Spaniards, and it certainly appears that he added the testimonies of others to his own observations. Nevertheless, the general picture Solís de Merás presents is similar to that of Menéndez's briefer report, which it possibly embellishes but certainly does not contradict in substance.

Mendoza Grajales took no part in the capture of Fort Caroline, since he had remained at St. Augustine, and he was not present at the second Matanzas massacre. He was, however, a crucial eyewitness at the first incident at Matanzas on September 28, when he accompanied the first expedition at Menéndez's request. Mendoza's account of the first executions is recounted in the last paragraphs of his memoir, even though his account of the incident is surprisingly brief compared to the attention he devoted to some less significant events. As with Solís de Merás's description of the second massacre, Mendoza's testimony strongly substantiates Menéndez's version of the first.

Overall, there are serious points of incompatibility between the Spanish and French versions of the massacres. Most egregious, perhaps, is the French insistence that only one massacre of shipwrecked Frenchmen took place, instead of the two consistently reported by Spanish sources. A closely related second point of explicit disagreement is the question of where the Frenchmen were killed. Since it is impossible to accept that either the French or Spanish writers were so badly informed about either of these issues that they made an honest mistake, intentional fabrication by one side or the other is the only possibility.

To explain these differences, we must first ask who had a motivation to relate these matters falsely. There is no apparent good reason why Spaniards might wish to claim the occurrence of an additional massacre or that the massacres took place in a different location. Regarding Menéndez's account in particular, it would have been an extraordinary machination to have added a false "postscript" in his October 15 letter that "added" a second massacre. If Ribault and all of his men were already dead—according to Le Challeux's version, they were killed at least twenty days prior to the posting of Menéndez's letter—such a deception (to the king, no less) would have been especially pointless. Even less explicable is why all three Spanish sources might have colluded upon such a fiction.

In contrast, there certainly are reasons why either Le Challeux and Le Moyne might have desired to present these two massacres as one. A single massacre certainly has more dramatic effect. In describing such an event, French writers could more easily portray Ribault as the heroic leader of a tragic quest. Having somehow regrouped his dispersed forces, and leading them on a courageous march to the north, Ribault was stopped tantalizingly close to his goal of Fort Caroline, but only by Spanish villainy. As a story, this version of events demonstrates the French leader as a man of fortitude, honor, conviction, and determination, instead of as a victim of the elements and his own indecisiveness—which, as we have seen, more closely resembles the reality of this case.

A third major point of disagreement concerns the supposed promise of clemency given by Menéndez to induce a surrender. Le Moyne supports Le Challeux on this point, though his details are somewhat different; meanwhile, the Spanish witnesses had very good reason to deny this. On the surface this appears a case of whom one wishes to believe. Two valid points can be made that support the Spanish testimony. First, of course, one can fall back on the unreliability of the French witnesses, a weakness compounded by the probable motives of Le Challeux and Le Moyne. Second, and perhaps equally compelling, is that Menéndez described his actions to King Philip prior to any criticism he had received, and there is little reason to believe that he expected any in the future. He related the incidents in a clearly worded explanation that was in no sense a denial or apology. Moreover, Mendoza Grajales and Solís de Merás fully support Menéndez's claim that he had made the situation quite clear to the French without resorting to deception. One must conclude that, while it is possible that Menéndez reneged on a promise of clemency and that his companions falsified their statements to support him, the burden of proof must fall on the French in this matter, and their proof is nonexistent.

A similar case is the fourth and final major point of disagreement between the French and Spanish versions. This is the question of the mutilation of Ribault and the other dead Frenchmen that was described in such gory detail by Le Moyne and Le Challeux. While we can again question the sources and motives of both French writers, the Spanish witnesses would have had excellent reason not to mention these alleged events. As with the question of the promise of clemency, this assertion by the French can be neither proved nor disproved, and we must admit that it is possible that it was true. My own conclusion, admittedly a subjective one, is that it would have been entirely out of character for Menéndez to have either ordered or permitted such atrocities. Even while his men were in a state of exhaustion and fear, the Spanish commander remained firmly in control of the situation throughout these events. While there can be little question of how he felt about "Lutherans," he was also a decisive leader who was able to think rationally under the most trying of circumstances.

Such are the two distinct and conflicting versions of what happened, in the end, to Ribault's fleet. In closing our analysis of the evidence surrounding these unhappy episodes, let us compare the respective versions of the total French casualties, which makes the judgment of the relative truths of these two incompatible versions even easier. If we believe the Spanish witnesses, there were some 330 Frenchmen executed or killed by Menéndez; perhaps 260 who drowned; 150 or so, including 50 women and children, who were captured; and anywhere from 100 to 150 who escaped by various means. This outcome qualifies as a colonial disaster of the first magnitude.

In contrast, Le Challeux and his literary successors would have us believe that the French attempt on Florida resulted in about 20 Frenchmen captured, 100 who escaped, one who drowned, and as many as 900, including babies, who were murdered with bloodthirsty glee by Menéndez's soldiers. This version of events avoids the embarrassment of having to admit that more Frenchmen probably drowned than were executed by Menéndez. It also enables these writers to claim that the French defeat was the result of neither the elements nor honorable battle. Only by emphasizing Spanish brutality and treachery could they make these dead Frenchmen into the heroic martyrs that the Calvinist cause required. These writers were not describing a colonial disaster. They were creating a myth, one that has unfortunately persisted into the twentieth century.

These two partisan works of Le Challeux and Le Moyne spawned a virtual corpus of French historical writing that distorted these events very soon after their occurrence. To appreciate the context of this literature, one must keep in mind that for more than thirty years after these events took place, ideological and political conflict dominated Reformation Europe. Following the St. Bartholomew's Day Massacres in 1572, French writers including François de Belleforest, André Thevet, Urbain Chauveton, and Lancelot Voisin de La Popelinière published historical treatments of Florida that all relied exclusively on Le Challeux's testimony.[17] During the next few years, the output of French anti-Catholic literature expanded enormously, and one can only regard these early treatments of the Florida defeat in a context of a rapid polarization of religious and political views. During the 1580s, Protestant publishers throughout Europe adopted a more specifically anti-Spanish tone, as the Netherlands conflict deepened and England braced for war with Spain.[18] By 1591, when Le Moyne's account finally appeared in print in Frankfurt, Spanish armies, allied to the French Catholic League, were invading France itself.

As one might expect, French contemporary writers portrayed their countrymen as blameless and innocent, and their Spanish conquerors as barbaric and treacherous. It is no coincidence that Protestants, such as Chauveton and La Popelinière, or *politique* Catholics such as Belleforest, wrote most of the early French treatments of the Florida debacle. Yet even André Thevet, a staunch Catholic Leaguer, was forced to rely on Le Challeux, for want of other sources. Although Thevet minimized the religious motives behind the executions, it is not entirely surprising that he followed Le Challeux's other details quite precisely, since he evidently had no other sources available to consult. As late as fifty years after the Florida defeat, when Jacques-Auguste de Thou, Agrippa d'Aubigné, and Marc Lescarbot composed their respective works, evidence about these events remained scarce and one-sided. Of these three later writers, only Lescarbot was even the least bit skeptical of his sources, but he could offer no alternative interpretation besides speculation.[19]

In contrast, the Spanish sources remained unpublished for centuries. The letters of Menéndez and the friar Mendoza were never intended for a wide audience, and they remained buried in Spanish archives until the nineteenth century. Neither Solís de Merás's chronicle nor a 1568 biography of Menéndez made it into print until relatively modern times.[20] This lack of easily accessible Spanish testimony, combined with the apparent abundance of sixteenth-century French sources, resulted in unbalanced later historical treatments. However, even after most of the relevant Spanish material became accessible, writers such as Paul Gaffarel and Francis Parkman, among others, disparaged its veracity.[21] For example,

Gaffarel directly rebuts the work of the Spanish writer Andrés Gonzalez de Barcia Carballido y Zuñiga, whose *Ensayo cronológico para la historia general de Florida,* published in 1723, is a gross exaggeration of these events from the opposite perspective.[22] Though Gaffarel consulted Menéndez, Mendoza Grajales and Solís de Merás about other events, he largely dismisses their contrary descriptions of the massacres. Parkman, in his 1865 *Pioneers of France in the New World,* simply misrepresents the Spanish testimony, such as claiming that Solís de Merás had written that Menéndez broke a promise of clemency, when in fact that author had specifically stated the contrary.[23]

Even in this century, most French and French-Canadian scholars, including Charles de La Roncière, Charles-André Julien, Marc Trudel, and Frank Lestringant, have not significantly altered this interpretation. They have usually either regarded the sixteenth-century French historians as authoritative or, what is even worse, accepted Le Challeux's and Le Moyne's publications as genuine eyewitness testimony.[24] They have seldom given the Spanish sources proper attention, and the result is that even modern historical accounts of this episode have been uniformly vague and confusing. However, it is possible to use the abundant surviving material with care. Doing so reveals a compelling story of how the servants of two powerful kingdoms waged a bitter and desperate battle in an uncharted land, for rewards that were, at best, uncertain.

NOTES

1. Introduction

1. Useful surveys of the process of European expansion include J. H. Parry, *The Age of Reconnaissance: Discovery, Exploration, and Settlement 1450 to 1650*, and G. V. Scammell, *The First Imperial Age: European Overseas Expansion, c. 1400–1715*.

2. The literature on the rise of English maritime power is voluminous; two of the best studies include David Waters, *The Art of Navigation in England in Elizabethan and Early Stuart Times*, and Kenneth Andrews, *Trade, Plunder, and Settlement: Maritime Enterprise and the Genesis of the British Empire, 1480–1630*.

3. On the Dutch, see Charles Boxer, *The Dutch Seaborne Empire, 1600–1800*.

4. For example, see Michel de Mollat du Jourdain, *Europe and the Sea*, 101–24, or Thomas A. Brady, Jr., et al., *Handbook of European History, 1400–1600*, 1:643–56. A different sort of inaccurate generalization can be found in Kris Lane, *Pillaging the Empire: Piracy in the Americas, 1500–1750*, 25–28.

5. Frank Lestringant, *Le Huguenot et le sauvage*, and numerous articles stress the idea of a "Protestant refuge" as the primary motivation behind the French initiatives in Brazil and Florida.

6. The standard works on these events include Francis Parkman, *Pioneers of France in the New World*, vol. 1, *France and England in North America*; Samuel Eliot Morison, *The European Discovery of America: The Southern Voyages, A.D.1492–1616*; and Paul Gaffarel, *Histoire de la Floride française*.

7. Works that discuss the impact of this technology upon European culture, religion, and politics are Elizabeth Eisenstein, *The Printing Press as an Agent of Change: Communications and Cultural Transformations in Early Modern Europe*, 2 vols., and Robert Kingdon, *Myths about the St. Bartholomew's Day Massacre, 1572–1576*.

8. An excellent historiographical essay on this subject is that of Lyle N. McAlister in his introduction to the reprint of Jeannette Thurber Connor's translation of *Pedro Menéndez de Avilés: Memorial*, by Gonzalo Solís de Merás, xiii–xxxi.

9. Nicolas Le Challeux, *Discours de l'histoire de la Floride, contenant la cruauté des Espagnols contre les subjets du roy en l'an mil cinq cens soixante cinq;* Jacques Le Moyne de Morgues, *Brevis Narratio eorum quae in Florida Americae provincia Gallis accider-*

unt, secunda in illam Navigationem duce Renato de Laudonniere classis praefecto anno MDLXIIII.

10. The effect of such published testimonies, including the Le Moyne and Le Challeux accounts, on later historical treatments of the subject is the focus of this author's doctoral dissertation, "France in America, 1555–1565: A Reevaluation of the Evidence."

2. Terra Florida

1. A concise description of Spanish concerns at Bayonne can be found in Henry Kamen, *Philip of Spain*, 101–3.

2. Good surveys of French events during the era immediately preceding these voyages include J. H. M. Salmon, *Society in Crisis: France in the Sixteenth Century*, 117–43; Frederic J. Baumgartner, *France in the Sixteenth Century*, 129–31, 151–61; R. J. Knecht, *The French Wars of Religion*; and Mack P. Holt, *The French Wars of Religion, 1562–1629*, 42–47.

3. See Stuart Carroll, *Noble Power during the French Wars of Religion: The Guise Affinity and the Catholic Cause in Normandy*, 100–104. In this work, the author demonstrates the complex kinship, political, and clientage factors that affected the court struggles of this era, persuasively demonstrating that religion was only one consideration that influenced court factions. On persecution during the reign of François II, see also R. J. Knecht, *Catherine de Medici*, 61–63.

4. The classic study of Calvin's efforts remains Robert M. Kingdon, *Geneva and the Coming of the Wars of Religion in France, 1555–1562*; another useful study dealing with the interplay of politics and religion is N. M. Sutherland's *The Huguenot Struggle for Recognition*.

5. A concise description of the first war can be found in Holt, *French Wars of Religion*, 49–55; see also Carroll, *Noble Power*, 116–23.

6. Kamen, *Philip of Spain*, 101–3; Salmon, *Society in Crisis*, 150–51.

7. Kamen, *Philip of Spain*, 82–83, 101; James Westfall Thompson, *The Wars of Religion in France, 1559–1576: The Huguenots, Catherine de Medici, Philip II*.

8. These events will be examined in more detail below in chapter 7.

9. On the early European maritime presence in the North Atlantic, see A. N. Ryan, "Bristol, the Atlantic, and North America," in *Maritime History*, ed. John B. Hattendorf, vol. 1, *The Age of Discovery*, 241–78.

10. Quoted by Arthur Heulhard, *Villegagnon, Roi d'Amérique*, 86. Though widely cited as a verbatim quote, this wording is in fact a thirdhand rendering of a statement François had made. See Paul Hoffman, "Diplomacy and the Papal Donation," 161n.31.

11. R. J. Knecht, *Francis I*, 305–25.

12. Hoffman, "Diplomacy and the Papal Donation," 156–58; Charles de La Roncière, *Histoire de la marine française*, 3:146.

13. Charles-André Julien, *Les voyages de découverte et les premiers établissements*, 86–89, 184.

14. Henri Harrisse, *Découverte et évolution cartographique de Terre-Neuve*, 103.

15. Lawrence Wroth, *The Voyages of Giovanni da Verrazzano, 1524–1528*, 14–16.

16. Paul Butel, *Les Caraïbes au temps des flibustiers*, 33–36; also Betsabe Caunedo del Potro, *Mercadores Castellanos en el Golfo de Vizcaya (1475–1492)*, 183–259.

17. A. Anthiaume, *Cartes marines, constructions navales, voyages de découverte chez les Normands, 1500–1650*, 184.

18. Kenneth Andrews, *The Spanish Caribbean: Trade and Plunder, 1530–1630*, 83–84; La Roncière, *Marine française*, 3:291–307; Julien, *Voyages*, 169–75.

19. Anthiaume, *Cartes marines*, 190–95; Louis Vitet, *Histoire de Dieppe*, 276–82.

20. Léon Guérin, *Ango et ses pilotes* (Paris, 1857) is the only full-length account of Ango's career. See also Vitet, *Histoire de Dieppe*, 280–82.

21. Henry Folmer, *The Franco-Spanish Rivalry in North America* (Glendale, Calif.: Arthur H. Clark, 1953), 53–58; La Roncière, *Marine française*, 3:307–47; "Memorandum of the Councils of State and of the Indies" (before June 26, 1541), in H. P. Biggar, *A Collection of Documents Relating to Jacques Cartier and the Sieur de Roberval*, no. 163, 320–26.

22. Knecht, *Francis I*, 333–43; Julien, *Voyages*, 147–57; Biggar, *Documents Cartier*, 244–45.

23. Olive Dickason, *The Myth of the Savage and the Beginnings of French Colonialism in the Americas*, chap. 9; Gayle Brunelle, "Sixteenth Century Perceptions of the New World," *Sixteenth Century Journal*; Philip Boucher, *Les Nouvelles Frances*, 6–7.

24. The first documented Norman voyage to Brazil was that of Paulmier de Gonneville in 1504, who reported Portuguese mentions of previous French ships to those shores. Charles and Paul Bréard, eds., *Documents relatifs à la marine normande au XVIe siècle* (Rouen, 1889), 203; Anthiaume, *Cartes marines*, 184–86.

25. Philip Benedict, *Rouen during the Wars of Religion*, 18–20; Emile Coornaert, *Les Français et le commerce international d'Anvers à la fin du XVe–XVIe siècle*, 23; Gayle Brunelle, *The New World Merchants of Rouen, 1559–1630*, 16–17.

26. E. Bradford Burns, *A History of Brazil*, 24–25.

27. La Roncière, *Marine française*, 3:455; Frederic Baumgartner, *Henry II, King of France*, 236–38.

28. Brunelle, "Sixteenth Century Perceptions," 75; Benedict, *Rouen*, 2.

29. See Frederic Baumgartner, "Adam's Will: Act II. Henry II and French Overseas Expansion," 137–47; see also Anthiaume, *Cartes marines*, 97–99.

30. A. Anthiaume, "Un pilote et cartographe Havrais au XVIe siècle, Guillaume Le Testu," 180–202.

31. Among the surviving written testimonies that directly concern Fort Coligny, there are at least four specific references to the Rio de la Plata region in connection with the goals of Villegagnon's mission. Among French writings of the era, the term "Perou" was usually employed as inexactly as was "les Indes" or "Brésil," and references to locations in America can often be difficult to interpret precisely. In contrast, mentions of more specific places, such as the "Rivière de la Plata," must be taken more literally.

32. For a more detailed hypothesis concerning the connection between the missions of Le Testu and Villegagnon, see Baumgartner, "Adam's Will." While his general conclusions seem sound, the reader is cautioned concerning some of the details, especially the dates, of the two missions.

33. See John McGrath, "Polemic and History in French Brazil"; Silvia Castro Shannon, "Military Outpost or Protestant Refuge: Villegagnon's Expedition to Brazil in 1555."

34. Huguette and Pierre Chaunu, *Seville et l'Atlantique (1504–1650)*, 8:399; David J. Weber, *The Spanish Frontier in North America*, 66.

35. Lyle McAlister, *Spain and Portugal in the New World*, 242–45; Clarence Haring, *The Spanish Empire in America*, 293–314; James Lang, *Conquest and Commerce: Spain and England in the Americas*, 47–51.

36. J. H. Parry, *The Spanish Seaborne Empire*, 53–57.

37. The classic and exhaustive study of the *flota* system can be found in Chaunu, *Seville et l'Atlantique*. More concise descriptions can be found in Haring, *Trade and Navigation between Spain and the Indies in the Time of the Hapsburgs*, and Butel, *Les Caraibes*, 27–29.

38. Paul Hoffman, *The Spanish Crown and the Defense of the Caribbean, 1535–1585*, 6. In this study, Hoffman gives a thorough description of the problems faced by outgoing and incoming Caribbean shipping during this era; see pp. 1–19 and 63–173. A more recent work that gives a nice description of these fleets and their problems is Pablo E. Pérez-Mallaína, *Spain's Men of the Sea: Daily Life and the Indies Fleets in the Sixteenth Century*, 9–15.

39. Pierre Chaunu, *Conquête et exploitation des nouveaux mondes*, no. 26, *Nouvelle Clio: L'histoire et ses problemes*, 283.

40. Chaunu and Chaunu, *Seville et l'Atlantique*, 8:396–99. See also Earl Hamilton, *American Treasure and the Price Revolution*, 34–43.

41. Hoffman's research on the influence of this idea on both the Spaniards and the French makes an invaluable contribution to our understanding of the motives of the planners of these missions. See "The Chicora Legend and Franco-Spanish Rivalry in La Florida," 419–32, and *A New Andalucia and a Way to the Orient*, 3–83.

42. Eugene Lyon discusses the primarily civilian nature of this undertaking in "Spain's Sixteenth Century Settlement Attempts: A Neglected Aspect."

43. The expression is Paul Hoffman's, and it usefully conveys the concept of the fertile, prosperous, temperate land that would-be colonists hoped to find. This idea may have had special significance to later Huguenot settlers, because of its religious connotation.

44. Cited by David B. Quinn, ed., *New American World: A Documentary History of North America to 1612*, 2:199.

45. Philip II to Luis de Velasco, December 29, 1557, cited by Quinn, *New American World*, 2:202.

46. Weber, *Spanish Frontier*, 67; Hoffman, *New Andalucia*, 144–81.

47. Luna to Philip II, November 1, 1558, cited by Quinn, *New American World*, 2:207–9.

48. Velasco to Philip II, May 25, 1559, cited ibid., 213–15.

49. Philip II to Luna, December 18, 1559, cited ibid., 221.

50. Philip II to Velasco, September 23, 1561, cited by Weber, *Spanish Frontier*, 68.

51. On Philip's attitude and policies toward his empire, including his American possessions, see Kamen, *Philip of Spain*, 61, 106–11, 137; Geoffrey Parker, *The Grand Strategy of Philip II*, 1–10.

52. Butel, *Les Caraïbes*, 26, 33–36; Haring, *Trade and Navigation*, 45–46.

53. "Treaty concluded between France and Spain, at Crépy-en-Laonnois, September 18, 1544, separate article relating to the Indies," cited by Frances Gardiner Davenport, ed., *European Treaties Bearing on the History of the United States and Its Dependencies*, 1, no. 18, 205–9; Hoffman, "Diplomacy and the Papal Donation," 162–65.

54. Julien, *Voyages*, 169–72.

55. Paul Hoffman, *Spanish Crown*, 12, 13, 66, 68. The author has quantified the available Spanish records into revealing tables that reflect the increase of corsair attacks against Spanish settlements and shipping between 1552 and 1559. This is consistent with the French evidence analyzed by Julien and La Roncière, cited below. On the actions of French corsairs after 1552, see Kris Lane, *Pillaging the Empire: Piracy in the Americas, 1500–1750*, 25–28.

56. La Roncière, *Marine française*, 3:579–84; Gabriel Marcel, *Les corsaires français au XVIe siècle dans les Antilles*, 18–19; Andrews, *Spanish Caribbean*, 83–84.

57. On the activities of French corsairs on American waters at midcentury, the most complete historical accounts can be found in La Roncière, *Marine française*, 3:520–89; see also Butel, *Les Caraïbes*, 33–36, and Julien, *Voyages*, 166–77.

58. Julien, *Voyages*, 173–74; Baumgartner, *Henry II*, 136–37.

59. Andrews, *Spanish Caribbean*, 83.

60. Ambassador Renard reportedly wrote to Philip at the time, "as to the article concerning the Indies, they have granted it with great difficulty, saying that by the preceding treaty (main body of truce) commerce is permitted to them." *Papiers d'etat du Cardinal Granvelle*, 4, 541, cited by Davenport, *Treaties*, 1:216n.6.

61. "Truce between France and Spain, concluded at Vaucelles, February 5, 1556," cited ibid., vol. 1, no. 20, 217.

62. At least two official communiqués survive that indicate French royal involvement in this project: "Michel de Seure to Henri II," January 30, 1559, BN Nouvelles acquisitions français 6638, fol. 4–6, and Nicot to Henri II, April 1559, ibid., fol. 166.

63. Cesáreo Fernández-Duro, *Armada Espanola desde la unión de los reinos de Castilla y de Aragón*, 2:464.

64. A number of diplomatic documents attest to the pervasiveness and extent of the Spanish concern about this matter. See Hoffman, *New Andalucia*, 160–68.

65. Ambassador to England Quadra to Margaret of Parma, December 20, 1561,

and Quadra to Cardinal de Granvelle, January 4, 1562, both cited by Heulhard, *Villegagnon*, 240. The preparations referred to seem to be those described in orders of August 23, 1561, and November 22, 1561, BN Fonds français 32614, fol. 279, 281; inventory of *artillerie de la marine*, October 13, 1561, BN Fonds français 15881, fol. 343.

66. The difficulty presented by conflicting interpretations of what constituted a "legitimate claim" to new territories is discussed in Anthony Pagden, *Lords of All the World*, 32–33, 46–48, and in John Juricek, "English Territorial Claims in North America under Elizabeth and the Early Stuarts," esp. 7–11. While Pagden insists that the legitimacy of the Papal Donation of 1493 remained the foundation of the Spanish diplomatic position through the sixteenth century, Juricek asserts that by the 1540s, this argument had become less important to Spain than the principle of "discovery and possession." Whenever Spanish diplomats offered the Papal Donation argument in the mid-sixteenth century, the French gave them a consistent response; as Pagden writes, "there is almost no French or English attack on the claims of Spanish sovereignty overseas which does not begin with a rejection of both the Bulls and the terms of the Treaty of Tordesillas" (48).

67. Davenport, in *Treaties*, 1:220n.9, asserts that ultimately, "an oral agreement was made, apparently to the effect that west of the prime meridian and south of the Tropic of Cancer might should make right." However, Hoffman places these negotiations in a more complete context and shows that this is misleading, since the diplomats never were able to agree to even that. See *New Andalucia*, 161–68, and "Diplomacy and the Papal Donation," 166–70. He concludes that although both sides desired a peaceful arrangement, much vagueness remained after 1561, and "each side remained free to define the Indies as it liked, and to try to back up its claims as best it might" ("Diplomacy and the Papal Donation," 169).

68. Hoffman, "Diplomacy and the Papal Donation," esp. 165–72.

69. Patricia Seed, *Ceremonies of Possession in Europe's Conquest of the New World, 1492–1640*, 9–13.

3. Gaspard de Coligny and the New World

1. A useful brief synthesis of the growth of French Protestantism during this period can be found in Holt, *French Wars of Religion*, 30–40; see also Kingdon, *Geneva and the Coming of the Wars of Religion in France*.

2. On the complications that arose from both political and religious factionalism after 1559, see Holt, *French Wars of Religion*, 41–49; Carroll, *Noble Power*, 89–159.

3. See especially Holt, *French Wars of Religion*, 50–53; Barbara Diefendorf, *Beneath the Cross: Catholics and Huguenots in Sixteenth Century Paris*, 57–65. The latter, which focuses on Paris, gives an eminently readable account of the many factors responsible for the conflicts that erupted both in the capital and elsewhere in the realm.

4. Junko Shimizu, *Conflict of Loyalties: Politics and Religion in the Career of Gaspard de Coligny, Admiral of France*, 43–56. Shimizu's study of the admiral's situation

during this crucial period is an invaluable contribution to our understanding of both Coligny and the political situation in France. Jules Delaborde's *Gaspard de Coligny, Amiral de France* is an invaluable resource for tracing the development of the admiral's career through documents, letters, and contemporary commentaries. A less flattering portrait of the admiral can be found in Carroll, *Noble Power,* esp. 89–131.

5. Baumgartner, *France in the Sixteenth Century,* 59.

6. A detailed explanation of the resumption of hostilities can be found in Lucien Romier, *Les origines politiques des guerres de religion,* 1:425–56; for a more concise summary, see Knecht, *Catherine de Medici,* 47–48.

7. Shimizu, *Conflict of Loyalties,* 33, though Carroll disagrees as to the extent that the capture of Calais helped the Guises at court (*Noble Power,* 91–93).

8. Salmon, *Society in Crisis,* 118, 123–24. Carroll cautions against overemphasizing religion as a singular determinant of factionalism after Henri's death (*Noble Power,* 90–93).

9. Delaborde, *Coligny,* 1:145.

10. There has been frequent disagreement about the timing of his conversion, though Shimizu's conclusion that Coligny had no direct exposure to Genevan Calvinism until 1558 is the most convincing. See Shimizu, *Conflict of Loyalties,* 18, 30–31; Romier, *Origines politiques,* 1:246–47; A. W. Whitehead, *Gaspard de Coligny, Admiral of France,* 61–70; Delaborde, *Coligny,* 1:380–81.

11. Shimizu, *Conflict of Loyalties,* 31.

12. The theme of a "Protestant refuge" is central to Frank Lestringant's *Huguenot et sauvage.* Others who accept this explanation include C. A. Julien, Marc Trudel, and A. W. Whitehead.

13. Salmon, *Society in Crisis,* 126–27; Shimizu, *Conflict of Loyalties,* 35–39.

14. Knecht, *Catherine de Medici,* 68–72.

15. This quotation is taken from Delaborde, *Coligny,* 1:464. Delaborde cites its origin as *Memoires de Condé,* 2:645–48. However, the edition consulted (London: DuBosse, de Nillor, 1740) contains this quote on p. 654, without clear attribution to Coligny. Shimizu notes that both Pierre de La Place, in *Commentaire de l'estat de la religion & republique soubs les rois Henri et François seconds & Charles neufieme* (n.p., 1565) and Regnier de la Planche, in his *Histoire de l'estat de France,* give approximate versions of Coligny's words, though the latter's account, at least, is not the same as the Delaborde quotation. In any case it is questionable whether any of the above authors could have faithfully presented Coligny's precise words. Nevertheless, Condé, La Planche, and Theodore Beza, while admittedly all Protestants, were consistent in their descriptions of Coligny's main points of emphasis at Fontainebleau, which the above-cited quote expresses quite succinctly. Thus, I have chosen to employ this quote, whatever its origin, as an illustration of the argument presented by Coligny at that assembly.

16. Shimizu, *Conflict of Loyalties,* 41.

17. Ibid., 43–47.

18. Ibid., 55–60.

19. See Knecht, *Catherine de Medici*, 72.

20. Queen to Throckmorton, March 31, 1562, United Kingdom, Public Record Office, *Calendar of State Papers, Foreign Series, Reign of Elizabeth* (hereafter cited as *CSPForeign, Elizabeth*), 4:no. 965, 570; Admiral of France to Cecil, April 1, 1562, ibid., 4:no. 975, 578; Prince Condé to Queen, April 2, 1562, ibid., 4:no. 976, 579; Admiral Chatillon to Queen, April 11, 1562, 4:no. 1002, 600; see also Thompson, *Wars of Religion in France*, 162. In "The Origins of Queen Elizabeth's Relations with the Huguenots," N. M. Sutherland argues that these Huguenot / English overtures would have taken place even earlier except for the lack of an identifiable Protestant political faction in France prior to François's death.

21. Throckmorton reported negotiations designed to jointly exterminate Protestants by December 31, 1560: Throckmorton to the Lords of the Council, December 31, 1560, *CSPForeign, Elizabeth*, 3:no. 833, 471–74. See also Thompson, *Wars of Religion in France*, 131–33, on relations between the Guises and Spain in 1561 and 1562, and Kamen, *Philip of Spain*, 106.

22. Salmon, *Society in Crisis*, 140–41; Delaborde, *Coligny*, 1:512–15.

23. Shimizu, *Conflict of Loyalties*, 43–56.

24. Delaborde, *Coligny*, 2:1–4; Knecht, *Catherine de Medici*, 83–87.

25. While there are no extant ships' registers or other documents that list the passengers or specify their religious affiliations, this seems clear from the published accounts and correspondence concerned with these enterprises.

26. G. Le Hardy, *Histoire de Protestantisme en Normandie*, 1–7; David Nicholls, "Social Change and Early Protestantism in France: Normandy, 1520–1562," 285.

27. Benedict, *Rouen*, 51; Guillaume and Jean Daval, *Histoire de la réformation à Dieppe, 1557–1657*, 7–8. The Calvinist brothers Guillaume and Jean Daval composed *Histoire de la réformation à Dieppe* sometime prior to 1661.

28. Vitet, *Histoire de Dieppe*, 61–76. In addition to the book by the Daval brothers, a Catholic work also provides us with detailed accounts of the spread of the new religion. The Catholic priest David Asseline wrote *Les antiquitez et chroniques de la ville de Dieppe* in 1682, at least in part as a response to the Davals, but in most respects his history is consistent with the Protestant work, with the notable exception that Asseline feels that the Davals overestimate the number of conversions in the city.

29. Vitet, *Dieppe*, 61–62.

30. Carroll, *Noble Power*, 110–11.

31. Daval, *Réformation à Dieppe*, 11–12.

32. Delaborde, *Coligny*, 1:459–60.

33. Ibid., 475.

34. Nicholls, "Social Change," 289–90.

35. Samuel Mours, *Le Protestantisme en France au XVIe siècle*, 141–42.

36. Ibid., 144.

37. Daval, *Réformation à Dieppe*, 22.

38. For a discussion of the various currents at work in the conversions of the maritime communities of Normandy and the French Atlantic coast, see Alain Cabantous, *Le ciel dans la mer: Christianisme et civilisation maritime XVI–XIXe siècle,* esp. chaps. 4 and 7; and Michel de Mollat du Jourdain, *La vie quotidienne des gens de mer en Atlantique IXe–XVIe siècle,* 221–45. There is little quantitative evidence available regarding the growth of Protestantism in sixteenth-century French maritime communities, and contemporary testimonies are often contradictory. However, both of the above authors point out that the level of Catholic orthodoxy in these areas was inconsistent prior to reform. Moreover, Cabantous notes that among declared Calvinists in these communities in the last half of the sixteenth century, strict adherence to Calvinist teaching was rare. It appears that in the years between 1560 and 1562, many Norman mariners "converted" from a somewhat nominal Catholicism to an equally nominal Calvinism. More study needs to be done in this area.

39. Catholic Spanish sailors, too, seem to have relied more on superstition than upon conventional religious practices. See Pérez-Mallaína, *Spain's Men of the Sea,* 237–45.

40. Carroll, *Noble Power,* 108–13.

41. R. V. Tooley, *Landmarks of Mapmaking,* 212–21, and Cumming, Skelton, and Quinn, *The Discovery of North America,* are but two of the volumes that graphically illustrate the varying geographic ideas of North America that Europeans had during the sixteenth century.

42. Wroth, *Verrazzano,* 71–90.

43. R. A. Skelton, *Explorers' Maps,* 78–94, 118–57; Harrisse, *Découverte et évolution,* 93–99; L. A. Vigneras, "A Spanish Discovery of North Carolina in 1566," 401. Regarding the influence of Verrazzano's observations upon later French explorations, including his concept of an isthmus and "false sea," Wroth writes that "It can hardly be thought that the events and outcome of the Verrazzano voyage of 1524 sank like a stone into a sea of forgetfulness, that it bore no resemblance to the westward explorations of the French in succeeding years." Wroth, *Verrazzano,* 188.

44. Menéndez, "Memorial de Pedro Menéndez," in Eugenio Ruidiaz y Caravia, *La Florida: Sa conquista y colonizacíon por Pedro Menéndez de Avilés,* 2:320–26. Hoffman discusses Menéndez's belief in the likelihood of a South Sea Passage in *New Andalucia,* 226–27.

45. E.G.R. Taylor, *Tudor Geography, 1485–1583,* 75–102; John Logan Allen, "The Indrawing Sea: Imagination and Experience in the Search for the Northwest Passage, 1497–1632," 27.

46. See Wroth, *Verrazzano,* especially the categorizations of sixteenth-century maps on pp. 179–80 and the accompanying text, 178–216.

47. Harrisse, *Découverte et évolution,* 93–99.

48. Vigneras, "A Spanish Discovery of North Carolina," 308–11, outlines much of the Spanish confusion over the possibility of a passage to the Pacific prior to Menéndez's voyage of 1565.

49. Seed, *Ceremonies of Possession*, 189–90.

50. This concept seems especially evident in the era immediately preceding Ribault's voyage of 1562. For example, even a Spanish map printed at Antwerp in 1562 depicts a large area of "Tierra Francisca," while in 1560, the Italian edition of Gomara's *History of the Indies* shows "Provincia di Nova Francia." Harrisse, *Découverte et évolution*, 93–99, 160–61, 185–88.

51. On the influence of Münster's maps on the European view of Florida, see Peter A. Cowdrey, Jr.'s notes on Münster in Dana Ste. Clair, ed., *Borders of Paradise: A History of Florida Through New World Maps*, 24–25, 58–59.

52. For example, the vastly influential Ribero map of 1529 (reproduced in Cummings et al., *Discovery of North America*, 106–7) or the Gutierrez map from prior to 1554 (reproduced in Tooley, *Landmarks of Mapmaking*, 213). On the influence of these maps, see also Vigneras, "A Spanish Discovery of North Carolina," 310.

53. The Le Testu atlas represented North America on the basis of reports of Norman mariners and existing Portuguese and Norman charts, not upon firsthand observation, since at that point Le Testu had not personally visited North America. As a result of this, as well as of his projection technique, his depiction of Florida and the east coast, by modern standards, is misleading in shape and size. The land of *"Floride"* is labeled, as distinct from the northern area of *"Anoerogua"* (perhaps a derivative of Norumbega). The direction of the coastline is depicted as primarily east-west and continuing in a generally straight line to Mexico; part, but not all, of the territory referred to as *"Floride"* is a small peninsula jutting out from this coast, roughly halfway between *"Anoerogua"* and *"Nouvelle Hispana."* In Le Testu's later map of 1566, the coast of *"Floride"* is more detailed, but it is still shown as adjacent to what Le Testu then labeled *"Regio de Bacaillus"* (area of the cod). Neither geographical features nor political labels in either map indicate a clear separation between *"Floride"* and either of its two adjacent areas. For a better understanding of Le Testu's concept of North America, see Anthiaume, "Le Testu," 180–202.

54. Wroth, *Verrazzano*, 193.

55. Waters, *Art of Navigation*, esp. 78–99, 144–46; Allen, "The Indrawing Sea," 27–33.

56. On the impact of the "Verrazzanian Sea" on the English, see David Beers Quinn, *England and the Discovery of America*, 171–74; Wroth, *Verrazzano*, 165–68.

57. As Paul Hoffman remarked, "relatively speaking, Coligny and Ribault had a wealth of information about the east coast of North America, but it was information that was contradictory on specific details even if full of promises of riches" (*New Andalucia*, 207).

4. The French Intent

1. His name is also commonly spelled "Ribaut" by the French, and in a bewildering number of ways in other languages. In contemporary English mentions, it most often appears as "Rybawde" or "Rybaud," which may explain the apparent difficulty some historians have had in locating Ribault in the indices for the vari-

ous English Calendars of State Papers. Two short biographies of Ribault have been written: Paul Bertrand de la Grassière, *Jean Ribault, marin dieppois et lieutenant du roi en Neuve-France*, and Benjamin-Remy Moquet, *Jean Ribault et ses compagnons glorifiés en Amérique*. Neither of these authors is particularly careful in his citations, nor has either one devoted much attention to Ribault's eight years in England, a serious omission that leads both writers to the simplistic conclusion that Ribault was merely a skilled mariner with few other attributes.

2. Taylor, *Tudor Geography*, 59–74.

3. La Grassière concludes on the basis of the correspondence of the French ambassador, Odet de Selve, that Ribault had been captured by the English in 1543, but an examination of these letters, cited in note 4, does not clearly support this conclusion. Compare with Taylor, *Tudor Geography*, 71; La Roncière, *Marine française*, 3:453n.2; and Moquet, *Ribault et ses compagnons*, 3–4. Each of these authors gives a different explanation for the circumstances that found Ribault in England in 1547. On Ribault's commission in 1546, see E.G.R. Taylor, ed., preface to *A Brief Summe of Geographie*, by Roger Barlowe, lii–liii.

4. *Correspondence Politique de Odet de Selve*, ed. Germain Lefèvre-Pontalis: "Selve à l'Amiral," October 12, 1546, no. 43, 41–43; "MM. de Selve et de La Garde au Roi," February 9, 1547, no. 117, 100–101; "Selve au Roi," March 18, 1547, no. 134, 117–19; "Selve au Connétable," July 14, 1547, no. 178, 164–65; "Selve au Roi," July 23, 1546, no. 193, 169–72; "Selve au Connétable," August 13, 1547, no. 207, 183–84; "Selve au Roi," October 18, 1547, no. 242, 218–21; "Selve au Roi," November 24, 1547, no. 257, 242–43.

5. United Kingdom, Public Record Office, *Calendar of State Papers, Negotiations between England and Spain: Researches in Foreign Archives* (hereafter cited as *CSPSpanish*), vol. 10, ed. Royal Tyler (Nendeln: Kraus Reprint, 1969), "Jehan Scheyfve to the Queen Dowager," June 24, 1550, 115.

6. Taylor, *Tudor Geography*, 93.

7. There are numerous references to Ribault in this capacity in studies of English navigation and cartography of the era, including E.G.R. Taylor, *The Haven-Finding Art: A History of Navigation from Odysseus to Captain Cook*, 194–95; David B. Quinn, *Sebastian Cabot and Bristol Exploration*, 22–23; and Franklin T. McCann, *The English Discovery of America to 1585*, 100–101. These authors mostly rely upon the same Privy Council records and personal correspondence that is cited in E. G. R. Taylor's introduction to Roger Barlowe's *A Brief Summe of Geographie*, first published in 1541 and reprinted by the Hakluyt Society, lii–lvi.

8. Waters, *Art of Navigation*, 78–99. This author establishes the heavy debt that English maritime development owes to Sebastian Cabot, especially because of Cabot's large-scale "borrowing" of Spanish technological and geographical knowledge. See also Quinn, *England and the Discovery of America*, 131–59.

9. In his article "The Chicora Legend and Franco-Spanish Rivalry in La Florida," Paul Hoffman wonders where Ribault might have been exposed to the Chicora legend associated with Lucas Vásquez de Ayllón (432–33). Ribault's close relationship with Cabot allowed him to have access to virtually all of the geo-

graphical ideas of the Spanish *Casa,* which probably included mention of the possible existence of Ayllón's "Chicora." In 1555 Richard Eden published the first English translation of Peter Martyr's *Decades,* a work that had already played an important role in propagating the Chicora idea in Spain, and this too may have influenced Ribault. See also Waters, *Art of Navigation,* 83–87.

10. Moquet, *Ribault et ses compagnons,* 6; La Grassière believes Ribault converted in 1556 but also believes that Coligny had converted by that time, which was probably not the case. *Ribault, marin dieppois,* 43.

11. Cited by La Grassière, *Ribault, marin dieppois,* 31–32.

12. Asseline, *Les antiquitez,* 251–68; Moquet, *Ribault et ses compagnons,* 5; La Grassière, *Ribault, marin dieppois,* 37–39.

13. Quoted by La Grassière, *Ribault, marin dieppois,* 39.

14. For Menéndez's involvement in these conflicts, see Solís de Merás, *Menéndez,* 45–63; see also Constantino Bayle, S.I., *Pedro Menéndez de Avilés,* 13–14.

15. La Grassière, *Ribault, marin dieppois,* 39–41; Moquet, *Ribault et ses compagnons,* 6.

16. Cecil to Throckmorton, July 9, 1559, *CSPForeign, Elizabeth,* 1:no. 962, 367.

17. Throckmorton to Cecil, July 19, 1559, *CSPForeign, Elizabeth,* 1:no. 1025, 394–95.

18. French Ambassador Noailles to queen regent, December 21, 1559, *CSPForeign, Elizabeth,* 1:no. 467, 211n.11.

19. In addition to the above documents, see also the following references: Dr. Wotton to Mary, April 27, 1557, United Kingdom, Public Record Office, *Calendar of State Papers, Foreign Series, Reign of Mary* (hereafter cited as *CSPForeign, Mary*), no. 568, 298–99; Document of Parlement of Rouen, April 20, 1558, ibid., no. 753, 369; Throckmorton to Council, June 1559, *CSPForeign, Elizabeth,* 1:no. 868 (21), 328; Throckmorton to Cecil, September 30, 1559, ibid., 1:no. 1406, 586; Throckmorton to Elizabeth, October 7, 1559, ibid., 2:no. 50 [8], 28; Throckmorton to Queen, October 9, 1559, ibid., 2:no. 57 [2], 29; Throckmorton to Cecil, March 7, 1560, ibid., 2:no. 837 (5), 437; Throckmorton to Cecil, March 9, 1560, ibid., 2:no. 845 (3), 443; Throckmorton to Queen, March 15, 1560, ibid., 2:no. 859 [13], 451–52; Throckmorton to Council, March 21, 1560, ibid., 2:no. 881 [8], 463.

20. It should be noted that Throckmorton was a committed Protestant who had been implicated in Wyatt's Rebellion against the accession of Mary Tudor but had escaped the death penalty imposed upon most of his co-conspirators. In service at the French court during this period, he relied upon Admiral Coligny and his staff for much of his information. *CSPForeign, Elizabeth,* vol. 2, contains numerous dispatches from Throckmorton in Paris, on a number of topics, often mentioning the admiral and various Protestants as sources. In 1562 Throckmorton was instrumental in arranging English intervention in Normandy during the first War of Religion. On his background, see Wallace McCaffrey, *The Shaping of the Elizabethan Regime,* 40–41; John Guy, *Tudor England,* 267, 274, 275. For a detailed analysis of Throckmorton's actions as ambassador to France between 1559 and 1562, see N.

M. Sutherland, "The Origins of Queen Elizabeth's Relations with the Huguenots," 73–96.

21. See La Grassière, *Ribault, marin dieppois*, 43–44. Since this author clearly misses the significance of Throckmorton's dispatches from the summer of 1559, one cannot regard his explanation of Ribault's presence in England to be anything more than speculation. Apparently the author is unable or unwilling to acknowledge the extent to which Ribault was connected to the intelligence networks of both France and England; moreover, if Ribault was merely involved in the planning of a Scottish expedition from France, it would make more sense that he had been in London to gather information regarding Scotland, from either Noailles or his English connections. If so, we still cannot be certain for whom he was gathering this information.

22. Carroll, *Noble Power*, 97–100.

23. Shimizu, *Conflict of Loyalties*, 34–37.

24. Delaborde, *Coligny*, 1:511–12.

25. Julien, for example, asserts that Coligny desired to avert civil war at home by reopening hostilities against Spain, as a means of "uniting the French, Catholics and Protestants, against the common enemy" (*Voyages*, 227). Other historians who have claimed that Coligny had a blatantly aggressive intent include Lestringant, *Huguenot et sauvage*, 24; Boucher, *Les Nouvelles Frances*, 9; Marc Trudel, *Les vains tentatives*, 1:194; and Gaffarel, *Floride française*, 6–7.

26. See Kamen, *Philip of Spain*, 65–71.

27. Sutherland, *The Huguenot Struggle for Recognition*, 110–16.

28. Carroll, *Noble Power*, 105–26.

29. As claimed by Julien, *Voyages*, 226–27.

30. Le Challeux's description of the recruitment of colonists appears in his first book, "Livre Premier," 9–44.

31. This had been planned in 1558, although it was never carried out, probably because of Henri's death. La Roncière, *Marine française*, 3:587–88.

32. Perhaps the most careful analysis of the ideological foundations of European overseas empires is Pagden's *Lords of All the World*, esp. chap. 3, in which he looks at French, British, and Spanish motives comparatively.

33. Ribault's *Whole and True Discouerye of Terra Florida* was published in England by Thomas Hacket in 1563, but whether it was published first in France is uncertain. See Jeannine Jacquemin, "La colonisation protestante en Floride et la politique européene au XVIe siècle," 185; compare with La Roncière, *Marine française*, 4:48n.2; Taylor, *Tudor Geography*, 28n.1. La Roncière believes that the work was first published in London, in French, but states that "we no longer have the work." Considering Ribault's subsequent actions after his arrival in England, Jacquemin's explanation makes more sense: that although this work was first *composed* in French as a report to Admiral Coligny (as indicated clearly by its initial passages), it was first *published* in English, at the end of May 1563, in London. It was republished in Richard Hakluyt's *Divers Voyages touching the discoverie of*

America and the Islands adiacent unto the same, made first of all by our Englishmen and afterwards by the Frenchmen and Britons. While we cannot know how much the published version differed from the original, this writer's guess is little if at all, since the published one maintains the quality of a report throughout. Citations from this work will be as Ribault, *Whole and True,* and refer to the version reprinted by Quinn, *New American World,* 2:285–95.

34. Later we will examine more precisely Catherine's reaction after the events in Florida of 1565, which reflect her conviction that Florida was "fair game" for French colonization. Not only do the accounts written by Ribault and Laudonnière echo this principle, but later explanations by French writers, especially François de Belleforest (1575) and Urbain Chauveton (1578–79), justify the French claim to Florida from a legalistic perspective. There seems little doubt that this viewpoint was sincerely held by a significant number of Frenchmen, and probably by most of the principals involved in this initiative. Unfortunately we have no written expression of this idea from Coligny.

35. On Laudonnière's background, see Léon Guérin, *Les navigateurs français,* 180–81, and Charles E. Bennett, *Laudonnière and Fort Caroline.*

36. "Report of Manrique de Rojas," in Bennett, *Laudonnière,* 107–24.

37. Ribault, *Whole and True,* 285. "Head of Britons" or Cape Breton was a prominent feature at mid-century in both Spanish and Norman maps. In the Desceliers planisphere of 1550, the name refers to a large region of eastern North America. See Harrisse, *Découverte,* 122–31, 169–76, 227–31.

38. René Goulaine de Laudonnière, *L'Histoire notable de la Floride situee en les Indes Occidentales, contenant les trois voyages faits en icelle par certains Capitaines et Pilotes françois,* which also appears as *A Notable Historie containing foure voyages made by certayne French Captaynes unto Florida Wherin the great riches and fruitfulnes of the countrey* in Richard Hakluyt, ed., *The Principal Navigations, Voyages, Traffiques and Discoveries of the English Nation,* 8:446–48. Hakluyt titled these works separately as *The Voyage of Captain John Ribault to Florida, 1562; The voiage of captaine René Laudonniere to Florida 1564;* and *A second voyage of captaine John Ribault to Florida 1565.* The Hakluyt edition of 1589 is utilized here, found in vols. 8 and 9 of *The Principal Navigations, Voyages, Traffiques and Discoveries of the English Nation.* These three works will be referred to subsequently in citations and text as *1562, 1564,* and *1565,* respectively. On the interesting history of the publication of Laudonnière's work, see David B. Quinn, *The Hakluyt Handbook,* 1:248–49, 285; Lestringant, *Huguenot et sauvage,* 163–81; William S. Maltby, *The Black Legend in England,* 65–68.

39. Laudonnière, *Description of the West Indies,* Hakluyt, 8:449–50.

40. Ibid., 450.

41. Both La Roncière and Julien give the impression that this first expedition had a distinct Protestant character and intent, and this in turn has influenced others to repeat this. La Roncière, at the beginning of this century, wrote that "singing the psalms of David, our Huguenots set foot on the banks of the river that they baptised the Jordan" (*Marine française,* 4:49). Later, Julien cited La Roncière in re-

peating the assertion that the party sang psalms at Port Royal, and he even expands upon the supposed religious nature of this initial expedition (*Voyages*, 229–
30). However, an examination of the original sources does not support this idea.
The two accounts by Ribault and Laudonnière (the only citations given by La
Roncière) make no mention whatsoever of singing psalms, at this point or at any
other, nor did Rouffin report anything of the sort to his Spanish captors. None of
these accounts indicate that religious activities besides spontaneous prayers and
"thanks to God" were undertaken by the voyagers at any time during this expedition.

42. "Report of Manrique de Rojas," in Bennett, *Laudonnière*, 118.

43. Hoffman also questions the accuracy of Rouffin's answers and concludes
that "the evidence closest in date to the events suggests that Ribault's principal
task was to explore the coast and determine which parts of the conflicting geographic information available in France were correct" (*New Andalucia*, 208).

5. Charlesfort

1. The galleass as a ship of war was generally slower but with more mounted
artillery than other ships of comparable tonnage. During this era there were few
formal ship types, and the words used to decribe different ships, especially "galleon" and "galleass," tended to be more inexact than they would be a century later.
See Felipe Fernández-Armesto, *The Spanish Armada: The Experience of War in 1588*,
18–19, 61, 286; Richard Woodman, *The History of the Ship*, 21–23, 341–44.

2. Later in his career, Spanish *adelantado* Pedro Menéndez had constructed a
fleet of galleys for harbor defense in the Caribbean as part of his effort to augment
the safety of Spanish towns and shipping.

3. M. Oppenheim, in *A History of the Administration of the Royal Navy and of
Merchant Shipping in Relation to the Navy from MDIX to MDCLX*, notes that in the
Tudor navy in midcentury, the terms "galleass," "galleon," and "ship" were often
used interchangeably to describe the same vessels. Ribault and Laudonnière were
probably describing vessels that would later be called "galleons," instead of the
Mediterranean type of "galleass" employed by the Spanish Armada in 1588.

4. See letters referenced below, chapter 7.

5. Laudonnière, 1562, 457. By "old" (olde) he probably meant experienced.

6. The soldiers on the first ship were described as *arquebusiers*.

7. "The Report of Manrique de Rojas," Bennett, *Laudonnière*, 118. Vendôme was
probably Louis Bourbon-Vendôme, Prince de Condé, instead of Antoine de Bourbon, King of Navarre and the Duke of Vendôme. This interpretation is indicated by
the testimony of the prisoner Meleneche, cited below.

8. One should not accept a Spanish description of *Luteranos* (or Lutherans) too
literally; such was the generally employed Spanish term for Protestants of all descriptions.

9. Ribault, *Whole and True*, 286.

10. See D. W. Meinig, *The Shaping of America: A Geographical Perspective on 500*

Years of History, 5–7, 55–65, and Frédéric Mauro, *Le Portugal et l'Atlantique au XVIIe siècle,* 11–27, for their explanations of how Atlantic conditions determined sailing routes and influenced colonization patterns.

11. One wishes that Ribault had provided more technical detail of how he accomplished this sailing, specifically exactly where he turned west and how often he had to change course en route. He was able to improve on his time in 1565, though he may have had faster ships, but it is interesting that Laudonnière's 1564 expedition did not follow the new route. One might conclude that Laudonnière did not feel confident enough to attempt it. Ribault, *Whole and True,* 286–87.

12. Ibid., 287.

13. On mid-sixteenth-century Timucuan culture, see Jerald Milanich, *The Timucua,* esp. 56–64, 82–89, 150–66; John E. Worth, *Timucuan Chiefdoms of Spanish Florida,* 1:5–18; and John W. Griffin, "The Men Who Met Menéndez," in *The Oldest City: St. Augustine—A Saga of Survival,* 1–25.

14. Ribault, *Whole and True,* 290.

15. Ibid., 289. This would seem to indicate that Ribault believed that the continent at that latitude was not very wide.

16. Ibid., 290. A surviving copy of a map drawn by Nicolas Barré roughly indicates the itinerary taken, as well as the possible location of the fort established. See William Cumming, "The Parreus Map of French Florida."

17. Paul Hoffman points out that Ribault's placing of markers was similar to the Portuguese practice of leaving stone markers to signify the last points of successive voyages along the west coast of Africa during the fifteenth century, and he suggests that "Ribault may have been following their example" (*New Andalucia,* 209).

18. Ibid., 292.

19. This is amply demonstrated by Ribault and Laudonnière's accounts. Rouffin, who had been in Florida for two years prior to his capture, was responding to direct questions that did not inquire as to his impressions of the country, which in any case by that time were probably less than optimistic.

20. Ribault, *Whole and True,* 293.

21. *1562,* 468.

22. *1562,* 471. Laudonnière provides a recounting of Ribault's speech, of indeterminate accuracy, in which the latter promised that those who remained would gain fame and royal favor, and which was apparently quite persuasive.

23. Ribault reports that thirty men remained, while Laudonnière and Rouffin say twenty-six. Rouffin is quite specific that three of the company died before departure from Charlesfort and that he was the only one left behind, leaving twenty-two who set sail and twenty-one who survived the crossing. However, this does not account for the drummer, Guarnache, whom Laudonnière reported as later having been hanged.

24. See Baumgartner, "Adams's Will," 137–41.

25. Ribault, *Whole and True,* 294.

26. Rouffin had remained at Charlesfort but was the only Frenchman who re-

mained behind when the rest of the garrison returned to France. His deposition has little to do with the events that occurred at Charlesfort after the main body of the expedition departed.

27. An archaeological team from the University of South Carolina, under the direction of Chester DePratter and Stanley South, has recently established the location of Charlesfort, which is on Parris Island, the site of the U.S. Marine Corps base.

28. *1562*, 15–16. Interestingly, the reason Rouffin gave for having stayed behind was that "there would not be anyone in the boat who understood navigation."

29. *1562*, 16.

30. Regarding the fate of Dieppe in the summer and fall of 1562, see Benedict, *Rouen*, 96–99; McCaffrey, *Elizabeth I*, 76–81; Vitet, *Histoire de Dieppe*, 68–86; Daval, *Réforme à Dieppe*, 22–35.

31. This date is given by Laudonnière, *1564*, 18.

32. Clarke to Killegrew, July 21, 1562, *CSPForeign, Elizabeth*, 5:no. 340 (3), 171.

33. The first contact with the English Crown was initiated by Condé as early as March 9, possibly prior to the arrival of the news of Vassy to Paris. See Throckmorton to Cecil, March 9, 1562, *CSPForeign, Elizabeth*, vol. 4, no. 931, 552–53. In May Coligny appealed directly to Elizabeth for military help in Normandy (Delaborde, *Coligny*, 2:92); specific plans developed by the English in July can be found in Memoranda by Cecil [July 1562], *CSPForeign, Elizabeth*, 5:no. 268, 141–42.

34. Somers to Throckmorton, August 18, 1562, *CSPForeign, Elizabeth*, 5:no. 499, 253; Sir William Woodhouse to Lord Clinton, August 18, 1562, ibid., 5:no. 500, 253–54.

35. On the diplomacy surrounding the exchange of Le Havre for Calais and the French efforts to recapture Le Havre, see Shimizu, *Conflict of Loyalties*, 95–96n.49; Thompson, *Wars of Religion*, 198–99; Delaborde, *Coligny*, 2:151, for the terms of this treaty, and 266–67 for later interpretations by the English. On Throckmorton's role in this affair, see McCaffrey, *Shaping of the Elizabethan Regime*, 124–25. The question of whether the admiral was actually aware of a quid pro quo of Le Havre for Calais is addressed in Whitehead, *Coligny*, 149 and 359–71. Whitehead concludes that Coligny's acquiescence to Hampton Court was based upon his understanding that this latter agreement gave the English the right to hold Le Havre only as a surety toward the later return of Calais. It is impossible to know with certainty what sorts of oral assurances Coligny may have given to his English counterparts, especially regarding the timing of either returning Le Havre to the French or Calais to the English. It may be that only the final draft of the treaty—probably unexamined by Coligny—contained a clause guaranteeing the English the right to make an outright exchange at any time prior to 1567, at their discretion. Whitehead concludes that "Coligny and Condé never proposed, nor knew of until too late, nor acknowledged, the objectionable article in the treaty of Hampton Court," a finding which Shimizu supports. Perhaps not, but at the very least both were guilty of haste and indiscretion brought on by their extreme anxiety over their military reversals at Rouen.

36. John Young to Cecil, November 2, 1562, *CSPForeign, Elizabeth,* 5:no. 969 (3), 423.

37. Daval, *Réforme à Dieppe,* 35; Vitet, *Histoire de Dieppe,* 82–86. Warwick to Queen, October 30, *CSPForeign, Elizabeth,* 5:no. 938, 409; Warwick to Cecil, October 30, ibid., 940, 410.

38. For Coligny's specific whereabouts during this period, see Delaborde, *Coligny,* 2:60–64.

39. French Ambassador's Declaration to the Council, November 10, 1562, *CSPForeign, Elizabeth,* 5:no. 1032, 450.

40. Knecht, *Catherine de Medici,* 93.

41. Report of November 6, 1562, United Kingdom, Public Record Office, *CSPDomestic Series, Reigns of Edward VI, Mary, and Elizabeth,* no. 41, 210.

42. John Izon, *Thomas Stucley, ca. 1525–1578, Traitor Extraordinary,* 21; J. Leitch Wright, *Anglo-Spanish Rivalry in North America,* 23–25. Izon's book is the only biography of Thomas Stucley; unfortunately it suffers from a lack of citations. One gets the impression that the author has sacrificed historical accuracy for the sake of dramatic narrative. In doing so he has extrapolated gaps in the historical evidence concerning this individual, and confirmation of some details Izon presents concerning Stucley's career is difficult. Wright writes that Ribault and Stucley may have been acquainted in France, since "Stucley probably had been in France with English troops aiding the Huguenots in 1562." The evidence for this claim is uncertain, as are the circumstances under which Ribault and Stucley met.

43. Guzman de Silva to King, October 22, 1565, *CSPSpanish,* vol. 1, *Elizabeth 1558–1567,* no. 328, 494–95.

44. Izon, *Stucley,* 21–22. Royal involvement for this expedition can be seen in diplomatic dispatches: Vaughan to Cecil, May 10, 1563, *CSPForeign, Elizabeth,* 6:no. 731 (1), 330; Henry Cobham to Challoner, May 14, 1563, ibid., 6:no. 743 (4), 337–38; Bromfield to Cecil, June 5, 1563, ibid., 6:no. 851 (2), 859.

45. Bishop Quadra to the King, May 1, 1563, *CSPSpanish,* 1:no. 222, 322–23.

46. Izon, *Stucley,* 21–23.

47. Smith to Queen, November 8, *CSPForeign, Elizabeth,* 5:no. 998, 434–35.

48. Thompson, *Wars of Religion,* 183–86; Warwick and others to the Privy Council, January 6, 1563, *CSPForeign, Elizabeth,* 6:no. 36, 21–22; Poulet to Dudley and Cecil, January 6, 1563, ibid., 6:no. 37 (1), 22; Montgomery to Queen, January 9, 1563, ibid., 6:no. 66, 34.

49. Queen to Charles IX, May 7, 1563, ibid., 6:no. 714, 324; Henry Cobham to Challoner, May 14, 1563, ibid., 6:no. 743 (4), 337–38; Delaborde, *Coligny,* 2:266–68.

50. This is the most persuasive explanation for Ribault's attempted flight to France. See Jacquemin, "La colonisation protestante en Floride," 181–208.

51. These details are recounted in Izon, *Stucley,* 38–43; except for the last, they cannot be verified.

52. Bishop Quadra to King, June 19, 1563, *CSPSpanish,* 1:no. 233, 335.

53. Guzman de Silva to Philip II, October 22, 1563, ibid., 1:no. 328, 495.

54. *1562,* 486.

55. Izon reports this as fact in *Stucley*, 41–42, without citation. Though there may have been scores of English vessels in the waters between Brittany and southern England at that time, it seems impossible that any other would have had one of Ribault's pilots on board.

56. "Deposition of Stefano de Rojamonte," in Bennett, *Laudonnière*, 97. This French prisoner who accompanied Laudonnière's 1564 mission told his Spanish captors that the Charlesfort survivors had returned to France in March 1564.

57. French Articles, October 1563, *CSPForeign, Elizabeth*, 6:no. 1353, 578; Memorial of the French Ambassador, November 2, 1564, ibid., 7:no. 769, 234; Memorial of M. de l'Aubespine, November 28, 1564, ibid., 7:no. 826 (2), 250; Reply to above, November 29, 1564, ibid., 7:no. 828 (2), 251; Queen to Smith, January 1, 1565, ibid., 7:no. 908, 278.

58. Smith to Queen, December 19, 1563, ibid., 6:no. 1505 (10) 626–29. In Throckmorton to Cecil, April 8, 1564, ibid., 7:no. 298 (2), 98, Throckmorton attributes the imprisonment of Englishmen in France to Ribault's continued captivity; see also Proposed by the French, June 12, 1564, ibid., 7:no. 476, 155. It is this last—a proposed swap of prisoners, one of whom was Ribault, made by the French—that La Grassière assumes was accepted and led to the release of Ribault shortly afterward (*Ribault*, 76). Though there is no indication that this was accepted, any more than were the previous offers, it is reasonable to assume that Ribault was released at the latest by early fall, especially in light of the improved relations between the two realms.

59. Wright, *Anglo-Spanish Rivalry in North America*, 24–25; Izon, *Stucley*, 49–50.

60. Eugene Lyon, *The Enterprise of Florida: Pedro Menéndez de Avilés and the Spanish Conquest 1565–1568*, 24.

61. Some historians have written that Ribault was led by a Portuguese pilot in 1562 (e.g., Lowery, *Spanish Settlements*, 2:31); this is impossible to substantiate from French sources.

62. "Chantonnay y Frances de Alava a Felipe II," January 9, 1563, Real Academia de la Historia, *Archivo Documental Español* (hereafter cited as *A.D.E.*), vol. 5, *Negociaciones con Francia (1563–1564)*, no. 616, 18; "Chantonnay à Felipe II," January 18, 1563, ibid., 5:no. 624, 36–41.

63. Lyon, *Enterprise of Florida*, 24–25.

64. "Perrenot [Chantonnay] to Philip," December 19, 1563, *A.D.E.*, vol. 5, no. 792, 521–22.

65. "Report of Manrique de Rojas," in Bennett, *Laudonnière*, 107; "Expedition of Hernando Manrique de Rojas," *Archivo General das Indias*, Seville Santo Domingo, 99 (54/1/15), trans. Lucy L. Wenhold, cited in Quinn, *New American World*, 2:308–16.

66. See Lyon, *Enterprise of Florida*, 36n.40.

6. Fort Caroline

1. "Deposition of Robert Meleneche," in Bennett, *Laudonnière*, 87–93; "Deposition of Stefano de Rojamonte," in Bennett, *Laudonnière*, 94–98. These were con-

tained in the dispatch sent from Santo Domingo to Seville at the end of January 1565, which arrived March 26. They were then included in Juan Rodriguez de Noriega's report to the king on March 29 of that year. See Lyon, *Enterprise of Florida*, 41.

2. *1564*, 1.

3. Le Moyne, *Brevis Narratio*, 119.

4. *1564*, 1–2. Three other accounts confirm that there were three vessels involved, though there is some disagreement about their sizes. They are the two depositions of Meleneche and Rojamonte, in Bennett, *Laudonnière*, 87–98; see also Anon., *Copie d'une lettre venant de la Floride envoyée à Rouen et depuis au Seigneur d'Everon*. This has been reprinted by Bennett, *Laudonnière*, 65–70, and by Quinn, *New American World*, 2:361–63.

5. Edouard Gosselin, *Documents authentiques et inédits*, 13–14nn.1, 2. Gosselin, however, misconstrues the stated destination of "Nouvelle France" as Canada, and he presents these documents as evidence that the French were planning an expedition to Canada, not to Florida. The same document, presented with the same explanation, appears in Gosselin's *Nouvelles glanes historiques normandes*, 8–9. La Roncière, *Marine française*, 4:54–55, misunderstands it to refer to Ribault's 1565 mission to Florida, not the 1564 mission, though it is clear that it is from the earlier year.

6. Salmon, *Society in Crisis*, 147; Carroll, *Noble Power*, 124–27.

7. "Deposition of Robert Meleneche," in Bennett, *Laudonnière*, 88; "Deposition of Stefano de Rojamonte," ibid., 95.

8. John Sparkes, "The Voyage Made by M. John Hawkins, Esquire, 1565," 122.

9. Le Moyne, *Brevis Narratio*, 119.

10. *1564*, 86.

11. Carroll, *Noble Power*, 122–23.

12. Those unhappy with the treaty apparently included the dying John Calvin and his key ministers in Geneva; Salmon, *Society in Crisis*, 147–48; Knecht, *Catherine de Medici*, 94.

13. Shimizu, *Conflict of Loyalties*, 113–14.

14. Knecht, *Catherine de Medici*, 92–95.

15. Benedict, *Rouen*, 114–18.

16. Daval, *Réformation à Dieppe*, 22–42; Thompson, *Wars of Religion*, 195; Carroll, *Noble Power*, 116–23.

17. Bernard Cottret, *The Huguenots in England: Immigration and Settlement, c. 1550–1700*, 47.

18. Ibid., 45–70, esp. 68.

19. *1564*, 14–15.

20. Worth, *Timucuan Chiefdoms*, 1:19–23.

21. Ibid., 21–23.

22. According to Le Moyne, the largest ship returned almost immediately upon arrival. We can determine that this is when the letter was returned by comparing

two accounts; the expedition of Captain Vasseur took place "on the 15th of this month" [*Copie d'une lettre*] and just prior to the return of the ships [*1564, 26*].

23. The precise location of the fort remains a matter of dispute. See Paul H. Gassandaner, "Proposed Location of the 1565 Huguenot Fort Le Caroline."

24. Le Moyne, *Brevis Narratio*, 120.

25. Ibid., 121.

26. *Copie d'une lettre venant de la Floride envoyée à Rouen et depuis au seigneur d'Everon*, in Bennett, *Laudonnière*, 65–70, and in Quinn, *New American World*, 2:361–63.

27. Laudonnière describes these as "Barkes," small open ships with both sails and oars, sometimes towed behind larger vessels as "ship's boats," useful for coastal sailing; Woodman, *History of the Ship*, 341. The colony had also kept one of the barks that had accompanied their fleet, which they put into use for river exploration immediately upon arrival.

28. *1564*, 49–50; Le Moyne, *Brevis Narratio*, 122. Neither Laudonnière nor Le Moyne makes specific mention of "Chicora" as a place they were seeking, though Le Moyne's map (published in 1591) does name an Indian village of Chicola near where Ayllón had sought it. On Le Moyne's map, see R. A. Skelton, "The LeMoyne-DeBry Map," in Paul Hulton, *The Work of Jacques Le Moyne de Morgues: A Huguenot Artist in France and England*, 1:45–54, esp. 48–49 on the likely sources of LeMoyne's information.

29. *Whole and True*, 289.

30. *1564*, 53–55; this is also mentioned by Le Moyne, *Brevis Narratio*, 124. It seems to be the same place mentioned by the Indians to Ribault in 1562, *Whole and True*, 290.

31. Le Moyne, *Brevis Narratio*, 121.

32. *1564*, 37.

33. Giles de Pysière, "Discours de l'enterprise et saccagement que les forsaires de l'isle Floride avoient conclud de faire à leurs capitaines et gouverneurs, estans unis en liberté," cited in Bennett, *Laudonnière*, 71–75.

34. Ibid., 125.

35. *1564*, 40.

36. The Spanish version of events found in the fifty-one-page official report sent to Seville in March 1565 is summarized by Lyon, *Enterprise of Florida*, 38–39, esp. 38n.1. This report included Meleneche's and Rojamonte's depositions, cited by Bennett. The information received by the Spanish about the activities of these mutineers is compatible with the information presented by Laudonnière in *1564*, 41–45, and Le Moyne, *Brevis Narratio*, 130.

37. Le Moyne, *Brevis Narratio*, 130–31.

38. *1564*, 66–69; Worth, *Timucuan Chiefdoms*, 1:22–23.

39. *1564*, 59–76. On p. 59 Laudonnière relates that "my men had store until the end of April (which was the time when at the uttermost, we hoped to have had succour out of France)." Meleneche's deposition stated that "it is believed that by

next May [the original ships that departed in June] will have returned with the people and all the other things requested," which included an additional five hundred men (Bennett, *Laudonnière*, 90). Rojamonte stated that reinforcements were due in March (Bennett, *Laudonnière*, 95–96).

40. *1564*, 67.

41. *1564*, 76.

42. Hawkins had taken custody of this man, Martin Atinas of Dieppe, after his brother, William Hawkins, had repaid some of Thomas Stucley's outstanding debts (Izon, *Stucley*, 42–43).

43. Sparkes, in Burrage, *Early English and French Voyages*, 119–22.

44. Ibid., 124.

45. *1564*, 79–80; Guzman de Silva to King, October 1, 1565, *CSPSpanish*, 1:no. 323, 485–86.

46. *1564*, 80–81.

47. Ibid., 81.

48. For studies of Menéndez's background prior to the 1560s, see John Frederick Schwaller, "Nobility, Family, and Service: Menéndez and His Men." Other details, though perhaps less objective, are found in the contemporary biography composed by Menéndez's brother-in-law, Solís de Merás, *Pedro Menéndez*. This is an invaluable source for the events in Florida. Avilés is a small Asturian port on the coast of the Bay of Biscay, not to be confused with the larger inland Léonese town of Avila. French and English historians have often "corrected" his name to be Pedro Menéndez "de Avila" or "Davila"; this is incorrect.

49. See Betsabe Caunedo del Potro, *Mercadores Castellanos en el Golfo de Vizcvaya*, 196–257.

50. Lyon, *Enterprise of Florida*, 12–13.

51. Solís de Merás, *Menéndez*, 45–63, describes his assignments in Flanders and the subsequent honors bestowed upon him. See also Ruidíaz y Caravia, *La Florida*, 2:739–40.

52. Fernandez-Duro, *Armada Española*, 2:462.

53. Chamberlain to Throckmorton, July 31, 1561, no. 356 (3), 216; Merchants of Bristol, December 31, 1561, *CSPForeign, Elizabeth*, 4:no. 756, 464–65; King Philip to Menéndez, February 3, 1562, ibid., 4:no. 866, 516; Provision to Peter Mellendez, February 21, 1562, ibid., 4:no. 898, 532.

54. Lyon, *Enterprise of Florida*, 21.

55. Instructions to General Pedro Menéndez, 1562, AGI, *Indiferente General* 415, cited by Lyon, *Enterprise of Florida*, 22n.6.

56. Crown to Luis de Velasco, September 23, 1561, AGI, *Patronato* 19, *ramo* 12, cited by Lyon, *Enterprise of Florida*, 22n.4.

57. Lyon, *Enterprise of Florida*, 23.

58. Ibid., 26–29.

7. The Race to Florida

1. Lyon, *Enterprise of Florida*, 34–36; Hoffman, *New Andalucia*, 199–202.

2. Oliver Leson to Challoner, August 24, 1565, *CSPForeign, Elizabeth*, vol. 7, no. 633, 192.

3. AGI, *Patronato* 254, cited by Lyon, *Enterprise of Florida*, 36; on Mimoso and other rumors, see also Hoffman, *New Andalucia*, 215–16, and Woodbury Lowery, *The Spanish Settlements within the Present Limits of the United States*, vol. 1, *Florida 1562–1574*, 101–2.

4. These regulations, to which Menéndez contributed many ideas, governed the schedules and procedures of the *Armada de la Guardia de la Carrera de Indias*, the formal name of the royally supported fleet that protected Spanish commerce in the New World. See Andrews, *Spanish Caribbean*, 66–67, and McAlister, *Spain and Portugal in the New World*, 430–31.

5. The "Memorial" of Menéndez is cited in full in Ruidíaz y Caravia, *La Florida*, 2:320–26. Though it is not dated, Lyon concludes on the basis of internal evidence that it must have been written between February 1 and March 15 of 1565; see *Enterprise of Florida*, 41n.8. Cf. Lowery, *Spanish Settlements*, 104n.2, in which he concludes that it was written in 1562 or early 1563; but this would make no sense considering the recommendations included in the report.

6. "Memorial of Pedro Menéndez," Ruidíaz y Caravia, *La Florida*, 2:321.

7. Ibid., 326.

8. "Capitulations and Asiento between Philip II and Pedro Menéndez de Avilés," March 20, 1565, cited by Quinn, *New American World*, 2:no. 308, 384.

9. Ibid.

10. See Lyon, *Enterprise of Florida*, 54–55, in which he compares Menéndez's privileges with similar grants awarded by the Crown. His conclusion is that the terms of this *asiento* were unusually lucrative, especially the trade privileges, perhaps owing to the immediacy of the situation and the past failures in Florida of previous *adelantados*.

11. "Capitulations and Asiento between Philip II and Pedro Menéndez de Avilés," March 20, 1565, cited by Quinn, *New American World*, 2:no. 308, 388.

12. Lyon, *Enterprise of Florida*, 41.

13. "Deposition of Robert Meleneche," cited in Bennett, *Laudonnière*, 90; "Deposition of Stefano de Rojamonte," cited ibid., 96. These depositions, along with the testimonies of various Spaniards, were included in this detailed report.

14. Le Challeux, *Discours de l'histoire de la Floride*, 9–10.

15. Ibid., 12–13.

16. Although we cannot be sure of the date of Ribault's return to France, it could have been any time after June 12, 1564, the date of the latest proposal to swap hostages made that we know of. See Proposed by the French, June 12, 1564, *CSPForeign, Elizabeth*, 6:no. 476, 155. Ribault's biographer La Grassière (*Ribault*, 76) believes that this proposal led to his release, but it is unclear on what basis he draws this conclusion. It is true that by this time, relations between France and England had improved.

17. Delaborde, *Coligny*, 2:344–59, 391–92; Shimizu, *Conflict of Loyalties*, 113–16.

18. "Francés de Alava à Felipe II," May 7, 1565, *A.D.E.*, 7:no. 1046, 313–14: the

Spanish ambassador in France, Francés de Alava y Beaumont, specifically investigated Coligny's whereabouts during the preparations for Ribault's second voyage, for the purpose of determining the admiral's level of involvement. He reported to Philip on May 7, 1565, that Coligny had not been in Normandy "for many months." Also, the admiral personally signed each of the artillery inventories from late April 1565 while at Châtillon.

19. Le Challeux, *Discours de l'histoire de la Floride*, 13.

20. On these commissions, La Roncière, *Marine française*, 4:54–55, cites P. Fournier, *Hydrographie* (1667), 257; sections of this document are reproduced by La Grassière, *Ribault*, 84.

21. Had the fleet sailed in early April, Meleneche's testimony that five hundred reinforcements would arrive during May (the less-reliable Rojomonte had said March) would have been accurate within a few weeks.

22. *L'Ambassade de St. Sulpice*, 364, cited by Thompson, *Wars of Religion*, 299.

23. "Inventories of the Artillery of the Marine," April to May 1565, BN Fonds français 21544, fol. 31–57.

24. "Parecer del Duque de Alba sobre varios puntos," April 11, 1565, *A.D.E.*, 7:no. 1028, 238.

25. Le Challeux, *Discours de l'histoire de la Floride*, 13–14.

26. Antonio Tibesar, ed., "A Spy's Report on the Expedition of Jean Ribault to Florida, 1565."

27. This is consistent with Le Challeux's estimate that the final number of civilians, after desertions, was three hundred.

28. Le Challeux, *Discours de l'histoire de la Floride*, 11–12.

29. Ibid., 13.

30. "Spy's Report," 591.

31. The twenty-six-page "Inventories of the Artillery of the Marine" lists the weapons by type, and they were mostly army weapons, not naval ones. On the types of weapons and their uses, see James B. Wood, *The King's Army: Warfare, Soldiers, and Society during the French Wars of Religion, 1562–1576*, esp. 111, 157–58. Aside from the nature of the weapons themselves, this is apparent from the way they were distributed among the ships as cargo. For example, the two largest ships, Ribault's flagship *Trinité* and the *Esmerillon*, carried almost all of the artillery, gunpowder, and cannonballs—these in addition to their separately listed shipmounted cannon, which they had in abundance, being galleasses. The smaller ships, especially *La Perle* under Ribault's son Jacques, carried almost all of the smaller armaments and tools as cargo, mostly distributed according to type.

32. "Inventories of the Artillery of the Marine," 35–37. It may also be that some of these weapons were intended for boarding actions between ships. Pérez-Mallaína, *Spain's Men of the Sea*, 184, describes the uses of some of these weapons that appear in the inventory.

33. Solís de Merás, *Menéndez*, 69.

34. Ibid., 70.

35. Lyon, *Enterprise of Florida*, 56–58.

36. Ibid., 59–60.

37. "Consulta hecha al Rey por el Consejo Real de las Indias en 5 de Mayo de 1565," cited by Lowery, *Spanish Settlements*, 109.

38. "Francés de Alava à Felipe II," May 7, 1565, *A.D.E.*, 7:no. 1046, 313–14; also "Francés de Alava al Secretario Francisco de Eraso," ibid., 7:no. 1047, 315. Ambassador Francis de Alava y Beaumont, referred to in these documents as Alava, is not to be confused with the Duke of Alva (or Alba).

39. Jacques-August de Thou first asserted this in 1609, and it has been repeated in "Ribaut," Haag and Haag, *France protestante, ou vies des Protestants français*, 8:428; it is also reported as likely by Shimizu, *Conflict of Loyalties*, 114–15.

40. Tibesar asserts that Ambassador Chantonnay had reported preparations being made by Ribault for Florida as early as February; see "A Spy's Report," 589. However, there is no citation and he may have been confused by a later dispatch, "Parecer del Duque de Alba sobre varios puntos," April 11, 1565, *A.D.E.*, 7:no. 1028, 235–37. In any case, the original contract drawn up between the king and Menéndez, of March 20, clearly refers to the latter's report and recommendations and gives no indication that the expedition was based upon any information coming out of France. See Ruidíaz y Caravia, *La Florida*, 2:415–27, for a full transcription of the *asiento*.

41. Lyon provides us with a complete documentary history of the negotiations between the Crown, the *Casa,* and Menéndez during the period from April to June (*Enterprise of Florida*, 55–70). Solís de Merás's account largely supports Lyon's interpretation but somewhat understandably emphasizes the extent of Menéndez's helplessness, due to his financial problems, to raise a suitable fleet.

42. Solís de Merás tells us that the total number of ships was 34, of which 19 left from Cadiz and the rest from the north coast, carrying a total of 2,646 persons (*Menéndez*, 74). The number of ships apparently included some very small vessels, and he seems to contradict himself later.

43. For an interesting analysis of the role played by Menéndez's relatives, see Schwaller, "Nobility, Family, and Service," 298–310; see also Pérez-Mallaína, *Spain's Men of the Sea*, 30–32.

44. In anticipation of this matter, Alva prepared a document outlining the Spanish claim to Florida: "Parecer del Consejo de Indias acerca de los derechos de la Corona de España sobre la Florida," June 18, 1565, *A.D.E.*, 7, no. 1088, 421–23. See also Lyon, *Enterprise of Florida*, 58–60, 108; Lowery, *Settlement of Florida*, 1:110.

45. Cited by La Grassière, *Ribault*, 89.

46. Guzman de Silva to Philip II, June 25, 1565, *CSPSpanish*, 1:no. 304, 441–42. Although Lyon believes that this dispatch may have confused the Spanish as to whether there was a second fleet, it is impossible to agree with that considering the last line. It is clear from this report that the Spanish learned that Ribault had definitely not left by the thirteenth, and that perhaps by the date of the letter he was still on the English coast. It is doubtful that his dispatch could have arrived in Bayonne—via Philip in Madrid—before the Bayonne meeting ended on June 29.

8. In the Eye of the Hurricane

1. Lyon, *Enterprise of Florida*, 97–99, gives the most reasonable approximation of the size of the fleet and describes the difficulties of making an accurate estimate of the size of the forces under Menéndez's command.

2. Mendoza Grajales, "Memoire of a Happy Result," in Bennett, *Laudonnière*, 145–46.

3. In the various Spanish accounts, there is frequent disagreement on the exact dates. Menéndez's dates are probably more reliable and will be employed here.

4. Menéndez to the king, August 13, 1565, cited in "Letters of Pedro Menéndez de Avilés," 417; and "Correspondencia de Pedro Menéndez de Avilés (1565–1568)," vol. 2, *Colección de diarios y relations para la historia de los viajes et descubrimientos*, 48. Subsequent citations for this series of Menéndez's letters to the king will be identified by the date of the letter, with the corresponding pages for each edition, *MHS* and Navarrete, respectively. Quotations will be taken from the *MHS* translation unless otherwise noted.

5. Menéndez, August 13, 1565, *MHS*, 418; Navarrete, 48.

6. Solís de Merás, *Menéndez*, 78.

7. Menéndez, September 11, 1565, *MHS*, 419; Navarrete, 50.

8. Solís de Merás, *Menéndez*, 79.

9. Menéndez, September 11, *MHS*, 419; Navarrete, 50.

10. Ibid. Both Mendoza Grajales and Solís de Méras give the date August 28 for the landfall (Mendoza Grajales, "Memoire," 150; Solís de Merás, *Menéndez*, 80), but they also indicate that they were then anywhere from twenty to eighty leagues (at least sixty miles) from Fort Caroline. If they are right, then it makes problematical Menéndez's later claim that he had discovered the present-day harbor of St. Augustine, described as eight leagues to the south of Fort Caroline, on St. Augustine's feast day. Menéndez seems to be most reliable; he wrote that they learned from the Timucuans the precise location of the French fort on August 28, when ashore at the place that he would later name St. Augustine.

11. Le Challeux, *Discours de l'histoire de la Floride*, 15, 16–17, gives the dates of the 14th and 27th; Laudonnière gives the date of the fleet's arrival as the 28th. Whether it was thirteen or fifteen days, the amount of time taken was clearly excessive. Even with a stop for resupply, it would have been easily possible for Ribault to reach Fort Caroline (with a favorable current through the Bahama Strait) within a week. His transatlantic voyage had averaged sixty to seventy nautical miles per day.

12. *1565*, 100.

13. The letter Ribault presented to Laudonnière, authorizing the former to take command of Fort Caroline, clearly states this. See ibid., 85–86.

14. *1565*, 82. This account is the most detailed about the arrival of Ribault's fleet. Le Moyne's version, though it does not mention the delay in Ribault's identifying himself, is otherwise consistent (*Brevis Narratio*, 131–32). Le Challeux clearly was not aware of the situation faced by either Ribault or the settlers at Fort Caroline.

One suspects that Laudonnière's account presents his own actions in the best possible light, but it is difficult to conclude that he is actually fabricating details. In particular, the delay in disembarking by Ribault's fleet seems to have been reasonable under the circumstances.

15. The various charges—most of them probably fictitious or exaggerated—are described by Laudonnière in *1565*, 85–86.

16. *1565*, 53.

17. *1565*, 85–87.

18. Solís de Merás, *Menéndez*, 84. This author, who was on board the *San Pelayo*, presents more detail than do Menéndez's letters to the king about the *adelantado*'s reasoning and the various options discussed. In general, this account, composed after the passage of a year or more, must be analyzed carefully in regard to its accuracy. Although we know from other sources that the author was present at many of the events he describes, his avoidance of using the first person makes it very difficult to determine which events he is reporting strictly firsthand and which he is basing on the testimonies of others, some perhaps gathered well after the fact.

19. Menéndez letter, September 11, *MHS*, 420; Navarrete, 51. Solís de Merás quotes Menéndez delivering precisely the same message in only slightly different words, 87.

20. Ibid., *MHS*, 420–21; Navarrete, 51.

21. Le Moyne, *Brevis Narratio*, 132–33. Le Moyne's narrative provides us with a detailed account of this meeting which we can regard as more objective than that offered by Laudonnière.

22. Ibid. Le Moyne adds that, except for contrary winds, this attack would have been undertaken immediately on September 6 or 7. His explanation seems to make more sense than Laudonnière's assertion that Ribault intentionally delayed his pursuit to ready his forces for a land attack on the Spanish.

23. According to Le Moyne, the only objection Laudonnière presented to Ribault was the weather. Compare *Brevis Narratio*, 133, and *1565*, 90–91. One may be slightly skeptical here as to whether Laudonnière was as prescient as he would like us to believe.

24. Since Ribault's fleet had seven ships and there were two others at Fort Caroline, we must conclude that six pursued the Spaniards, though Laudonnière is less clear about this and we are not sure which ships these were. This one can infer from Menéndez's account of how many later appeared at St. Augustine ("four French galleons . . . together with two or three pinnaces astern," Menéndez letter, October 15, *MHS*, 425; Navarrete, 55), and from later accounts that state there were three French ships at Fort Caroline on September 28 (*1565*, 95–97; Solís de Merás, 101–2; Menéndez letter, October 15, *MHS*, 426–27; Navarrete, 55). In Le Challeux's second book (*Discours de l'histoire de la Floride*, 45), he claims that there were only four ships and that they all sank, but this does not account for the ship later reported by Spanish authorities to have been at large in the Indies (see below, note 56).

25. During the discussion of their next move, Ribault showed Laudonnière his orders, which included the order "see that you suffer him not to encroach upon you, no more than he would that you encroach upon him." As Laudonnière reported it, this ended any further discussion of the matter (*1565*, 91).

26. Mendoza Grajales, "Memoire of a Happy Result," Bennett, *Laudonnière*, 154–55.

27. Menéndez's letter states "within two days," while Mendoza Grajales (155) indicates one day, and Solís de Merás says that they were there only a couple of hours, waiting for the tide to come in (90).

28. Lyon tells us that "the French, after sailing around briefly, went off to the southward, seeking to find and destroy the *San Pelayo*," which is what he believes they were doing when the hurricane struck (*Enterprise of Florida*, 120). It would make sense but is directly contradicted by all three Spanish eyewitnesses.

29. Menéndez letter, October 15, *MHS*, 426; Navarrete, 55.

30. Le Challeux (*Discours de l'histoire de la Floride*, 26) tells us it rained continuously until September 23, though other accounts indicate brief breaks in the storm during that period.

31. Solís de Merás, who was present and was in a better position to overhear the complaints of the men, gives a rather full and detailed account of the resistance of the Spanish officers and soldiers to this plan, which continued until the attack on Fort Caroline (*Menéndez*, 93–97).

32. In his September 10 letter to Philip, cited above, Menéndez indicated his belief at that point that Fort Caroline was only "six leagues" or eighteen miles away. By that point, he had made the trip twice, and this gives a good indication of the extent of his disorientation.

33. Solís de Merás, *Menéndez*, 95–96.

34. Laudonnière writes that the officer in charge of the sentries, La Vigne, "thinking the Spanyardes would not come at such a strange time, he let [the sentries] depart, and to say the truth, he went himself unto his lodging" (*1565*, 94).

35. Menéndez letter, October 15, *MHS*, 426; Navarrete, 55.

36. Menéndez letter, October 15, *MHS*, 427; Navarrete, 56; Solís de Merás, *Menéndez*, 101.

37. Le Challeux, *Discours de l'histoire de la Floride*, 26.

38. Ibid., 26–27.

39. Ibid., 32: "furent esgorgez et massacrez."

40. In the last few pages of *1565* (94–100), Laudonnière becomes defensive about his own actions and accusatory toward others, including La Vigne, the captain of the guard; Jean François, a captured Frenchman who may have served as Menéndez's guide; Jacques Ribault, who refused to give Laudonnière one of his pilots for the return voyage; and Jean Ribault himself. At no point does he accuse Menéndez of either treachery or brutality during the attack.

41. Le Moyne, *Brevis Narratio*, 134.

42. Laudonnière indicated in *1565* (95–97) that there were three French ships still at Fort Caroline but that they sank one themselves to keep it out of Spanish

hands. Menéndez confirmed this, referring to "the three ships that they [the French] had in front of the fort," one of which the French sunk, when he attacked Fort Caroline. Solís de Merás also reported three ships but claimed one was sunk by Spanish artillery (*Menéndez*, 102–3).

43. It appears that these two vessels were among the three that had stayed behind when the other six went to St. Augustine. Since Laudonnière claimed that Jean Ribault had ordered "that all soldiers that were under his charge should presently with their weapons embarke" (*1565*, 90–91), leaving him with only civilians and women and children (ibid., 93–94), one would conclude that Jacques Ribault commanded one of the ships that had pursued the Spaniards south. This implies that the younger Ribault must have been able to return to the north during the storm. It is not only unlikely but would have meant that there were four ships at Fort Caroline when the Spanish attacked, which is contradicted by the other sources. More probably, then, Laudonnière exaggerated the defenselessness of Fort Caroline, and Jacques Ribault and some of his troops had indeed remained behind.

44. Solís de Merás, *Menéndez*, 103–4. Menéndez's own letter indicates that for at least a couple of days after taking the fort, his prime concern was hunting down any Frenchmen who had escaped and trying to capture the two remaining ships.

45. One can infer from Solís de Merás's account that he was not among these thirty-five, although he supplies many details of this return journey (*Menéndez*, 106–9). Menéndez himself did not describe to the king this overland journey back to St. Augustine.

46. Solís de Merás says there were forty Spanish soldiers; Menéndez and Mendoza Grajales say fifty.

47. Menéndez letter of October 15, *MHS*, 428; Navarrete, 57.

48. Ibid., *MHS*, 428–29; Navarrete, 57.

49. Solís de Merás, *Menéndez*, 113.

50. Mendoza Grajales, "Memoire of a Happy Result," Bennett, *Laudonnière*, 163.

51. Ibid.

52. Menéndez recounts that he was told by the French that they numbered 140, of whom he spared sixteen and killed the rest (Menéndez letter of October 15, *MHS*, 438; Navarrete, 65). Mendoza Grajales gives the number as 111 killed and ten or twelve spared ("Memoire of a Happy Result," Bennett, *Laudonnière*, 163), while Solís de Merás gives the number of captured Frenchmen as 208 (*Menéndez*, 115). It is conceivable that the last, who also gives us the lowest estimate of the number of Spanish troops, desired to emphasize the extent to which the Menéndez's force was outnumbered. Probably the true total of Frenchmen is somewhere between the two lower estimates.

53. Menéndez letter, October 15, *MHS*, 429–31; Navarrete, 57–59. Among other things, he writes of a French/English agreement to jointly raid the silver fleet, that Ribault planned to build a fort on the coast of Cuba, and that the French would provoke a slave uprising throughout the Spanish Indies.

54. Solís de Merás reported 350 Frenchmen in the group, of whom 150 were

executed (*Menéndez*, 117, 121); Menéndez (*MHS*, 438; Navarrete, 65–66) reported 200 and 70, respectively. As to numbers, probably the *adelantado* is more reliable, though it is possible that he wanted to minimize the extent of his cruelty. In either case, the apparent fact that many Frenchmen refused to surrender adds credibility to the claims of both witnesses that Menéndez refused to promise mercy to this second group if they did so.

55. Menéndez letter, October 15, *MHS*, 438–39; Navarrete, 65.

56. One of these ships reportedly survived the storm and headed south to raid Spanish shipping before being captured. The other ship is unaccounted for, unless it was the *Perle* under Jacques Ribault's command, which was somehow able to return to Fort Caroline. See Lyon, *Enterprise of Florida*, 124n.41.

57. Menéndez letter, December 5, 1565, *MHS*, 439; Navarrete, 67.

58. Ibid., *MHS*, 440; Navarrete, 67; Solís de Merás, *Menéndez*, 124–30.

59. Menéndez letter, December 5, 1565, *MHS*, 440; Navarrete, 67.

60. A number of these prisoners, perhaps even most of them, were repatriated to France within two years, thanks to the efforts of Catherine and Admiral Coligny. In August 1566, Coligny wrote to King Charles IX of his hope that the king would be able to negotiate the freedom of Aligre d'Uilly (or d'Huilly), mentioned in the Inventorie des Artilleries as among Ribault's officers on the *Trinité*. Cited in Delaborde, *Coligny*, 2:454. See also La Roncière, *Marine française*, 4, 55n.2. Catherine and her ambassador, Fourquevaux, continued diplomatic efforts to free these prisoners through the fall of 1566, with uncertain results. By 1570 it appears that some of these prisoners were still held by the Spanish; BN Fonds français 16103, fol. 639, mentions diplomatic attempts to free them. Their subsequent fate is unknown.

9. Aftermath

1. Gaffarel cites Jacques-August de Thou, Agrippa d'Aubigné, and Louis Vitet as historians whose criticism of Catherine's supposed indifference have misled modern historians, and he argues that this was simply untrue (*Floride française*, 237–43). On this point, at least, the present author is in agreement with M. Gaffarel.

2. On December 13, English diplomat Thomas Smith, with the traveling French court (then at Moulins), relayed the information that "the Spaniards have met Jean Ribault and his son and others going to Florida, and discomforted them. He and his saved themselves, asking the Spaniards why they assailed them. Answer was made that the King of Spain had war against the French King. This report was written to him by Jean Ribault's son." Smith to Leicester and Cecil, December 13, 1565, *CSPForeign, Elizabeth*, 7:no. 1734, 536–37. This is the first known reference to this news reaching the French court; it is not known whether the report reached Spain.

3. Although Gaffarel reprints most of the relevant letters, the most complete collection of Catherine's correspondence regarding this matter is found in Hector de La Ferrière, *Lettres de Catherine de Medici*, vol. 2, 1563–66, *Documents inedits sur l'histoire de France*, 328–61.

4. Lyon, *Enterprise of Florida*, 144.

5. Fourquevaux to Charles IX, December 24, 1565, cited in Gaffarel, *Floride française*, 414–15, and in La Ferrière, *Lettres de Catherine de Medici*, 337n.1. The duke's reported words seem unequivocal: "déjà les François y vont mal pour la descente des Espagnols qui y furent envoyés l'esté dernier." It remains possible that Alva was bluffing to test Fourquevaux's response.

6. Delaborde, *Coligny*, 2:394–404.

7. Fourquevaux to Catherine de Medici, January 17, 1566, cited by Gaffarel, *Floride française*, 416–17.

8. Fourquevaux to Charles IX, January 22, 1566, cited by Gaffarel, *Floride française*, 417; Fourquevaux to Charles IX, February 4, 1566, ibid., 417–18; Fourquevaux to Charles IX, February 11, 1566, ibid., 420.

9. Catherine to Fourquevaux, January 20, 1566, La Ferrière, *Catherine de Medici*, 341–43.

10. Advices from Sir Thomas Smith to the Earl of Leicester, January 23, 1566, *CSPForeign, Elizabeth*, 8:no. 41 (3), 9.

11. Fourquevaux to Charles IX, February 18, 1566, cited by Gaffarel, *Floride française*, 421–22. Philip's reaction to the news is also described in Kamen, *Philip of Spain*, 110.

12. What Fourquevaux reported at that time agrees with the versions of Menéndez and Solís de Merás, with only a few insignificant differences of numbers; ibid., 422.

13. Fourquevaux to Charles IX, March 6, 1566, cited by Gaffarel, *Floride française*, 424–26.

14. These may well have been the same royal orders that Laudonnière wrote that he had been shown by Ribault.

15. Catherine to Fourquevaux, March 17, 1566, cited by Gaffarel, *Floride française*, 426–28.

16. Philip to Menéndez, May 12, 1566, Ruidíaz y Caravia, *La Florida*, 2:363.

17. Fourquevaux to Catherine, April 9, 1566, cited by Gaffarel, *Floride française*, 433.

18. The latter is a major issue of subsequent diplomatic dispatches between Fourquevaux in Spain and Catherine and Charles in France between July 1566 and May 1567 (Gaffarel, *Floride française*, 440–49). See also Delaborde, *Coligny*, 2:453–60.

19. Vitet, *Histoire de Dieppe*, 284–85; La Roncière, *Marine française*, 4:64; Gaffarel, *Floride française*, 242–43.

20. Pierre Miquel, *Guerres de Religion*, 258–59; Thompson, *Wars of Religion*, 300.

21. Delaborde provides a sampling of contemporary French Protestant suspicions as to the agreement reached at the Bayonne meeting, in *Coligny*, 2:388–95. See also Jacques-Auguste de Thou, *Histoire universelle depuis 1543 jusqu'en 1607*, vol. 5 (1564–70), Livre XXXVII, 33–37.

22. Translated and reprinted by Bennett, *Laudonnière*, 167–70. As originally published, this appeared with a shorter work of uncertain authorship, the "Petition of the Widows and Orphans of Fort Caroline," which also described various

acts of savagery, appended as "Livre Troisième." This work was also republished thirteen years later as "Request to the King," as a supplement to Urbain Chauveton's foreword, *Brief discours et histoire d'un voyage de quelques François en la Floride: et du massacre autant injustement qur barbarement executé sur eux, par les Hespagnols*, to his translation of Girolamo Benzoni's *Histoire nouvelle du Nouveau Monde*, 97–99.

23. *Remonstrances très humble en forme d'avertissement des captaines de la marine*, BN Dupuy 464, fol. 48.

24. Lestringant regards this work as a Huguenot "polemic masterpiece" (*Huguenot et sauvage*, 102, 116, 153–55).

25. Chamberlain to Cecil, August 31, 1566, United Kingdom, Public Record Office, *CSPDomestic Series, Reigns of Edward VI, Mary, and Elizabeth, 1547–1580*, vol. 7 (Addendum), no. 27, 15; Amias Paulet to Sir Hugh Paulet, August 2, 1566, United Kingdom, Public Record Office, vol. 7 (Addendum), no. 30 (1), 17.

26. The English reported his ultimate destination as Florida. Fitzwilliam to Queen, September 18, 1566, *CSPForeign, Elizabeth*, 8:no. 719, 130–31. His father's account is more ambiguous, in *Commentaires et lettres de Blaise du Monluc, Marechal de France*, 75–76. See also Julien, *Voyages*, 263–66.

27. Fourquevaux to Charles IX, November 2, 1566, cited by Gaffarel, *Floride française*, 447. The ambassador wrote, in explanation of these events, "at least the Portuguese accompanied Melendez to Florida and were those who committed the greatest butchery of the poor Frenchmen, whose vengeance begins at Madeira." The captive French sailor Jehan Memyn's deposition also asserted that Portuguese took part in the Florida massacres ("Deposition of Jehan Memyn," cited by Bennett, *Laudonnière*, 100). However, the Spanish sources make no specific mention of Portuguese participation.

28. Julien, *Voyages*, 265–66; Gaffarel, *Floride française*, 255.

29. These events were chronicled shortly afterward, in *Histoire memorable de la reprinse de l'isle de la Floride faicte par les François sous la conduite du capitaine Gourgues gentil-homme Bourdelais*. This account was published anonymously in April 1568, written apparently by de Gourgues himself almost immediately upon his return to France. In 1586 it was published by Martin Basanier in Paris; the following year, it was translated into English and published by Richard Hakluyt, with some minor abridgement, as *The Fourth Voyage of the Frenchmen into Florida, under the conduct of Captain Gourgues, in the yeere, 1567*. Subsequently it appeared in *Principal Navigations*, 9:100–112. De Gourgues's background is recounted on the first and last two pages of this account.

30. Quote taken from *Fourth Voyage*, Hakluyt, *Principal Navigations*, 9:109. The phrase "nor as unto Mariners" has been the focus of some misunderstanding. Gaffarel, *Floride française*, 304n.1, reports that the term employed was "Marranes," which he believes was used in this case as an ethnic slur. This idea has been repeated by both La Roncière (*Marine française*, 4:68) and Julien (*Voyages*, 260). Gaffarel is mistaken; in the original French version, the word used is "Marriniers,"

the meaning of which seems clear enough. [De Gourgues], *Histoire memorable de la Reprinse de l'isle de la Florida*. The same term is employed in the Basanier edition of 1586. *Histoire memorable de la reprinse de la Floride* (Paris: Martin Basanier, 1586).

31. Solís de Merás, *Menéndez*, 124. For a brief but revealing examination of the question of de Gourgues's religion, see Charles-André Julien, "Note sur la religion de Dominique de Gourgues."

32. *Fourth Voyage*, 111; see also Gaffarel, *Floride française*, 314–19; Julien, *Voyages*, 262.

33. These were the account by Solís de Merás and a more formal work by Bartolomé Barrientos, a professor of Latin at the University of Salamanca.

34. This is a point made by Lyle McAlister in his introduction to Solís de Merás, *Menéndez*, xiii–xv.

35. Lyon's *Enterprise of Florida* is the authoritative work on the subsequent fate of Menéndez's Florida; see esp. 131–219.

36. Lyon, *Enterprise of Florida*, 128n.48. As it turned out, later Spanish documents attest to this ship's being taken by "heretic mutineers" and eventually being shipwrecked off the coast of Denmark. This story is recounted by Pérez-Mallaína, *Spain's Men of the Sea*, 56.

37. Kamen, *Philip of Spain*, 113–20.

38. Salmon, *Society in Crisis*, 169; Shimizu, *Conflict of Loyalties*, 124–25.

39. Shimizu, *Conflict of Loyalties*, 121–22; Carroll, *Noble Power*, 131–34; Thompson, *Wars of Religion*, 299.

40. Salmon, *Society in Crisis*, 168–69; Holt, *French Wars of Religion*, 63–66.

41. Delaborde, *Coligny*, 2:457–60.

42. Shimizu, *Conflict of Loyalties*, 121–28.

43. Delaborde, *Coligny*, 2:479–80.

44. Kingdon, *Myths about the St. Bartholomew's Day Massacre*, 24; Holt, *French Wars of Religion*, 81; Shimizu, *Conflict of Loyalties*, 135–56.

45. Cited in both Spanish and French as "L'Amiral Jacques Sores vu par les Espagnols."

46. Lestringant, *Huguenot et sauvage*, 159–63.

47. "Inventory of the Artillery of the Marine," August 1570, BN Fonds français 21544, fol. 65.

48. A concise and reliable description of this raid is found in Andrews, *Trade, Plunder, and Settlement*, 130–31. See also Anthiaume, "Le Testu," 139–40. A full account was published in 1626 by Drake's nephew (also Sir Francis Drake), entitled *Sir Francis Drake Revived*. Hakluyt devotes scarce attention to this incident; in *Principal Navigations*, there is only a brief chapter entitled "The first voyage attempted and set foorth by the expert captaine M. Francis Drake . . . to Nombre de Dios and Panama, about the yeere 1572" (vol. 9, 75–76).

49. See Andrews, *Trade, Plunder, and Settlement*, 252–54, on the impact of the Treaty of London on English colonization in North America.

50. Kamen, *Philip of Spain*, 108–12; Parker, *Grand Strategy*, 118–22.

Appendix: A Note on the Sources

1. The eyewitness accounts of these events include the two letters written by Menéndez to King Philip, of September 11, 1565, and October 15, 1565, cited in MHR (419–25 and 425–39) and Navarrete 49–55 and 55–66; Solís de Merás, *Menéndez*, 84–90; "Memoire of a Happy Result" (report of Mendoza Grajales, Menéndez's chaplain), cited in Bennett, *Laudonnière*, 141–63; Mendoza Grajales was present from September 4 to September 10 but did not accompany the Spanish troops to Fort Caroline.

The French accounts that qualify as eyewitness testimonies are Laudonnière's *L'Histoire notable de la Floride* published under the collective title *L'histoire notable de la Floride située en les Indes Occidentales, contenant les trois voyages fait en icelle par certains capitaines & pilotes François . . . a lequelle a esté adiousté un quatriesme voyage fait par le capitaine Gourgues, mis en lumière par M. Basanier;* and the first book ["Livre Premier"] of Nicolas Le Challeux's *Discours de l'histoire de la Floride contenant la cruauté de Espagnols, contre les sujets du roy, en l'an mil cinq cens soixante cinq,* 9–44. Le Challeux accompanied Ribault's 1565 mission to Florida and narrowly escaped from Fort Caroline to provide us with one of the most influential accounts of the French defeat. *Discours de l'histoire de la Floride* was published in Dieppe, by J. Le Sellier, in May 1566. During the same year it was republished twice by Le Sellier in Dieppe and once each in Paris and Lyon by I. Saugrain. The last two, which were identical to the original except for the typeface and pagination, were entitled *La Floride, ou histoire memorable, de ce qui est advenu au dernier voyage du capitaine Jean Ribaud.* Citations here will be from the original Dieppe edition in the John Carter Brown Library, Brown University, Providence, Rhode Island. Le Challeux's description of the recruitment of colonists appears in his first book, "Livre Premier," pages 9–44. The entire work has also been reprinted by Suzanne Lussagnet, ed., *Les Français en Amerique pendant la seconde moitié du XVIe siècle;* and the first section of Jacques Le Moyne de Morgues's *Brevis Narratio.* This appears in English translation as "Narrative of Jacques Le Moyne de Morgues," in Hulton, *Work of Jacques Le Moyne de Morgues.*

2. Le Moyne, *Brevis Narratio,* 135.

3. Le Moyne wrote that "Ribault summoned his senior men to a conference consisting of nearly thirty officers, in addition to noblemen, officials, and other administrators." Le Moyne indicates that he was present at this meeting, not unlikely since he was Ribault's chief cartographer (ibid., 132).

4. In fact, according to Solís de Merás, the *adelantado* was so anxious to get rid of them that he offered some of the French who were aboard ship in the harbor a better ship, supplies, and a passport to return to France safely if they would take the women and children off his hands (*Menéndez,* 102). Amazingly, this offer, if true, was refused. In mid-October, these captives were sent by ship to Puerto Rico. Concerning the later fates of these individuals, see *Menéndez,* 106, 111, 124. Eugene Lyon also cites later official Spanish documents attesting to the capture of close to fifty French women and children (*Enterprise of Florida,* 123n.404).

5. The second section of Le Challeux's "Livre Deuxième" is found between pages 45–52 of *Discours de l'histoire de la Floride*. This is followed by a third section, also of separate authorship, entitled "Une Requeste au roy, faite en forme de complainte par les vesves, petits enfans orphelins, & autres leurs amis, parens, & alliez de ceux qui ont esté cruellement envahis par les Espagnols en la France Anthartique dit la Floride." This last part will be referred to henceforth as "Petition of the Widows and Orphans."

6. Ibid., 52.

7. See Eugene Lyon, "Captives of Florida," 13–21. Lyon concludes, in fact, that all of the male adult prisoners taken by Menéndez at Fort Caroline and Matanzas were put to work at St. Augustine and San Mateo until at least mid-1567 and were released by Menéndez to the custody of royal officials at Seville only with great reluctance.

8. Le Moyne, *Brevis Narratio*, 137–38.

9. Le Moyne says these were "a certain drummer named Dronet, and someone else from Dieppe, named Masselin, who was a flute-player and lutanist. These two were saved to play for them at their revels" (ibid., 137). There may be an element of truth here, since Menéndez also mentioned sparing a "drummer, fifer, and trumpeter," along with a few others, at the second massacre he describes (Menéndez letter of October 15, *MHS*, 438; Navarrete, 65).

10. Parkman, *Pioneers of France*, 112.

11. *Discours de l'histoire de la Floride*, 45.

12. *Discours de l'histoire de la Floride* never specifically mentions the number of Frenchmen, though Le Moyne tells us it was "more than eight hundred tough and experienced arquebusiers" (Le Moyne, *Brevis Narratio*, 136).

13. *Discours de l'histoire de la Floride*, 51. Le Moyne expands upon this supposed promise of clemency, going as far as to assert that Ribault was given a written guarantee, described as a "gracefully penned letter" (*Brevis Narratio*, 21). The alleged violated promise was later publicized as the ultimate example of Menéndez's "treachery."

14. In fact, the arrival of this letter to Seville was delayed until after the beginning of the year, arriving in Spain at virtually the same time as some of the Spanish soldiers coming back from Florida. See Lyon, *Enterprise of Florida*, 144–45.

15. Solís de Merás, in contrast, credits Menéndez's individual initiatives as the prime factor in making possible a Spanish victory. Perhaps the *adelantado's* responsibility lies somewhere in between, but there is surprisingly little indication in this October 15 letter that he is trying to win praise from the king for his actions.

16. Many historians accept the claim of Menéndez's biographer Barrientos, composed in 1568, that Solís de Merás was not only at Matanzas on October 10, but was one of the two Spaniards who executed Ribault. Since Solís de Merás never specifically claims that he was present, and there is no mention of his presence by Menéndez, this leaves room for doubt. See McAlister, preface to Solís de Merás, *Menéndez*, 12.

17. These accounts include, in chronological order, Belleforest's French edition of Sebastian Münster's 1555 *La cosmographie universelle* (1575); André Thevet's *La cosmographie universelle* (also 1575); Urbain Chauveton's introduction to his translation of Girolamo Benzoni's *Histoire nouvelle du nouveau monde* (1579); La Popelinière's *Les trois mondes* (1582). For an analysis of the origins of their information, see my Ph.D. dissertation, "France in America, 1555–1565," esp. chap. 9.

18. Good treatments of this literature and its impact include Maltby, *The Black Legend in England*; Pierre Chaunu, "La légende noire antihispanique," *Revue de psychologie des peuples*, no. 2 (1964): 188–223; Kingdon, *Myths about the St. Bartholomew's Day Massacre*.

19. De Thou, *Histoire universelle* (1609) (Basel, 1743), vol. 4, book 44, 110–21; Marc Lescarbot, *Histoire de la Nouvelle France* (1609) (reprint, New York, 1968), 331; and Agrippa d'Aubigné, *Histoire universelle* (1616), 2:342–44.

20. Solís de Merás's account was written in 1567; the following year Bartolomé Barrientos, a professor at the University of Salamanca, composed *Vida y hechos de Pero Menéndez de Avilés*, which relied heavily on the former work. This was published in 1902 in *Dos Antiguas Relacions de la Florida* and more recently in English as *Pedro Menéndez de Avilés: Founder of Florida*.

21. Gaffarel, *Floride française*.

22. Andrés Gonzalez de Barcia Carballido y Zuñiga, *Ensayo cronológico para la historia general de Florida*; Gaffarel, *Floride Française*, 225–40.

23. Parkman, *Pioneers of France*, 108–15.

24. These treatments include La Roncière's *Marine française*, vol. 4; Julien's *Voyages*; vol. 1 of Marc Trudel's *Histoire de la Nouvelle France*, entitled *Les vains tentatives*; and Lestringant's *Huguenot et sauvage*.

BIBLIOGRAPHY

Bibliothèque Nationale, Paris: Manuscripts
    Fonds Français 15881, 16103, 21544, 32614
    Dupuy 464
    Nouvelles Acquisitions Français 6638

Allen, John Logan. "The Indrawing Sea: Imagination and Experience in the Search for the Northwest Passage, 1497–1632." In *American Beginnings*, ed. Emerson W. Baker et al., 8–35. Lincoln: University of Nebraska Press, 1994.

Andrews, Kenneth. *The Spanish Caribbean: Trade and Plunder, 1530–1630*. New Haven: Yale University Press, 1978.

————. *Trade, Plunder, and Settlement: Maritime Enterprise and the Genesis of the British Empire, 1480–1630*. Cambridge: Cambridge University Press, 1984.

Anon. *Copie d'une lettre venant de la Floride, envoyée à Rouen, et depuis au Seigneur d'Everon*. Paris: N. and J. Bruneau, 1565.

Anthiaume, A. *Cartes marines, constructions navales, voyages de découverte chez les Normands, 1500–1650*. Paris: E. Dumont, 1916.

————. "Un pilote et cartographe Havrais au XVIe siècle, Guillaume Le Testu." *Bulletin de Géographie Historique et Déscriptive*. Paris: Comité des Travaux Historiques et Scientifiques, 1911.

Asseline, David. *Antiquitez et chroniques de la ville de Dieppe*. Vol. 2. Edited by Michel Hardy. Dieppe, 1874.

Barcia Carballido y Zúñiga, Andrés Gonzalez de. *Ensayo cronológico para la historia general de Florida*. Translated and edited by Anthony Kerrigan, with notes and foreword by Herbert E. Bolton. Gainesville: University of Florida Press, 1951.

Barrientos, Bartolomé. *Pedro Menéndez de Avilés: Founder of Florida*. Translated and edited by Anthony Kerrigan. Gainesville: University of Florida Press, 1965.

————. "Vida y hechos de Pero Menéndez de Avilés, Cavallero de la Hordem de Sanctiago, Adelantado de Florida." In *Dos Antiguas Relacions de la Florida, publicadas por primera vez*, ed. Genaro García. Mexico City: J. Aguilar, 1902.

Baumgartner, Frederic. "Adam's Will: Act II. Henry II and French Overseas Expansion." In *Proceedings of the 11th Meeting of the French Colonial History Society Held in Quebec, May 1985*, ed. Philip Boucher, 137–47. New York: University Press of America, 1986.

———. *France in the Sixteenth Century.* New York: St. Martin's Press, 1995.

———. *Henry II, King of France.* Durham, N.C.: Duke University Press, 1987.

Bayle, Constantino. *Pedro Menéndez de Avilés.* Vol. 16: *Grandezas Españolas.* Madrid: Administración de Razón y Fé, 1928.

Belleforest, François de, ed. *Cosmographie universelle de tout le monde, . . . by* Sebastian Münster. Paris: Nicolas Chesneau et Michel Sonnius, 1575.

Benedict, Philip. *Rouen during the Wars of Religion.* Cambridge Studies in Early Modern History. New York: Cambridge University Press, 1981.

Bennett, Charles E. *Laudonnière and Ft. Caroline.* Gainesville: University of Florida Press, 1975.

Biggar, H. P. *A Collection of Documents Relating to Jacques Cartier and the Sieur de Roberval.* Ottawa: Public Archives of Canada, 1930.

Boucher, Philip. *Les Nouvelles Frances.* Providence, R.I.: John Carter Brown Library, 1989.

Boxer, Charles. *The Dutch Seaborne Empire, 1600–1800.* New York: Alfred Knopf, 1965.

Brady, Thomas A., Jr., et al. *Handbook of European History, 1400–1600.* Leiden: Brill, 1995.

Brunelle, Gayle. *The New World Merchants of Rouen, 1559–1630.* Vol. 16, *Sixteenth Century Essays and Studies.* Kirksville, Mo.: Sixteenth Century Journal Publishers, 1991.

———. "Sixteenth Century Perceptions of the New World." *Sixteenth Century Journal* 20, no. 2 (April 1990): 75–79.

Burns, E. Bradford. *A History of Brazil.* New York: Columbia University Press, 1970.

Butel, Paul. *Les Caraibes au temps des flibustiers, XVIe–XVIIe siècles.* Paris: Aubier Montaigne, 1982.

Cabantous, Alain. *Le ciel dans la mer: Christianisme et civilisation maritime XVIe–XIXe siècle.* Paris: Fayard, 1990.

Carroll, Stuart. *Noble Power during the French Wars of Religion: The Guise Affinity and the Catholic Cause in Normandy.* Cambridge: Cambridge University Press, 1998.

Caunedo del Potro, Betsabe. *Mercadores Castellanos en el Golfo de Vizcvaya (1474–1492).* Madrid: Universidad Autonoma, 1983.

Chaunu, Huguette, and Pierre Chaunu. *Seville et l'Atlantique (1504–1650).* Paris: Armand Colin, 1955.

Chaunu, Pierre. *Conquête et exploitation des nouveaux mondes.* Nouvelle Clio: L'histoire et ses problemes, no. 26. 3d ed. Paris: Presses Universitaires de France, 1987.

———. "La légende noire antihispanique." *Revue de psychologie des peuples* 2 (Le Havre, 1964): 188–223.

Chauveton, Urbain. *Brief discours et histoire d'un voyage de quelques François en la Floride: Et du massacre autant injustement que barbarement exécuté sur eux, par les*

Hespagnols, l'an mil cinq cens soixante cinq. . . . Prefatory section to first French edition of *Histoire nouvelle du nouveau monde*, by Girolamo Benzoni. Translated by Chauveton. Geneva: Eustache Vignon, 1579.

Condé, Louis Bourbon-Vendôme, Prince de. *Memoires de Condé ou recueil pour servir à l'histoire de France.* Vol. 2. London, 1740.

Connor, Jeannette Thurber, ed. *Colonial Records of Spanish Florida.* Vol. 1. Florida State Historical Society Publications, no. 5. DeLand: Florida State Historical Society, 1925.

Coornaert, Emile. *Les Français et le commerce international d'Anvers, à la fin du XVe–XVIe siècle.* Paris: Marcel Rivière, 1961.

Cottret, Bernard. *The Huguenots in England: Immigration and Settlement, c. 1550–1700.* Cambridge: Cambridge University Press, 1991.

Cumming, William. "The Parreus Map of French Florida." *Imago Mundi* 17 (1963): 27–40.

Cumming, W. P., R. A. Skelton, and D. B. Quinn. *The Discovery of North America.* New York: American Heritage Press, 1971.

D'Aubigné, Agrippa. *Histoire universelle.* Edited by André Thierry. Vols. 1 and 2. Geneva: Droz, 1981.

Daval, Guillaume, and Jean Daval. *Histoire de la réforme à Dieppe, 1557–1657.* Edited by Emile Lesens. Rouen, 1878.

Davenport, Frances Gardiner, ed. *European Treaties Bearing on the History of the United States and Its Dependencies.* Vol. 1. Washington: Carnegie Institution, 1917–37.

Delaborde, Jules. *Gaspard de Coligny, Amiral de France.* 3 vols. Paris, 1882.

Dickason, Olive. *The Myth of the Savage and Early French Colonialism in the Americas.* Edmonton: University of Alberta Press, 1983.

Diefendorf, Barbara. *Beneath the Cross: Catholics and Huguenots in Sixteenth-Century Paris.* Oxford: Oxford University Press, 1991.

Eisenstein, Elizabeth. *The Printing Press as an Agent of Change: Communications and Cultural Transformations in Early Modern Europe.* 2 vols. Cambridge: Cambridge University Press, 1980.

Fernández-Armesto, Felipe. *The Spanish Armada: The Experience of War in 1588.* New York: Oxford University Press, 1988.

Fernández-Duro, Cesáreo. *Armada Española desde la unión de los reinos de Castilla y de Aragón.* Vol. 2. Madrid, 1896. Reprint, Madrid: Museo Naval, 1972–73.

Folmer, Henry. *Franco-Spanish Rivalry in North America, 1524–1763.* Glendale, Calif.: Arthur C. Clark, 1953.

Gaffarel, Paul. *Histoire de la Floride française.* Paris: Fermin-Didot, 1875.

Gassandaner, Paul H. "Proposed Location of the 1565 Huguenot Fort Le Caroline." *Florida Anthropologist* 49, no. 3 (September 1996): 131–48.

Gosselin, Edouard, ed. *Documents authentiques et inédits pour servir à l'histoire de la marine normande.* Rouen, 1876.

———. *Nouvelles glanes historiques normandes.* Rouen: Boissel, 1873.

[Gourgues, Dominique de]. *Histoire memorable de la reprinse de l'isle de la Floride, faicte par les Français, sous la conduite de Capitaine Gourgues.* N.p., 1568.

Griffin, John W. "The Men Who Met Menéndez." In *The Oldest City: St. Augustine, Saga of Survival,* ed. Jean Parker Waterbury, 1–25. St. Augustine: St. Augustine Historical Society, 1983.

Guérin, Léon. *Ango et ses pilotes.* Paris: Bertrand, 1857.

———. *Les navigateurs français.* Paris: Bertrand, 1846.

Guy, John. *Tudor England.* Oxford: Oxford University Press, 1988.

Haag, Eugène, and Emile Haag. *La France protestante, ou vies des Protestants français.* 10 vols. Paris: 1846–54.

Hakluyt, Richard, ed. *Divers Voyages touching the discoverie of America and the Islands adiacent unto the same, made first of all by our Englishmen and afterwards by the Frenchmen and Britons.* London: T. Dawson, 1582.

———. *The Principal Navigations, Voyages, Traffiques and Discoveries of the English Nation.* Vols. 8–10. 3d ed. Glasgow: James MacLehose and Son, 1903–5. Reprint, New York: Augustus M. Kelley, 1969.

Hamilton, Earl. *American Treasure and the Price Revolution.* Cambridge: Harvard University Press, 1934.

Haring, Clarence. *The Spanish Empire in America.* New York: Oxford University Press, 1947. Reprint, New York: Harcourt Brace and World, 1963.

———. *Trade and Navigation between Spain and the Indies in the Time of the Hapsburgs.* Harvard Economic Studies, no. 19. Cambridge: Harvard University Press, 1918.

Harrisse, Henri. *Découverte et évolution cartographique de Terre-Neuve et des pays circonvoisins, 1497–1501–1769.* London: 1890. Reprint, Ridgewood N.J., 1968.

Heulhard, Arthur. *Villegagnon, Roi d'Amérique: Un gens de mer du XVIe siècle.* Paris: E. Leroux, 1897.

Hoffman, Paul E. "The Chicora Legend and Franco-Spanish Rivalry." *Florida Historical Quarterly* 62 (April 1984): 419–38.

———. "Diplomacy and the Papal Donation, 1493–1585." *The Americas* 30, no. 2 (October 1973): 151–83.

———. *A New Andalucia and a Way to the Orient: The American Southeast during the Sixteenth Century.* Baton Rouge: Louisiana State University Press, 1990.

———. *The Spanish Crown and the Defense of the Caribbean, 1535–1585: Precedent, Patrimonialism, and Royal Parsimony.* Baton Rouge: Louisiana State University Press, 1980.

Holt, Mack P. *The French Wars of Religion, 1562–1629.* New York: Cambridge University Press, 1995.

Hudson, Charles. *The Southeastern Indians.* Nashville: University of Tennessee Press, 1976.

Hulton, Paul, ed. *The Work of Jacques Le Moyne de Morgues: A Huguenot Artist in France and England.* 2 vols. London: British Museum Publications, 1977.

Izon, John. *Thomas Stucley, ca. 1525–1578, Traitor Extraordinary.* London: Andrew Melrose, 1956.

Jacquemin, Jeannine. "La colonisation protestante en Floride et la politique européene au XVIe siècle." *Bulletin de la Société de l'Histoire Protestantisme Française* 101 (1955): 181–208.

Julien, Charles-André. "Note sur la religion de Dominique de Gourgues." *Bulletin de la Société Protestantisme Française* 101 (October–December 1955): 5–7.

———. *Les voyages de découverte et les premiers établissements.* Paris: Gérard Montfort, 1948.

Juricek, John T. "English Territorial Claims in North America under Elizabeth and the Early Stuarts." *Terrae Incognitae* 7 (1976): 7–22.

Kamen, Henry. *Philip of Spain.* New Haven: Yale University Press, 1997.

Kingdon, Robert. *Geneva and the Coming of the Wars of Religion in France, 1555–1562.* Geneva: Droz, 1956.

———. *Myths about the St. Bartholomew's Day Massacre, 1572–1576.* Cambridge: Harvard University Press, 1988.

Knecht, R. J. *Catherine de Medici.* New York: Longman, 1998.

———. *Francis I.* New York: Cambridge University Press, 1982.

———. *The French Wars of Religion.* 2d ed. London: Addison Wesley Longman, 1996.

La Ferrière, Hector de, ed. *Lettres de Catherine de Medici.* Vol. 2. Paris, 1885.

La Grassière, Paul Bertrand de. *Jean Ribault, marin dieppois et lieutenant du roi en Neuve-France.* Paris: La Pensée Universelle, 1971.

Lane, Kris. *Pillaging the Empire: Piracy in the Americas, 1500–1750.* Armonk, N.Y.: M. E. Sharpe, 1998.

Lang, James. *Conquest and Commerce: Spain and England in the Americas.* New York: Academic Press, 1975.

La Popelinière, Lancelot Voisin de. *Les trois mondes par le seigneur de la Popelliniere.* Paris: Pierre Le Huillier, 1582.

La Roncière, Charles de. *Histoire de la marine française.* Vols. 3 and 4. Paris: Librairie Plon, 1909–32.

Laudonnière, René Goulaine de. *L'Histoire notable de la Floride située en les Indes Occidentales, contenant les trois voyages faits en icelle par certains capitaines et pilotes françois. . . .* Paris: Guillaume Auvray, 1586.

———. *A Notable Historie containing foure voyages made by certayne French Captaynes unto Florida Wherin the great riches and fruitfulnes of the countrey. . . .* In Richard Hakluyt, ed., *The Principal Navigations, Voyages, Traffiques and Discoveries of the English Nation,* vols. 8 and 9. 3d ed. Glasgow: James MacLehose and Son, 1903–5. Reprint, New York: Augustus M. Kelley, 1969.

Le Challeux, Nicolas. *Discours de l'histoire de la Floride, contenant la cruauté des Espagnols contre les subjets du roy en l'an mil cinq cens soixante cinq.* Dieppe: J. Le Sellier, 1566.

———. "Discours de l'histoire de la Floride." In *Les Français en Amérique pendant la seconde moitié du XVIe siècle,* ed. Suzanne Lussagnet. Paris: Presses Universitaires de France, 1953.

Lefèvre-Pontalis, Germain, ed. *Correspondence politique de Odet de Selve, ambassadeur de France en Angleterre (1546–1549).* Paris: Germer Baillière, 1888.

Le Hardy, G. *Histoire du Protestantisme en Normandie.* Caen: 1869.

Le Moyne de Morgues, Jacques. *Brevis Narratio eorum quae in Florida Americae provincia Gallis acciderunt, secunda in illam Navigationem duce Renato de Laudonniere classis praefecto anno MDLXIIII.* Frankfurt: Theodore de Bry, 1591.

Lescarbot, Marc. *Histoire de la Nouvelle France, contenant les navigations, découvertes et habitations faites par les François en les Indes Occidentales et Nouvelle France.* Translated by W. L. Grant (*History of New France*). Toronto: Champlain Society, 1907. Reprint, New York: Greenwood Press, 1968.

————. *Histoire de la Nouvelle France, contenant les navigations, découvertes et habitations faites par les François en les Indes Occidentales et Nouvelle France.* 3d ed. Paris: A. Perier, 1618.

Lestringant, Frank. *Le huguenot et le sauvage.* Paris: Aux Amateurs des Livres, 1990.

Lowery, Woodbury. *The Spanish Settlements within the Present Limits of the United States.* Vol. 1, *Florida, 1562–1574.* New York: G. P. Putnam's Sons, 1905.

Lyon, Eugene. "Captives of Florida." *Florida Historical Quarterly* 50, no. 1 (July 1971): 1–24.

————. *The Enterprise of Florida: Pedro Menéndez de Avilés and the Spanish Conquest, 1565–1568.* Gainesville: University of Florida Press, 1976.

————. "Spain's Sixteenth-Century Settlement Attempts: A Neglected Aspect." *Florida Historical Quarterly* 59 (January 1981): 275–91.

Maltby, William S. *The Black Legend in England.* Durham. N.C.: Duke University Press, 1971.

Manucy, Albert. *Menéndez: Pedro Menéndez de Avilés, Captain General of the Ocean Sea.* Sarasota: Pineapple Press, 1992.

Marcel, Gabriel. *Les corsaires français au XVIe siècle dans les Antilles.* Paris: E. Leroux, 1902.

Mauro, Frédéric. *Le Portugal et l'Atlantique au XVIIe siècle.* Paris: SEVPEN, 1960.

McAlister, Lyle N. *Spain and Portugal in the New World, 1492–1700.* Vol. 3, *Europe and the World in the Age of Discoveries.* Minneapolis: University of Minnesota Press, 1984.

McCaffrey, Wallace. *The Shaping of the Elizabethan Regime.* Princeton: Princeton University Press, 1968.

McCann, Franklin T. *The English Discovery of America to 1585.* New York: Octagon Books, 1969.

McGrath, John T. "France in America, 1555–1565: A Reevaluation of the Evidence." Ph.D. dissertation, Boston University, 1994.

————. "History and Polemic in French Brazil." *Sixteenth Century Journal* 27, no. 2 (Summer 1996): 385–97.

Meinig, D. W. *The Shaping of America: A Geographical Perspective on 500 Years of History*. Vol. 1 of *Atlantic America, 1492–1800*. New Haven: Yale University Press, 1986.

Menéndez de Avilés, Pedro. "L'Amiral Jacques Sores vu par les Espagnols." *Bulletin de la Société de l'Histoire de Protestantisme Française* 101 (October–December 1955): 209–13.

———. "Correspondencia de Pedro Menéndez de Avilés (1565–1568)." Vol. 2: *Colección de diarios y relations para la historia de los viajes et descubrimientos*. Edited by M. F. Navarrete. Madrid: Instituto Histórico de Marina, 1943.

———. "Letters of Pedro Menéndez de Avilés." Edited and translated by Horace E. Ware. *Proceedings of the Massachusetts Historical Society* 8 (1892–94), 2nd series, January 1894. 416-68.

Milanich, Gerald. *The Timucua*. Oxford: Blackwell, 1996.

Miquel, Pierre. *Les guerres de religion*. Paris: Fayard, 1980.

Mollat du Jourdain, Michel de. *Europe and the Sea*. Translated by Teresa Lavender Fagan. Oxford: Blackwell, 1993.

———. *La vie quotidienne des gens de mer en l'Atlantique, IXe-XVIe siècle*. Paris: Fayard, 1983.

Monluc, Blaise de. *Commentaires et lettres de Blaise de Monluc, Marechal de France*. Vol. 3. Edited by Alphonse de Ruble. Paris: 1867.

Moquet, Benjamin-Remy. *Jean Ribault et ses compagnons glorifiés en Amérique*. Dieppe: Imprimerie Dieppoise, 1926.

Morison, Samuel Eliot. *The European Discovery of America: The Southern Voyages, A.D. 1492–1616*. New York: Oxford University Press, 1974.

Mours, Samuel. *Le Protestantisme en France au XVIe siècle*. Paris: Librairie Protestante, 1959.

Nicholls, David. "Social Change and Early Protestantism in France: Normandy, 1520–1562." *European Studies Review* 10 (1980): 279–308.

Oppenheim, M. *A History of the Administration of the Royal Navy and of Merchant Shipping in Relation to the Navy from MDIX to MDCLX*. London: Bodley Head, 1896.

Pagden, Anthony. *Lords of All the World*. New Haven: Yale University Press, 1995.

Parker, Geoffrey. *The Grand Strategy of Philip II*. New Haven: Yale University Press, 1998.

Parkman, Francis. *Pioneers of France in the New World*. Vol. 1: *France and England in North America*. New York: Library of America, 1983.

Parry, J. H. *The Age of Reconnaissance: Discovery, Exploration, and Settlement 1450 to 1650*. Berkeley: University of California Press, 1981.

———. *The Spanish Seaborne Empire*. London: Hutchinson, 1966.

Pérez-Mallaína, Pablo E. *Spain's Men of the Sea: Daily Life on the Indies Fleets in the Sixteenth Century*. Translated by Carla Rahn Phillips. Baltimore: Johns Hopkins University Press, 1998.

Pigeonneau, H. *Histoire du Commerce de la France.* Vol. 2. New York: Burt Franklin Reprint, 1970.

Pysière, Giles de. "Discours de l'enterprise et saccagement que les Forsaires de l'isle Floride avoient conclud de faire à leurs capitaines et gouverneurs . . . par Giles de Pysière, natif de la ville de Rouen." In Charles E. Bennett, *Laudonnière and Ft. Caroline.* Gainesville: University Presses of Florida, 1975.

Quinn, David Beers. *England and the Discovery of America.* New York: Oxford University Press, 1974.

———. *Sebastian Cabot and Bristol Exploration.* Bristol: Historical Association of the University of Bristol, 1968.

Quinn, David Beers, ed. *The Hakluyt Handbook.* Vol. 1. London: Hakluyt Society, 1974.

———. *New American World: A Documentary History of North America to 1612.* Vol. 2. New York: Arno Press and Hector Bye, 1979.

Real Academia de la Historia. *Archivo Documental Español.* Vols. 4–8. Madrid: Real Academia de la Historia, 1951–63.

Ribault, Jean. *The Whole and True Discouerye of Terra Florida.* London: Thomas Hacket, 1563.

Romier, Lucien. *Les origines politiques des guerres de religion.* 2 vols. Paris: Perrin, 1913–14.

Ruídiaz y Caravia, Eugenio. *La Florida: Su conquista y colonizacíon por Pedro Menéndez de Avilés.* 2 vols. Madrid: Real Academia de la Historia, 1843.

Ryan, A. N. "Bristol, the Atlantic, and North America." In *Maritime History,* ed. John B. Hattendorf. Vol. 1: *The Age of Discovery.* Malabar, Fla.: Krieger, 1996.

Ste. Claire, Dana, ed. *Borders of Paradise: A History of Florida through New World Maps.* Gainesville: University Press of Florida, 1995.

Salmon, J. H. M. *Society in Crisis: France in the Sixteenth Century.* New York: St. Martin's Press, 1975.

Scammell, G. V. *The First Imperial Age: European Overseas Expansion c. 1400–1715.* London: Unwin Hyman, 1989.

Schwaller, John. "Nobility, Family, and Service." *Florida Historical Quarterly* 66 (January 1988): 298–310.

Seed, Patricia. *Ceremonies of Possession in Europe's Conquest of the New World, 1492–1640.* Cambridge: Cambridge University Press, 1995.

Shannon, Silvia Castro. "Military Outpost or Protestant Refuge? Villegagnon's Expedition to Brazil in 1555." In *Essays in French Colonial History,* ed. A. J. B. Johnston. Lansing, Mich.: 1997.

Shimizu, Junko. *Conflict of Loyalties: Politics and Religion in the Career of Gaspard de Coligny, Admiral of France.* Travaux d'humanisme et renaissance, vol. 114. Geneva: Droz, 1970.

Skelton, R. A. *Explorers' Maps: Chapters in the Cartographic Record of Geographic Discovery.* New York: Praeger, 1958.

Solís de Merás, Gonzalo. *Pedro Menéndez de Avilés, Adelantado, Governor and Cap-*

tain-General of Florida: Memorial. Edited and translated by Jeannette Thurber Connor, with a preface by Lyle McAlister. DeLand: Florida State Historical Society, 1923.

Sparkes, John. "The Voyage Made by M. John Hawkins, Esquire, 1565." In *Early English and French Voyages Chiefly by Hakluyt 1534–1608*, ed. Henry S. Burrage. New York: Charles Scribner, 1906. Reprint, New York: Barnes and Noble, 1967.

Sutherland, N. M. *The Huguenot Struggle for Recognition*. New Haven: Yale University Press, 1980.

———. "The Origins of Queen Elizabeth's Relations with the Huguenots." In *Princes, Politics, and Religion*, ed. N. M. Sutherland, 73–96. London: Hambledon Press, 1984.

Taylor, E. G. R. Preface to *A Brief Summe of Geographie*, by Roger Barlowe. Publications of the Hakluyt Society, 2nd series, no. 69. London: Hakluyt Society, 1932.

———. *The Haven-Finding Art: A History of Navigation from Odysseus to Captain Cook*. London: Hollis and Carter, 1971.

———. *Tudor Geography*. New York: Octagon Books, 1968.

Thevet, André. *Cosmographie universelle de André Thevet, Cosmographe du Roy*. Paris: Pierre d'Huillier, 1575.

Thompson, James Westfall. *The Wars of Religion in France, 1559–1576: The Huguenots, Catherine de Medici, Philip II*. New York: Frederick Ungar, 1958.

Thou, Jacques-August de. *Histoire universelle depuis 1543 jusqu'en 1607*. Vols. 4, 5, and 6. London: 1734.

Tibesar, Antonio. "A Spy's Report on the Expedition of Jean Ribault to Florida, 1565." *The Americas* 11, no. 4 (April 1955): 589–92.

Tooley, R. V. *Landmarks of Mapmaking*. London: Wordsworth Editions, 1989.

Trudel, Marc. *Les vains tentatives*. Vol. 1: *Histoire de la Nouvelle France*. Montreal: Fides, 1963.

United Kingdom. Public Record Office. *Calendar of State Papers, Foreign Series. Reign of Mary* (1553–58). Edited by William Turnbull. 12 vols. Nendeln, Liechtenstein: Kraus Reprint, 1967.

———. *Calendar of State Papers, Foreign Series. Reign of Elizabeth* (1558–88). Edited by Joseph Stevenson. Vols. 1–8. Nendeln, Liechtenstein: Kraus Reprint, 1966.

———. *Calendar of State Papers, Domestic Series. Reigns of Edward VI, Mary, and Elizabeth* (1547–80). Edited by Robert Lemon. Vols. 7 and 13. Nendeln, Liechtenstein: Kraus Reprint, 1967.

———. *Calendar of State Papers, Negotiations between England and Spain: Researches in Foreign Archives*. Vol. 1, edited by Martin Hume. Vol. 10, edited by Royal Tyler. Nendeln, Liechtenstein: Kraus Reprint, 1969, 1971.

Vigneras, Louis-André. "A Spanish Discovery of North Carolina, 1566." *North Carolina Historical Review* 46, no. 4 (October 1969): 398–414.

Vitet, Louis. *Histoire de Dieppe*. Paris: 1844.

Waters, David W. *The Art of Navigation in England in Elizabethan and Early Stuart Times*. London: Hollis and Carter, 1958.

Weber, David J. *The Spanish Frontier in North America*. New Haven: Yale University Press, 1992.

Wernham, R. B. *The Making of Elizabethan Foreign Policy, 1558–1603*. Berkeley: University of California Press, 1980.

Whitehead, A. W. *Gaspard de Coligny, Admiral of France*. London: Methuen and Co., 1904.

Wood, James B. *The King's Army: Warfare, Soldiers, and Society during the French Wars of Religion, 1562–1576*. Oxford: Blackwell, 1996.

Woodman, Richard. *The History of the Ship*. London: Conway Maritime Press, 1997.

Worth, John E. *Timucuan Chiefdoms of Spanish Florida*. Vol. 1. Gainesville: University Press of Florida, 1998.

Wright, J. Leitch. *Anglo-Spanish Rivalry in North America*. Athens: University of Georgia Press, 1971.

Wroth, Lawrence. *The Voyages of Giovanni da Verrazzano*. New Haven: Yale University Press, 1970.

INDEX

John T. McGrath is assistant professor of social science at Boston University's College of General Studies, where he teaches courses in social change and world history. He has written two textbooks for McGraw-Hill's custom publishing series and is the author of an article in the *Sixteenth Century Journal*.